PENDLETON ROUND-UP AT 100

OREGON'S LEGENDARY RODEO

BY MICHAEL BALES
AND ANN TERRY HILL

Introductions by
Roberta Conner and
William F. Willingham

Edited by Karen Kirtley
Directed by Stephen Aldrich Forrester of
the East Oregonian Publishing Company

GRAPHIC ARTS™ BOOKS

EO Archive: East Oregonian Digital Archive
Hall of Fame Collection: Courtesy of the Pendleton Round-Up
   and Happy Canyon Hall of Fame, Pendleton, OR—all photos by Nicole
   Barker for the *East Oregonian*
Hamley Archive: Courtesy of Hamley & Company, Pendleton, OR
Helm Collection: Courtesy of Polly Helm, Portland, OR
Howdyshell Collection: Courtesy of the Howdyshell Collection, Pendleton,
   OR
Low Collection: Courtesy of Wayne Low, Pilot Rock, OR
OHS Collection: Courtesy of the Oregon Historical Society, Portland, OR
PWM Archive: Courtesy of the Pendleton Woolen Mills Archive, Portland,
   OR
Tamástslikt Collection: Courtesy of the Tamástslikt Cultural Institute,
   Confederated Tribes of the Umatilla Indian Reservation, Pendleton,
   OR—all photos by Nicole Barker for the *East Oregonia*n
Compilation © MMIX by Graphic Arts™ Books

Graphic Arts™ Books
An imprint of Graphic Arts Center Publishing Company
P.O. Box 10306
Portland, OR 97296-0306
(503) 226-2402 * www.gacpc.com

Library of Congress Cataloging-in-Publication Data

Bales, Michael.
   Pendleton Round-Up at 100 : Oregon's legendary rodeo / by Michael Bales
      and Ann Terry Hill ; with contributions by Roberta Conner and William F.
      Willingham ; foreword by Gordon Smith ; edited by Karen Kirtley.
      p. cm.
   Includes bibliographical references and index.
   ISBN 978-0-88240-773-9 (hardbound) — ISBN 978-0-88240-774-6
      (softbound) 1. Pendleton Round-Up—History. I. Hill, Ann Terry. II.
      Kirtley, Karen. III. Title.
   GV1834.55.O72P463 2009
   791.8'409795—dc22
                                                  2008042368

President: Charles M. Hopkins
Associate Publisher: Douglas A. Pfeiffer
Editorial Staff: Timothy W. Frew, Kathy Howard, Jean Bond-Slaughter
Editor: Karen Kirtley
Design: Elizabeth Watson
Production Coordinator: Vicki Knapton

Second printing 2009

Printed in China

▶ **Lula Matlock, queen of the 1917 Round-Up.** *Low Collection.*

CONTENTS

▲ **Vera McGinnis, ca. 1914.** *Low Collection.*

FOREWORD

BY U.S. SENATOR GORDON SMITH

Every community has a history that helps define its heart. That is especially true for the people of Pendleton, Oregon, during the second week of every September. That week, the hearts of Pendletonians beat a little faster and the shout of "Let'er Buck" sounds in every ear. It signals that the saga of the Pendleton Round-Up continues, that the pride and spirit of a community is alive and well, and that a weeklong celebration of Western culture, of the cowboy way of life, is again renewed.

Beginning in the fall of 1910, a group of cowboys and Native Americans, farmers and ranchers, men and women, and boys and girls, gathered to celebrate the harvest and to show off their skills. Stores closed early, and the whole town showed up. A rip-roaring western rodeo broke out, and the Pendleton Round-Up was born. The rest, as they say, is history.

Every Pendleton family has their favorite Round-Up memories, and the Smith family is no different. For over half a century, multiple generations of my family have sat in the same grandstand box on rodeo grounds. The Round-Up influence was so great that it followed my family across the country to Washington, D.C., when my father went to work for President Eisenhower in 1953. Dad would still travel to Pendleton for the Round-Up, and some of my earliest memories are of my nine brothers and sisters gathered around upon his return to watch his eight-millimeter home movies of the parade and rodeo.

When I moved back to Pendleton with my wife, Sharon, and new daughter, Brittany, the Round-Up again became part of my life. My business, Smith Frozen Foods, is a staunch corporate sponsor, and September would often find our home overflowing with out-of-town friends, who came to see for themselves what they had heard me brag about for years. Two sons, Garrett and Morgan, would complete our family, and there was nothing Sharon and I enjoyed more than watching the parade and rodeo through the excited eyes of our children.

Brittany would grow up to become part of Round-Up royalty, serving for one year as a princess in the Round-Up court and reigning for one year as queen. Watching my daughter ride her horse into the arena at breakneck speed while waving with both hands brought tears to my eyes then, and the memory of it still does so today.

As a United States Senator, I have had the opportunity to bring the United States Secretary of Agriculture to the Round-Up, and I still haven't given up on one day convincing the President of the United States that there is no better way to understand the history and culture of the western United States than by traveling to Pendleton the second week of September.

For one hundred years, the name and fame of the Pendleton Round-Up, fueled by the energy of generations of citizen volunteers, has spread around the world. May it ever be so for Pendleton, and may the shout ever be heard: "Let'er Buck"!

▼ Gordon and Sharon Smith, Round-Up queen Brittany, and Morgan, 2002. *By Don Cresswell in EO Archive.*

INDIANS AT THE ROUNDUP PENDLETON ORE

▲ Indians at the 1911 Round-Up. Poker Jim is second from left; Billy Joshua a.k.a. McKay and Small Hawk are at right. *By O. G. Allen in Low Collection.*

8

ACKNOWLEDGMENTS

Attempting to capture a hundred years of Round-Up history has required piecing together fragments from a multitude of treasured scrapbooks, photo albums, postcard and artifact collections, family memorabilia, and letters and e-mails telling well-remembered tales—the generous offerings of hundreds of hearts. It is not possible to list the names of everyone who has added to the richness of this account, but we owe thanks to each of you. Readers will find many of your names in the following pages.

Four major contributors have deep roots in Umatilla County, Oregon.

William F. Willingham, Oregon public historian, is the son of Floyd Willingham, who owned and ran the Curio Shop on Main Street, Pendleton, during Bill's growing-up years. Bill's grandfather William Gibbs was a rancher who supplied stock for the first Round-Up in 1910, and his great-grandparents were among the region's first white settlers. He tells their story in his 2006 book *Starting Over: Community Building on the Eastern Oregon Frontier*.

Roberta Conner, director of the Tamástslikt Cultural Institute in Pendleton, is a member of the Confederated Tribes of the Umatilla Indian Reservation and a longtime Round-Up devotee. Her mother and her aunt were Round-Up queens, and she appears regularly in the Happy Canyon show and helps with Saturday's Indian dance contests. She has contributed to numerous published works, including the 2006 *Lewis and Clark Through Indian Eyes*.

Ann Terry Hill, a writer who contributes to *American Cowboy*, *True West*, *Cowboys & Indians*, and *Persimmon Hill* magazines, comes from a pioneer Round-Up family. She is a former Round-Up princess and queen; her father, Fred Hill, a past Round-Up president, was inducted into the Pendleton Round-Up and Happy Canyon Hall of Fame in 2008. Terry has close ties to the Pendleton area, and a profound love for it. Without her wealth of family, friends, and resources, this book would not have come together.

Stephen Forrester, president of the East Oregonian Publishing Company and publisher of the *Daily Astorian*, grew up in Pendleton. He initiated this book, and his company's enthusiasm and financial support have sustained it. Steve has called on many friends and colleagues in the Pendleton area and across the state to open doors that may otherwise have remained closed.

Michael Bales and I are the newcomers on the centennial book team. Mike spent twenty-five years as a newspaper reporter and editor, mostly in Florida. He now lives in Portland, where he is completing a master's degree in writing at Portland State University and freelancing for the *Oregonian*. He is smitten—by the Round-Up, by the West—as only a newcomer can be. Mike's intense curiosity, his research skills, and his knack for conveying drama have contributed immeasurably to this book.

I grew up in Kentucky, where I saw many a thoroughbred race but never a rodeo. I'm a long-time editor (beginning with a seven-year stint in Manhattan) and a genuine webfoot, a Portlander for more than thirty years. Nine days at the 2007 Round-Up made me a convert. As everyone says, I love it, and there's nothing like it. I'm a fan for life—of the place, the people, and the inimitable Pendleton Round-Up.

From all the book team, very special thanks go to

Matt Johnson and the Howdyshell Collection

Wayne Low and the Wayne Low Collection

Polly Helm and the Helm Collection

Mort Bishop III, Steve Wright, and the Archives of the Pendleton Woolen Mills

Parley Pearce, Blair Woodfield, and the Archives of Hamley & Company

Tamástslikt Cultural Institute and the Confederated Tribes of the Umatilla Indian Reservation, especially the Collections staff

Betty Branstetter and the Pendleton Round-Up and Happy Canyon Hall of Fame

George Murdock, Kathryn Brown, and the staff of the *East Oregonian*

Julie Reese and the Umatilla Historical Society

Marsha Matthews and the Research Library of the Oregon Historical Society

Nicole Barker and Don Cresswell, *East Oregonian* photographers

George Anderson, Don Erickson, and David Ogilvie, Round-Up and Happy Canyon photographers

Jim Whiting, my photographer husband and rodeo companion

Directors of the Round-Up and Happy Canyon, 2006–2008—especially Doug Corey, Steve Corey, Kevin Hale, Tim Hawkins, Dennis Hunt, Mike Thorne, and Butch Thurman

All the crew at Graphic Arts Center Publishing Company, especially Mike Campbell, Tim Frew, Kathy Howard, Doug Pfeiffer, and Elizabeth Watson.

—Karen Kirtley, September 2008

THE FIRST 100 YEARS OF THE PENDLETON ROUND-UP

BY WILLIAM F. WILLINGHAM

This is not going to be any ordinary "Wild West" show. It will be the
best exhibition ever given in Pendleton or any other place also in
the west for that matter. It will be worth coming many miles to see.

—Roy Raley in *East Oregonian*, 1910

▼ Poster for Buffalo Bill Cody's
Wild West show.

When "*Let'er Buck*" rang out in Pendleton, Oregon, on a warm September day in 1910, the crowd gathered around the dusty arena could not have imagined that they were witnessing the beginning of one of the twentieth century's most successful rodeos. There were precedents, such as the Cheyenne Frontier Days in Wyoming, Buffalo Bill's Wild West shows, and other frontier exhibitions that showcased Native American pageantry. But the exhibitions of horsemanship and cowboy skills in the arena that day, the speed and sheer variety

BUFFALO BILL CODY

Buffalo Bill Cody, perhaps the most famous American world-wide during his lifetime, visited Pendleton on three separate occasions. In August 1902 he brought his Wild West show to town. Annie Oakley, the superstar "Little Sure Shot," was not with him, as she had been injured in a train accident the year before. According to the August 21, 1902, *East Oregonian*, the show was robust, but locals weren't impressed. After all, they were living the Wild West.

Cody was featured in the Sells-Floto Circus that came to Pendleton June 3, 1914, and again on June 10, 1915. He was under contract as part of an agreement to pay off debts accumulated by Buffalo Bill's Wild West Show, which had been auctioned off in 1913.

According to hand-me-down memories passed on to Parley Pearce, co-owner of Pendleton western store Hamley & Company, Cody came into Hamley's on both visits, dressed in full Buffalo Bill costume. He made several purchases, but what he bought is not recorded.

◄ **Buffalo Bill Cody, 1903.** *Prints and Photographs Division, Library of Congress.*

▲ Roy Raley, first Round-Up president.

Howdyshell Collection.

▶ ▲ Horse-drawn combine harvests wheat in

Umatilla County, 1910. *By Jim Whiting; original by*

W. S. Bowman, at St. Anthony Hospital, Pendleton.

▶ Cattle grazing on North Hill above

downtown Pendleton. *Low Collection.*

A man can find within our borders extremely fertile farming land, grazing land, timberland, mountain solitudes and patches and stretches that are good for nothing.

—J. P. Wager, 1885

of exhibition events, the wild abandon of the cowboys and cowgirls who competed and performed, thrilled the audience at Pendleton as never before. The excitement in the arena at that first Round-Up proved to be the start of a widely popular rodeo and Native American exhibition that would continue for another century. The Pendleton Round-Up has stood the test of time and gives every appearance of lasting as long as people enjoy reliving the daring spirit and rip-roaring action of the American frontier.

The precise origins of the Pendleton Round-Up are a matter of debate. Some place its beginnings in a demonstration of western horsemanship at a Fourth of July celebration at Pendleton in 1909, while others argue for a display of bronco riding and horse races, coupled with Native American dances, at the October 1909 Eastern Oregon District Fair in Pendleton. Whatever the show's impetus, Pendleton attorney Roy Raley and a group of young businessmen are credited with organizing the original 1910 frontier extravaganza that would become world famous as the Pendleton Round-Up.

From the start, Raley had big ideas of what the frontier exhibition could do for Pendleton. He announced that

> **if the present plans can be successfully carried out it will do more to keep Pendleton on the map, to bring people here and to send them away satisfied than any other form of entertainment which we could give. This is not going to be any ordinary "Wild West" show. It will be the best exhibition ever given in Pendleton or any other place also in the west for that matter. It will be worth coming many miles to see.**
> (*East Oregonian*, July 29, 1910)

Ironically, the Round-Up began as an entertainment that honored a way of life no longer typical of Umatilla County in 1910. Bronco-busting tournaments and Native American war dances described a time at least twenty-five years in the past, when cattle and cowboys dominated the rangeland of eastern Oregon and the so-called Bannock War of 1878 caused turmoil on the Umatilla Indian Reservation. In the 1880s, cattle buyers assembled thousands of head of cattle at Pendleton then drove them to markets in Montana and Wyoming. But even then, wheat farming and sheep raising were fast crowding out the rangeland cattle business of northeastern Oregon. By 1910, wheat and wool production and related businesses dominated the agricultural economy of northeastern Oregon. On the eve of the 1911 exhibition, the editor of the *East Oregonian* admitted as much when he wrote, "The show is not intended to depict the life in this country at this time, for the Round-Up is not

The dirt road has been paved, and generations of automobiles have replaced the horse-drawn coaches and wagons. Yet Main Street, Pendleton, remains the central thoroughfare it was in pioneer days.

▲ ▲ Main Street, ca. 1908. *Low Collection.*

▲ Main Street, ca. 1930s. *Low Collection.*

▲▲ Cowboys in
the arena, 1910.
Helm Collection.

▲ T. A. Spray
riding a steer,
1910 Round-Up.
Low Collection.

▶ Prize saddle,
1910. *Helm Collection.*

MAIN PRIZE OF THE ROUND-UP MADE BY HAMLEY & SON VALUE $250

Bert Kelly, saddle bronc champion of 1910, won an elaborately hand-tooled Hamley saddle, trimmed with gold and silver.

typical of Pendleton and of eastern Oregon these days." (*East Oregonian*, September 14, 1911)

Popular nostalgia for the fast-disappearing American West had already found an outlet in the frontier exhibition at Cheyenne, Wyoming, and in the numerous touring Wild West shows. Entertainments such as Buffalo Bill's extravaganza sought to present the settlement of the West as a triumph of civilization and domestic order over Native American savagery and wilderness conditions. Merging myth and memory, fiction and reality, they told their version of the conquest and domestication of the frontier West. In their dramatizations, the cowboy represented the vanguard of the white race, bringing progress and civilization to a chaotic territory. Through his skills of roping, riding, and shooting, the cowboy helped to tame the West.

The Wild West show emerged in the final years of frontier settlement by Euro-American emigrants and helped to crystallize myth and reality into a powerful memory that would dominate how millions of people remembered the winning of the American West. Audiences willingly accepted the exaggerated and idealized presentation of frontier life as the true story. By the time the Pendleton Round-Up was staged, millions of people throughout North America and Europe had embraced the cowboy as the ideal man, fearless, independent, hard-working, honest, and loyal.

The Round-Up could claim greater authenticity in its presentations of the cowboy skills because its performers were not mere actors recreating the distant past, but actual working cowboys—ranchers and cowhands who still broke wild horses and roped and branded cattle on ranches throughout the Northwest. The competitions in Pendleton represented more than mere nostalgia or fading memory. As Raley put it when describing the 1911 performance, the Round-Up "gathered together all the features which comprise the West of song and story." Most importantly, it did so in such a way that the spectator had

an opportunity to see the cowboys and cowgirls as they are and not as they are imitated, the Indians of the reservation and not of the circus; the untamed horse of the prairie, and best of all things which the open life of the range produces and each one at its best. (*East Oregonian*, September 14, 1911)

Pendleton Indian Robe Series—Pattern No. 406

This is some of our Boy Robes

▲▲ **Indian men and boys in traditional regalia, 1931.** *OHS Collection, CN 010571.*

▲ **Teepees at the Round-Up, ca. 1920.** *By R. Doubleday in Low Collection.*

◄ **Pendleton Mills postcard with note by Fannie Kay Bishop, 1910.** *PWM Archive.*

► **Beaded Indian moccasins, n.d.** *Hall of Fame Collection.*

15

Our home is on the plains, Let 'er buck,

Where the god of freedom reigns, Let 'er buck,

Where there's rugged joys and pains,

Where no law of man restrains, Let 'er buck.

—Merle Chessman, *East Oregonian*, September 1911

Another writer noted at the time,

The actor's is the realm of fiction, the Round-Up performer's the province of truth, and the cowboy's audience never experiences the disappointment of dropping from an imaginary to the actual world at the falling of a curtain, is never forced to sigh and say, when it is all over, "After all, it was not real." (*East Oregonian*, September 14, 1911)

In like manner, the Round-Up's depiction of Native Americans could legitimately claim greater authenticity than that attempted in the Wild West shows. The latter, for example, used the American Indian chiefly in historical re-enactments that purported to describe how the white settlers and the United States Army overcame Native American "savages" to bring Euro-American civilization to the West. Hence Buffalo Bill's Wild West show presented Native American attacks on wagon trains, stagecoaches, and a settler's frontier cabin, all of which Buffalo Bill repulsed with the aid of valiant cowboys, scouts, or the cavalry. Buffalo Bill's Wild West show also staged re-enactments of "Custer's Last Stand" and the battles of Wounded Knee and Summit Springs.

At the Round-Up, in contrast, Native Americans set up a teepee encampment and gave demonstrations of traditional dancing, horsemanship, and skills in beadwork, leatherwork, weaving, and basket making. They celebrated their Indian heritage without emphasizing hostilities between themselves and whites.

Thus it was with full knowledge of the popular Wild West entertainments and in the spirit of pioneer remembrance that in the summer of 1910, a group of young business and civic leaders in Pendleton announced the formation of the Northwestern Frontier Celebration Association and their intent to put on a show in the fall. Roy Raley took the lead in organizing the exhibition. Others provided key assistance, including Mark Moorhouse, insurance agent; Roy Ritner, banker and farmer; Lawrence Frazier, bookstore owner; Will Ingram, grocer; Max Baer, clothier; A. J. McAllister, druggist; and J. H. Gwinn, title abstracter. The group quickly filed articles of incorporation as a non-profit and set a budget of $2,860 for the fall show.

If the promoters were to put on a frontier exhibition in two months, money would have to be raised and a multitude of tasks accomplished. The incorporation papers allowed for the issuance of $5,000 in capital stock, five hundred shares at $10 each. Enthusiastic subscribers in the local community quickly claimed over half the shares. With sufficient money in hand to cover the initial budget, the exhibition board assigned the tasks necessary to pull off "a frontier exhibition of picturesque pastimes, Indian and military spectacles, cowboy racing and bronco busting for the championship of the Northwest." (Rupp, 1985)

With Raley as president of the association and providing overall leadership, several other prominent local men carried out key tasks. Lot Frazier assumed the job of getting the grounds in shape at the baseball field in the west end of the town, bordering the Umatilla River. Workers leveled a quarter-mile dirt track for the races and hastily threw up a wooden grandstand and bleachers to hold a few hundred spectators. Umatilla County sheriff Til Taylor and rancher James Sturgis gathered livestock. Lee Drake of the *East Oregonian* arranged publicity, and Paul Sperry organized a parade through town and named it "Westward Ho!" Will Ingram served as business manager. Harry Gray arranged special trains at reduced fares to bring rodeo fans to Pendleton from throughout the Northwest. A host of others helped with the myriad details that needed attention if Pendleton were to produce a successful show in record time. In the decades to come, volunteers would continue to show extraordinary commitment to the annual community enterprise.

Aware that Native American participation in the Round-Up would be a key element in representing frontier life, show organizers worked quickly to enlist Indian support. In early August, Roy Bishop of the Pendleton Woolen Mills and Major Lee Moorhouse, former superintendent of the Umatilla Reservation, attended a council of the three tribes making up the Umatilla Reservation. At the meeting, they won the backing of Chiefs Umapine of the Cayuse, No Shirt of the Walla Walla, and Amos Pond of the Umatilla; the council voted unanimously to take part. Soon, other Northwest tribes agreed to join the event. Most importantly, Poker Jim, a highly respected Walla Walla, promised to bring his string of race horses and to encourage other Indians to do so.

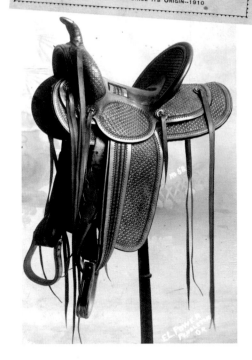

The Round-Up promoters shelved the "military spectacles" when the army at Vancouver Barracks refused to supply soldiers and the Indian participants refused to take part in a staged battle if they couldn't shoot back. The focus shifted to cowboy and cowgirl events, and a $250 Hamley saddle (from the Pendleton Hamley harness and saddle store) was promised as the top prize for the best bronco buster. Hamley's craftsmen used gold-headed nails and silver from silver dollars for trim, and they crafted hand-stamped leather of the finest quality. Promoters billed the prize as "the handsomest thing in the saddle line this city has ever seen." (*East Oregonian*, September 27, 1910)

The phrase "Let 'er Buck" adorned promotional buttons and press releases. Mark Moorhouse, exhibition manager, traveled to Cheyenne to see firsthand what made the frontier celebration so successful. Based on his observations, the promoters decided to add a wild horse race as a featured event.

When opening day of the Round-Up arrived on September 29, 1910, a crowd of seven thousand showed up, and organizers had to turn away hundred of spectators. Overnight, carpenters threw up bleachers for another three thousand. The *East Oregonian* reported that the first Round-Up was a "whirlwind success."

The Native Americans' encampment, dramatic war dances, and daring horsemanship in the races added "color and novelty" to create an "inspiring spectacle." The bronco riding excited the crowds, and the first horse race produced an unexpected thrill when one pony fell and ten more ponies and riders tumbled over it in a mass pile-up. Other

▲▲▲ **Saddlemakers in Hamley's shop,** 1910. *OHS Collection, OrHi 61768.*

▲▲ **Ad for E. L. Power, saddlemaker.** *Low Collection.*

▲ **Prize saddle by E. L. Power, 1910.** *By W. S. Bowman in Low Collection.*

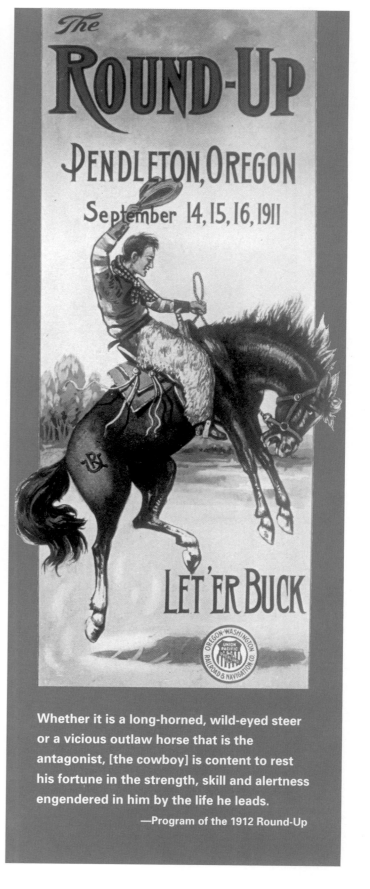

▲▲ Fans at the 1910 Round-Up pack the wooden grandstand and spill into the arena. *Howdyshell Collection.*

▲ Cowboys await their turn for the 1910 bucking contest. *By W. S. Bowman in Low Collection.*

▶ 1911 Round-Up poster. *OHS Collection, OrHi 91472.*

events included a wild horse race, trick riders, steer roping, steer wrestling, and a grand parade around the arena. Buffalo Vernon gave a memorable demonstration of bull-dogging a steer to the ground and holding the animal down by biting its lip in "a mighty classy exhibition." At the end of the three-day event, the *East Oregonian* boasted that "if Pendleton was ever off the map which is doubtful, she has been put back on with a vengeance and in letters so big that the whole country cannot help but see. The words "Pendleton" and "Round-Up" are on the lips of thousands and will continue to be for the months and years to come." (*East Oregonian*, September 28–October 1, 1910)

Whether it is a long-horned, wild-eyed steer or a vicious outlaw horse that is the antagonist, [the cowboy] is content to rest his fortune in the strength, skill and alertness engendered in him by the life he leads.

—Program of the 1912 Round-Up

In 1909, a small wool mill in Pendleton began producing blankets with intricate American Indian designs. Pendleton Woolen Mills supported the Round-Up from its start with advertising and with blanket prizes.

◄ Ad for Pendleton Woolen Mills in the 1913 program. *PWM Archive.*

▼ Cowboys and cowgirls race across the arena behind flag bearers, n.d. *By L. Moorhouse in OHS Collection, OrHi 95223.*

"Goin' Some"
Round Up Pendleton Oregon

Maj. Moorhouse.

UMATILLA BRAVES AT THE ROUNDUP

With the 1910 show widely considered a success, organizers began planning for the 1911 exhibition. The 1910 Round-Up had turned a profit of $3,000, and the $10 shares soon rose in value. The original backers refused to sell. Instead, shareholders plunged into renewed fund-raising in order to expand the show. Under the continued leadership of Roy Raley and Mark Moorhouse, the exhibition association decided to purchase fifteen acres of land between Court Street and the Umatilla River, where the 1910 Round-Up had taken place. The owner, William Matlock, sold the ground for $5,000. The association paid $1,000 down and gave a five-year note for the balance. The non-profit association then deeded the property to the City of Pendleton and signed a ten-year leaseback agreement for $1.00 a year.

By February 1911, the association had developed and begun to implement expansion plans. First they raised $12,000, which they put toward enlarging the grandstand to a capacity of ten thousand, building corrals, and expanding and improving the racetrack. Next they launched a major promotional campaign to attract spectators. As added attractions, they bought two stagecoaches to race, contracted with mounted cowboy and cowgirl bands to provide music, and hired trick riders and ropers. The great success in 1910 of the Westward Ho! Parade and the arena show of

▲▲ **Umatillas at early Round-Up.**

By W. S. Bowman in Low Collection.

▲ **Indians in Westward Ho! Parade, ca. 1911.**

By W. S. Bowman in Low Collection.

▶ **Beaded vest, ca. 1940.** *Tamástslikt Collection.*

FACING PAGE ▶ Top left: **Grand parade, 1911.** *By J. B. Burrell in Helm Collection.*

Bottom left: **Aerial view of the Round-Up grounds, ca. 1955.** *Low Collection.*

Top right: **Fans at the 1911 Round-Up.** *By J. B. Burrell in Low Collection.*

Bottom right: **W. F. Blancett rides "Hot Foot" in 1911 bucking contest.**

By W. S. Bowman in Helm Collection.

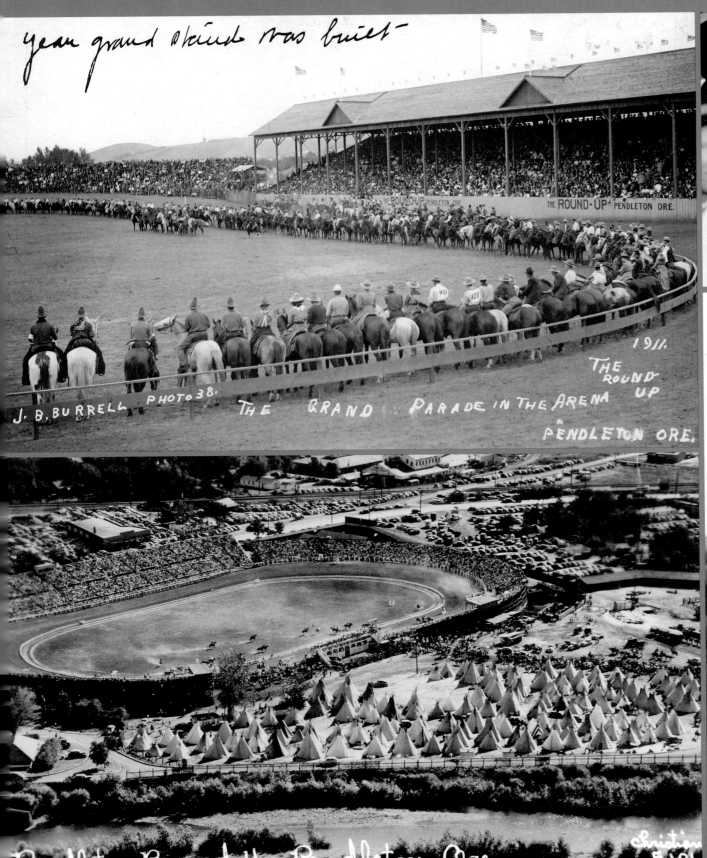

year grand stand was built —

J. B. BURRELL PHOTO 38. THE GRAND PARADE IN THE ARENA

1911. THE ROUND UP PENDLETON ORE.

Pendleton Round-Up Pendleton, Ore.

Christian E101

BURRELL PHOTO 15 EXPRSSIONS AT THE ROUND-UP

THE ROUND-UP 1911.

LET 'ER BUCK

▲ Directors of the Round-Up in 1913. Til Taylor is at left; Roy Bishop is fifth from right. *Low Collection.*

▶ Ben Jory rides "Hot Stuff," 1911. *By W. S. Bowman in Low Collection.*

▶▶ Men and boys waited all night to buy grandstand tickets, 1916. *Low Collection.*

Indian dancing assured their continuing place in future Round-Ups. An exciting show depended in large part on the quality of the stock, so association directors sought and purchased top steers and the best bucking and racehorses they could find. Once again, the directors visited the show at Cheyenne to make sure that Pendleton's Round-Up was not outdone by its chief competitor.

As the Round-Up's reputation rapidly spread throughout the West, contestants were eager to compete at the show. As the *East Oregonian* noted, "Pendleton is the mecca of the cowboys." (September 11, 1911) The 1911 Round-Up did not disappoint. Some thirty-one thousand spectators bought tickets, and twelve thousand showed up for the first of the three daylong shows.

The highlight of the 1911 Round-Up was the bucking finals, when Jackson Sundown, an Indian cowboy; George Fletcher, a black cowboy; and John Spain, a white cowboy, competed for the prize saddle. While the spectators in the stands clearly favored Fletcher, the judges in the arena, all

BEN JORY RIDING HOT STUFF

W.S.BOWMAN PHOTO No.116

THE ROUND UP. PENDLETON OR. 1911

GEORGE FLETCHER. AFTER WINNING SECOND IN THE BUCKING CONTEST

Oregon writer Ken Kesey's 1994 novel *Last Go Round: A Real Western* focuses on the 1911 contest between Fletcher, Spain, and Sundown. In the opening chapter, Kesey writes that "in one rare 8 x 10 copy of the trio together, the complexions are even hand-tinted, to make sure posterity gets the point: one rider's face is tinted Indian copper, one Caucasian pink, one a deep molasses brown."

▲◄ **George Fletcher, 1911.** *By W. S. Bowman in Low Collection.*

◄ **Buffalo Vernon, 1911.** *By W. S. Bowman in Howdyshell Collection.*

► **Pat Henry trick roping.** *Low Collection.*

ROUND UP. PENDLETON OR.

W.S.BOWMAN PHOTO No.135

BUFFALO VERNON CHAMPION STEER ROPER OF THE NORTH WEST

FLETCHER & VERNON

k Roping

▲ Winner's Certificate awarded to Lew W. Minor in 1912. *Hall of Fame Collection.*

▲▶ William McAdoo at front row center, ca. 1918. McAdoo was secretary of the treasury under President Woodrow Wilson and also Wilson's son-in-law. *By W. S. Bowman in Low Collection.*

▶ Pinky Gist, cowboy clown, 1930. *Low Collection.*

▼ The saddle of Lew W. Minor, 1912 saddle bronc champion. *Hall of Fame Collection.*

McADOO & GIST

◄ Indian dancers, including Mitchell Lloyd and Tom Shillal, perform as women form a semicircle around them. *OHS Collection, CN 010514.*

▼ Wreck in stagecoach race, 1911. *By W. S. Bowman in PWM Archive.*

▼▼ Umatillas at the Round-Up, believed to be (from left) Fish Hawk, Uma Sumkin, and Umapima, 1910. *By W. S. Bowman in Low Collection.*

experienced stockmen, awarded the prize to Spain. Fletcher had made a showy ride, but the judges thought Spain's form was better and his bronc harder to handle. According to the news accounts, when Fletcher "rode around the track after the contest was over he was greeted with a deafening roar of applause." (*East Oregonian*, September 18, 1911)

The controversial outcome of the contest proved to be a long-term boon to the Round-Up because it attracted wide attention and established early on that top cowboys came to the Pendleton Round-Up to deliver their very best performances. The *East Oregonian* captured that spirit:

The slogan of the Round-Up is a good one to remember. When things do not go right with you, when the circumstances seem to be against you and Fate deals you a blow between the eyes, remember what the cowboys say in the great Northwest. Just grit your teeth, get another hold, be a man and "Let 'er buck!" (*East Oregonian,* September 14, 1911)

Between 1912 and 1920, the directors of the Round-Up Association worked to fine-tune and build up the successful elements of the exhibition. In the process, they established

► Fancy roper Jane Burmoudy.
By R. Doubleday in Low Collection.

►▼ Cowgirls trick riding in 1921.
By R. Doubleday in Low Collection.

▼ Gold-trimmed vest and skirt made by Hamley & Co. for queen Mary Robison in 1936. *Hall of Fame Collection.*

COWGIRLS HEADED FOR THE ROUND-UP

COWGIRLS

the hallmarks that would make the show famous over the ensuing century. The outstanding features of the Round-Up included its fast pace and wild, daredevil performances by top-ranked horsemen. The bucking contests, in particular, tested the ability and stamina of the contestants, because there was no time limit on the rides. As Hoot Gibson, all-around cowboy champion at the 1912 Round-Up, later remarked, "When we got on a bronc we just stayed there until he quit bucking or we ran out of wind. Those horses kept it up for forty seconds sometimes, and believe me that's a lot of time when you're sitting on top of him." (Rupp, 1985)

Glamorous, tough-as-nails cowgirls added to the arena excitement. The women contestants' resourceful and spirited riding in relay races often brought the crowds to their feet.

Above all, the excitement of the unscripted show thrilled the spectators. As Mark Moorhouse explained,

the cowboys and cowgirls and Indians that go to make up the show do not come on and do their "turns" according to cues, neither do they or we know just what is going to happen, therefore situations arise that are neither planned nor expected, each situation must be met and handled in its own way, the show must go on. (*East Oregonian*, September 14, 1911)

The rapid flow of events at the Round-Up captured the audience's attention. The show opened and closed with wild horse bucking or racing events and offered plenty of action in between with stagecoach, relay, and pony express races. Bulldogging and steer and calf roping rounded out the competitive program. Trick riding, fancy roping, and clowning in the arena provided diversions.

The performers' appearance also caught the audience's fancy. The cowboys wore colorful shirts and scarves, decorated vests, woolly chaps, and big Stetsons. The cowgirls concocted their own elaborate costumes, reflecting the fashions of the day. Native American dancers performed in colorful regalia made of tanned deer and elk hides adorned with beads, shells, and bird feathers. The midpoint of each show was marked by the grand entrance of hundreds of cowboys and Native Americans, mounted and in splendid

▲ Cowgirls ready for the bucking contest, n.d. *Howdyshell Collection.*

◄ Champions of the 1922 Round-Up. From left: Hugo Strickland (steer roping), Ray Bell (second in saddle bronc riding), Howard Tegland (first in saddle bronc riding), Yakima Canutt (third in saddle bronc riding), and Mike Hastings (bulldogging). *Howdyshell Collection.*

Women have been stars at the Round-Up since it began. Round-Up royalty added glamour and panache, and women competitors faced the same dangers as men.

◀ Queen Jean McCarty, 1938. *OHS Collection, CN 002472.*
▲ Sheet music for Round-Up songs. *Hall of Fame Collection.*
▼ Nettie Hawn, women's bucking champion in 1913. *Howdyshell Collection.*

CHAMPION 1913.
NETTIE HAWN ON SNAKE

McCARTY & HAWN

traditional dress, led by the Mounted Cowboy Band and massed flags.

Both white and Indian women competed in the Round-Up from the beginning. Their main events included the cowgirls' relay and pony express races, Indian races, fancy roping, and trick riding. In the 1920s, Mabel Strickland became famous for her championship relay riding and exhibition steer roping, while red-headed Fox Hastings demonstrated steer bulldogging that challenged the best of the cowboy doggers. Bertha Blancett displayed her horsemanship by riding "slick," without the tied stirrups often used in women's events for safety. A fatal injury sustained by cowgirl Bonnie McCarroll in the 1929 saddle bronc contest led to the end of this event for women at the Round-Up, though women continued to compete in racing events.

From the very first Round-Up, a queen and a court of princesses have helped to promote the show. In the early years, the queens often performed as cowgirls in the rodeo; in later years they functioned primarily as good-will ambassadors, representing the community spirit and East Oregon roots the Round-Up exemplified.

To provide accommodations for the crowds that flocked to Pendleton for the Round-Up, the association soon expanded the grandstand and bleachers to hold twenty thousand spectators. It was scarcely enough, since up to fifty thousand in total attendance showed up each September. In 1913, fifty special trains converged in Pendleton for the Round-Up. Fortunately, the Pullman cars provided housing for thousands of arriving visitors.

Pendleton, a town with fewer than six thousand inhabitants, pulled out all the stops to welcome and entertain the throngs attracted to the Round-Up. The many ways in which the whole town worked together to put on each year's show contained the germ of the Round-Up's success and longevity: it was a community enterprise enriching to everyone involved. Year after year, the Round-Up Association spent the show's profits on maintenance or improvements and turned over any remaining funds to local charities or the city parks.

The Pendleton Round-Up had to excel, for it was not without competition. In 1912, for example, some fifty-two round-ups, rodeos, and frontier exhibitions appeared in the Northwest and Canada. But few had the staying power of

◀ Kathleen McClintock, 1929 queen. *By Rice in OHS Collection, CN 013266.*

▼ Beaded gauntlet gloves, frequent Indian trade and gift items, n.d. *Tamástslikt Collection.*

Happy Canyon was as real a place as Meadows, Cold Springs, and Butter Creek. Residents of a nine-mile stretch between Pendleton and Echo called their home Happy Canyon because of their frequent dances and pleasant existence there.

—Roberta Conner, 2007

the Round-Up. As a 1924 editorial in the *East Oregonian* put it: "Because the Round-Up is a community enterprise and because there is no private gain nor ever has been, the Round-Up survives and flourishes where other shows falter and die." (*East Oregonian*, September 20, 1924)

In 1913, the Round-Up added a night show to the annual festivities. Roy Raley wrote the first script for an outdoor pageant depicting the arrival of white pioneers and the settlement and development of the West. Two years later, Raley worked with Cayuse tribal member Anna E. Minthorn Wannassay to revise the script and incorporate the story of tribal life on the Columbia River Plateau before contact with white men. Enlivened through pantomime, musical score, and the appearance onstage of live animals, the Happy Canyon Pageant was a success from the start. A unique community production, it became a key feature of the annual Round-Up. Over time, the roles of the Native Americans and white westerners became the virtual property of the performers and were handed down within their families. Happy Canyon will celebrate its hundredth year in 2013.

On occasion, attempts have been made to rewrite portions of the show that became dated or out of step with current views of ethnic stereotyping. But the basic story lines seem to defy alteration. The Happy Canyon Pageant remains a cherished part of the Pendleton area's communal identity.

During World War I, the Round-Up took on distinctly patriotic overtones. As preparations got under way for the 1917 show, Troop D, Oregon Cavalry, left Pendleton in cowboy costumes and attracted much attention as their train passed through Portland. Captain Lee Caldwell, a star performer at the Round-Up and the troop commander, telegraphed from their North Carolina training camp with a request to begin the Round-Up with three yells for the absent cowboys. Liberty Loan appeals and an army band from Fort Lewis opened the show that September. The Round-Up netted $5,000 profit from the 1917 show and donated it to the Red Cross.

Cowboys and cowgirls participating in the Round-Up demonstrated their support for the troops in Europe. Yakima Canutt bulldogged a steer wearing his white U.S. Navy uniform. At the 1918 show, Bertha Blancett wore a black armband with a gold star as she took part in racing

The *Oregon Journal*, later enveloped into *The Oregonian*, sponsored a train bound specifically for the Pendleton Round-Up with Bishop Benjamin Dagwell as a leader. That's what you call draw!

—Gerry Frank, 2007

FACING PAGE ◄ Pioneer and Indian scenes from the Happy Canyon Pageant, n.d. *By W. S. Bowman in Howdyshell Collection.*

◄ Queen Donne Boylen and princesses greet an airplane in 1945. *Howdyshell Collection.*
▼◄ Members of the 1931 Round-Up court meet one of the trains that converged on Pendleton for Round-Up. *OHS Collection, CN 010501.*
▼ Bertha Blancett in 1918. She wears a black armband in memory of her husband, who was killed in the war in France. *By W. S. Bowman in Low Collection.*

MILDRED DOUGLAS

events and the Happy Canyon Pageant. Her husband, star Round-Up performer Dell Blancett, had been killed in action in France six months earlier.

Many observers considered the 1920s the golden era of the Round-Up. The level of performance, quality of livestock, and wealth of pageantry had grown, according to the *East Oregonian*, "into a spectacle that belongs to the entire United States." Hoot Gibson, a star performer at the Round-Up, filmed a movie called *Let'er Buck* that won favorable reviews and large audiences around the country. In 1924, a talented artist, Wallace Smith, created the bucking horse emblem that became the copyrighted symbol of the Round-Up.

Charles Wellington Furlong, an eminent professional lecturer, scientist, and adventurer, began attending the Round-Up and even took part in the show. In 1921 he added to its fame by writing a book entitled *Let'er Buck*. In somewhat purple prose, he tried to capture the essence of the Round-Up's popularity:

> Man ever seeks to perpetuate himself and his history. In almost all lands there are certain feasts and carnivals. . . . Each year at Pendleton, Oregon, there occurs in the fall a great carnival which epitomizes the most dramatic phases of the pioneer days of the West—and its spirit. There the real, practical work of the trail, cow camp and range is shown, through the sports of the pioneer; for the play of a people is usually but a normal outgrowth and expert expression of its work. . . . The Round-Up is an epitome of the end of the Great Migration on this continent and stands not only as typical of Pendleton, but of Oregon, of the West of America. (*Furlong*, 1921)

In 1927, the Round-Up Association added a Dress-Up Parade the Saturday before Round-Up week to mark the beginning of the show's festivities. The decade ended with a voter-approved city bond issue of $20,000 for enlarging the grandstand and improving the grounds. Most of the show's earnings were returned to the contestants in large purses for the competitive events, spent on physical improvements to the rodeo grounds, or expended on high-quality livestock. Yet by the end of the decade, the Round-Up had also contributed $108,061 to community betterment.

FACING PAGE ◄ Mildred Douglas trick riding. *Low Collection.*

◄ Cowboy champions, 1918. *Howdyshell Collection.*

▲ Round-Up program, 1926. Wallace Smith created the bucking horse emblem in 1925. *Low Collection.*

Pendleton Drug Co.

UMATILLA CHIEFS AT THE ROUND UP #9

UMATILLA CHIEFS

FACING PAGE ◄ Umatilla chiefs carry
the flag at the 1931 Round-Up.
OHS Collection, CN 010474.

◄▲ Cowboys in the grand march, 1930.
OHS Collection, bb003682.
▲ Oregon's governor Charles A. Sprague
in the Westward Ho! Parade, 1941.
OHS Collection, CN 014466.
◄ Les Johnson leaves the chute on
"Necktie," as a 1960s crew from ABC-TV
records the show. *Howdyshell Collection.*

▲ From left: Oregon governor Mark Hatfield at the 1962 Round-Up with his wife, Antoinette, and radio newscaster Frank Hemingway, of ABC in Los Angeles.
Howdyshell Collection.

During the 1930s and 1940s, first worldwide economic depression and then World War II caused considerable turmoil for the Round-Up. In the early 1930s, attendance declined, and the show suffered deficits and required underwriting by Pendleton individuals and businesses. The Round-Up's indebtedness almost led to the cancellation of the 1933 show. But the people of Pendleton and the surrounding area wanted the Round-Up to continue, and the association board decided to reorganize and keep going.

In May 1933, the new Pendleton Round-Up Association succeeded the original Northwest Frontier Celebration Association, and work on the September show began in earnest. Over the next five years, increased attendance and a close watch on expenses enabled the association to retire its accumulated debt of $16,000 and even continue contributing to the Pendleton Parks Commission.

A new crisis arose in 1937, when some prominent rodeo cowboys formed a union called the Cowboys Turtle Association and demanded that the Round-Up judges be Turtles and that certain livestock requirements be met. The Round-Up Association refused and would not permit Turtles to enter the 1937 show. In turn, the Turtles

boycotted the 1937 and 1938 shows. The standoff had little effect on either show, as plenty of contestants and large crowds came to Pendleton anyway. By the time of the 1939 event, the Turtles and the Round-Up Association had resolved their differences, and Turtles once again participated in the Round-Up.

On the eve of the 1940 event, just when it appeared that the Round-Up had successfully weathered the economic hard times of the Depression era, the show faced a new challenge. On August 15, 1940, a fire consumed the old wooden grandstand and all the wagons, coaches, and other horse-drawn equipment stored beneath it. The association directors and the entire community rose to the occasion. Cash donations of $35,000 poured in within days, and McCormack & Foley Construction Company volunteered to build a new grandstand at cost. A crew of seventy-three workers completed a three-thousand-seat concrete grandstand in time for the show. After the 1940 Round-Up, they added two more sections, for a total capacity of five thousand. According to accounts at the time, the show came off "bigger and better than ever."

Because of the wartime emergency, the Round-Up Association decided not to hold shows in 1942 and 1943. Performances resumed in 1944, with bull riding added as an official event. Over forty thousand spectators attended the 1944 Round-Up. The show thrived in the late 1940s, and the association added a west grandstand and bleachers to accommodate the growing crowds.

For the next fifty years, the main features of the Round-Up remained intact. At the same time, association directors were not afraid to experiment in order to keep the show fresh. In 1951, for instance, they added a chuck-wagon race to energize the show; the next year, they returned brahma bull riding to the action. Local riding clubs were allowed to put on relay and pony express races. The directors even experimented briefly with a Saturday night performance. Potential conflicts with the Happy Canyon show soon ended the nighttime Round-Up performance. Also in 1951, the Main Street Cowboys were formed to promote the Round-Up and to provide free evening entertainment in downtown Pendleton for the throngs attending the four-day rodeo.

The association continued to make physical improvements as funds allowed. These included roofing the south

◄ Fire destroyed the Round-Up stadium in August 1940. *Howdyshell Collection.*
◄ Lester Hamley awarding prize Hamley saddle, 1940s. *Low Collection.*

The brahma bull is a vicious opponent. His skin is loose over his hard-muscled body, and he hooks as he bucks high, crooked, and hard.

▶ **Bull rider Chuck Shelton hits the dirt in 1958.** *Howdyshell Collection.*
▶ ▼ **Aboard a fierce bucker, 1968.** *Howdyshell Collection.*

BULL RIDING

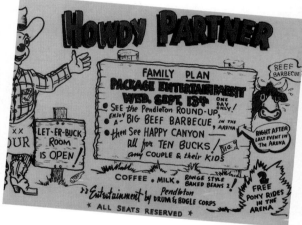

grandstand in 1954 and adding a new north grandstand with bucking chutes in 1957. Other additions over time were new livestock barns, corrals, fencing, and other grounds improvements.

Periodically, the Round-Up performances were televised, giving the show a national audience. Beginning in 1961, a family-style barbecue held in the arena at the conclusion of the first day's show became another popular event. To recognize past accomplishments by cowboy and cowgirl contestants, Round-Up directors and officers, and others who had served the Round-Up faithfully over the years, the association created a Round-Up and Happy Canyon Hall of Fame in 1969.

A key ongoing feature of the Round-Up has been the involvement of Native American tribes from throughout the Northwest. In the Round-Up's first year, the organizers allotted the participating tribes a portion of the grounds adjacent to the arena, where they could set up an encampment of teepees for the duration of the show and meet with friends and family from other tribes. As rodeo historian Joan Burbick has noted, "The temporary village of teepees was a great draw for tourists, but it also provided time and space for Indians to gather, exchange news, feast, and even trade." (Burbick, 2004, 83) Dancing and craft demonstrations, Indian beauty contests, and participation in races and the Westward Ho! Parade added elements to the Pendleton rodeo that few others could boast.

The colorful Happy Canyon Pageant could not exist without the full involvement of Umatilla tribal members. Over time, some Native Americans have expressed ambivalence about taking part in the events of the Round-Up. Yet the annual show has provided a way for members of the Indian and non-Indian communities to participate in each other's worlds and to honor their interconnected histories in the Northwest.

As the Pendleton Round-Up neared its one hundredth anniversary in 2010, it continued to exhibit the qualities that made it the most authentic show on the rodeo circuit.

▲◄ Crowd reacts with horror during the bull riding contest, n.d. *Howdyshell Collection.*

▲ Flier for the first family barbecue in 1961. *Courtesy of the Hill family.*

▲ Wallace Smith's 1925 bucking horse image is featured in the Round-Up's centennial logo.
▶ Randy Magers on "Whizbang," 1980.
Howdyshell Collection.

FACING PAGE ▶ Tyler Fowler, of Alabama, leaves "Broken Bones," 2002. *By Don Cresswell, EO Archive.*

W. K. Stratton, while researching a book on rodeo, spent 2003 visiting major shows around the country and decided that the Round-Up was the "finest rodeo" going. For him, the defining features were its lineage (traditional ties to the real West) and the quality of the competition. In Stratton's words,

> There's something akin to apostolic succession in the [Pendleton] rodeo arena. Today's ropers will be roping against older competitors who roped against ropers who roped against ropers who roped in a cowboy contest against a trail hand or two who once worked the range. . . . More than any other rodeo, the Pendleton Round-Up has an appreciation for its heritage. . . . Sadly, Pendleton is the only place remaining in America where you can see a big-time rodeo in such a sincere setting.

As he watched the grand entry into the Round-Up arena at the beginning of the show, Stratton noted that

> the six hundred or so contestants will include the top-ranked riders, ropers, and bulldoggers on the PRCA [Professional Rodeo Cowboys Association] circuit. . . . The grand thing is that they will be competing here in this old arena in front of people who cling to something indefinable yet important—call it quality—at a time when the rest of the country seems to be willing to flush it away. (Stratton, 2005, 231–233)

Nothing so evokes the commitment to long-standing traditions and the true skills of the cowboy and cowgirl as the grand entry of the Round-Up royalty at the beginning of each show. Preserving a tradition that began in 1934, flagbearers gallop into the arena followed by the queen and

There's an old saying in theater that when an animal steps on stage, something electric goes through the audience: we do not know what will happen. Now, make that a herd of steers, bucking bulls, horses at high speed, and amazing riders. At the Pendleton Round-Up, the energy goes wild from the first event.

—Kim Stafford, 2008

LET 'ER BUCK

her four attendants, who jump their horses over the fence between the track and the infield then race around the arena at full speed to thunderous applause from the spectators. Today's Round-Up royalty honor the authenticity of the Round-Up with their demonstration of fine horsemanship and their timeless western outfits. Generally the daughters of local businessmen and ranchers, they have been riding and honing their horsemanship for most of their lives.

Above all, the Round-Up continues to honor its founding commitment, established by Raley and his young cohorts, that the Round-Up would be a community effort. As Raley wrote in 1911,

The Round-Up is unique. Owned and controlled by the entire business population of the city, it is practically a municipal institution. It is run without profit, for the glory of Pendleton and the old West. . . . There is scarcely a man, woman or child in the City of Pendleton who has not freely done his part in bringing the Round-Up to a wonderful success. . . . The Round-Up has made Pendleton the capital of the great horseback country of the West. (*East Oregonian*, September 14, 1911)

The clarion call of the Pendleton Round-Up, as it continues to celebrate the frontier spirit and traditions one hundred years on, still says it all: Let 'er Buck!

FACING PAGE ◄ Left: Jason Hill, Indian director, attends the 2007 Junior Indian Beauty Contest with Happy Canyon princesses Chelsea Dick (left) and Monece Moses. *By Jim Whiting.*
Right: Father and son tour the arena at the 2007 qualifying rounds, known in Pendleton as "slack." *By Jim Whiting.*

◄▲ Traditional men's war dance, 2007. Left to right: Amos Pond, Stuart Harris, Clifford Stanger, and Randall Melton (in forefront). *EO Archive.*
▲ Annie Johnson on horse with travois in the Westward Ho! Parade, 1960s. *Howdyshell Collection.*
◄ Mennonite fans watch the action in 2007. *By Jim Whiting.*

▲ **Indians stream into the arena for the daily dance performance, 2007.** *By Jim Whiting.*

ROUND-UP REMINISCENCES:
"YOU CAN'T EAT LOUND-UP"

BY ROBERTA CONNER

Today, the Indian Village at Round-Up is the single largest encampment of tribal people locally as well as the largest Indian encampment on the professional rodeo circuit. It brings more tribal people together for more days than any other local event.

▼ Early Indian encampment. *PWM Archive.*

The Pendleton Round-Up has always been a hearkening back to another time. For local Cayuse, Umatilla, and Walla Walla tribal people, the 1910 Round-Up presented an opportunity to do what we had done countless times in our very long history—camp with relatives and friends, feast, gamble, race horses, parade, sing, and dance. The major difference, then as now, was that non-Indians were organizing the event—the directors of the newly formed Round-Up Association. That dynamic and some of the wild and wooliness, somewhat

▲ Informal round-up, pre-1910.

PWM Archive.

romanticized and sometimes authentic, that rears its head during Round-Up has resulted in a variety of tribal responses to Round-Up today. Many tribal families participate and enjoy; some avoid, endure, or are indifferent; and others detest Round-Up time.

Before the days of big livestock trucks and modern horse trailers, local tribesmen would round up wild horses in the spring, summer, and fall. Local Indian wranglers broke the horses to ride or broke them to lead in order to take them home. Eventually non-Indians would gather from miles around to get a good price on sound stock. And there were a lot of horses. In 1890, the local tribes were the largest livestock-producing tribes in the United States; according to

the Commissioner of Indian Affairs, "the Confederated Tribes surpassed all other tribes in the possession of horses." At tribal round-ups he witnessed, the late Pendleton saddle maker Duff Severe recalled seeing every color of horse known to man and a few that were novel combinations. According to our oral histories, the rigorous, festive, and sometimes rowdy tribal round-ups and our annual Fourth of July celebration, including games, parades, races, and dances, were inspiration for the Pendleton Round-Up. In the earliest years, some of the Round-Up bucking and wild horses were cayuses.

When the Pendleton Round-Up began in 1910, one hundred and five years had passed since Lewis and Clark arrived overland in the interior Northwest. Only sixty-three years earlier, our kinsmen had killed the Whitman missionaries, with whom we had many problems. Warnings from local Hudson's Bay employees suggested the tribes should be wary of these American missionaries who had designs on our country. Tensions had accumulated over the way the Whitmans treated some Indians and over Whitman aid to Oregon Trail immigrants who brought with them diseases to which the tribes had no immunity. Worst of all, Dr. Whitman seemed unable to cure diseased Indian patients when almost entire Cayuse villages were dying.

Only fifty-five years before Round-Up was launched, the Treaty of 1855 had reduced the lands we had the right to live on by 92 percent. Only thirty-three years had passed since the Nez Perce War of 1877, and only twenty-five years since the Joseph band returned from exile in the Oklahoma Indian Territory, where more than a hundred relatives were buried. Thirty years before Round-Up started, the federal policy of dividing tribally owned lands into individual Indian allotments began. The policy resulted in Congress opening up 140,000 acres of the Umatilla Reservation for "settlement" and the Pendleton Notch Act authorizing the sale of tribal lands to the city of Pendleton, which had been built partly on the reservation. Twenty years before the first Pendleton show, Indian agents were still issuing forms granting permission for an Indian to be absent from the respective agency to travel elsewhere, after the Indian disclosed the destination, duration, and purpose of the travel. In the decade immediately preceding the first Round-Up, Indians were still moving onto the reservation as encroachments ended any chance of living off reservation.

Wounds of forced assimilation and loss of land, freedom, and rights were still fresh in 1910. But for tribal people who camped together in great numbers at Cayuse, Johnson Creek, and the July Grounds, Round-Up was a kind of blessing. It was one more celebration where they could remember a different way of life, when they camped together with neighboring tribes and relatives at various camas prairies. It was a time to remember living peaceably.

Today, our encampment at Round-Up is the single largest encampment of tribal people locally as well as the largest Indian encampment on the professional rodeo circuit. While we have many traditional events and multi-day dance

▲ Indian Village and adjacent parking lot, 1930s. *Low Collection.*

contests that draw huge numbers of tribal people, Round-Up brings more tribal people together for more days than any other local event. Perhaps this is because we are fond of carrying on our ancestors' roles in the early Round-Ups, or because we are reminding ourselves of our universe when we used to camp in large gatherings frequently, or because we simply enjoy the modern festivities.

Cayuse tribal member Anna Minthorn Wannassay, who had participated in dramatic arts at the Carlisle Institute in Pennsylvania, helped Roy Raley revise the script for the Happy Canyon night pageant to include Indians. They began the pageant by depicting our traditional way of life: deer hunters, women working hides, digging roots, and grinding foods, the end of berry harvest, arrival of tribal neighbors, and a gathering for a wedding and subsequent trading. Living by the annual seasonal gathering cycles was still common when the Round-Up started.

When my mother, Leah Conner, received a Happy Canyon Appreciation Award in 1993, she said that her elders enjoyed participating in the village scene of Happy Canyon because they wanted to show others that our people had once lived very differently, in peace in our lands, where there was great abundance and happiness. In the early days

Recently, at the age of four, one of my nieces watched the whole Happy Canyon show for the first time. At the end of the evening she said to me, "Auntie, you have to do something. They're killing Indians and taking our land."

—Roberta Conner, 2008

of Round-Up, many Indian families used that week for salmon harvest in Weiser, Idaho, or at Celilo Falls on the Columbia. Yakama visitors would come to Round-Up rich in fresh huckleberries from Mount Adams and bring other fresh fruit as gifts to hometown campers. For many years, successful fisherman would arrive at Round-Up on Friday and Saturday with salmon to sell. Today, some tribal members still go fishing instead of coming to Round-Up, but the fishing mecca at Celilo is no more.

As a little girl, Warm Springs tribal member Nettie Queahpama Shawaway, born in 1900, remembered when her older sister Mae and her husband were headed by wagon from Simnasho to catch the train to Pendleton to go to one of the earliest Round-Ups. She was so excited at the prospect of going that she ran and asked her mother if she could go. Her mother told her to find her horse and get ready to go to the mountains to get food for winter. "She told me, 'you can't eat Lound-Up,'" Nettie recalled. (In Ichishkiin or Columbia River Sahaptin, there are no "r" sounds, so tribal members speaking English as a second language often pronounced *r*'s as *l*'s.) Nettie said she stumbled around looking for her horse and crying "like somebody died" because she was so sad she couldn't go. Her mother eventually acquiesced. Millie Queahpama, Nettie's mother, danced in the Round-Up arena with her daughters after she was honored for being the oldest Indian participating in the 1973 Round-Up, at the age of 105. Millie died in 1975 at the age of 107. Nettie lived to be nearly 102.

When asked about Nez Perce saddle bronc champ Jackson Sundown, Nettie remembered being afraid of him. The way she described it, he was an old married man and she was a teenager. Eye contact, let alone conversation, would have been improper.

The story of Jackson Sundown's 1916 Pendleton championship in the saddle bronc contest has become a Western legend. Part of Sundown's renown is because he and African-American bronc rider George Fletcher broke the color barrier in rodeo at Pendleton. Other aspects of his fame derive from being a survivor of the Nez Perce War of 1877 and from winning his championship at the age of fifty-three.

Many Indian cowboys after Sundown have competed and won at the Round-Up. Our champions at Pendleton

▲ From left: Cleda, Millie, and Sybil Queahpama and Darlene Mitchell, Warm Springs, ca. 1973. *Howdyshell Collection.*

As long as I can remember, we always moved down to Round-Up. For me it is a time for reunion of my family. They all come and camp and get to see each other. It's a good place to renew old acquaintances and make new friends. When people talk about the Round-Up, we invite them to come and see it and camp.

—Cecelia Bearchum, 2008

include Colville's Alex Dick, who won the bull riding title in 1946. Shoat Webster, Shawnee, is renowned as a timed-event champion of the 1940s and 1950s and is in the Round-Up and Happy Canyon Hall of Fame. Joe Chase, Mandan-Hidatsa, won the saddle bronc contest in 1960. Kenny McLean, Okanogan, was the saddle bronc champ in 1962 and 1963. Bob Gottfriedson, Shushwap-Okanogan, won the saddle bronc title in 1977.

Two local tribal cowboys, ropers and bulldoggers who were brothers to Clarence Burke—Bobby and Richard Burke—performed exhibition roping in Pendleton as well as on stages from Seattle to San Francisco. In addition to bulldogging, steer roping, and saddle bronc riding, Lucien Williams did trick and fancy roping and riding. Other local tribal cowboys included calf ropers Charlie Wocatsie and Victor Williams, steer roper Wilkins Williams, and bronc rider and wild horse racer Narcisse McKay. Local tribal Northwest Bucking contestants included Jesse Jones Sr., Bill Elk, and Walter Bonifer, as well as LaMose, William, Lee, Pinto, and Jack Edmo from the Shoshone-Bannock tribes and Colville's Louis Friedlander. Mose Sam competed in the bull riding in the 1940s, followed by Colville bull riders Larry Condon, Dave and Shawn Best, and Gary Sam. More recently, timed-event contestants included Bryson Liberty, Victor Williams, Summer Burke, and Jay Minthorn along with bronc riders Jasper Shippentower and Leonard Cree. Wild horse racing teams from the area included the names Minthorn, Conner, and Jones, as well as Smith and Wewa from Warm Springs, Edmo from Fort Hall, Benson from Yakama, and Meanus from Celilo—cowboys who camped and rodeoed for decades around the Northwest as well as at Pendleton.

If there were a Round-Up and Happy Canyon Hall of Fame for Indian horse racing, legacies of the Bronson, Jones, Minthorn, Burke, Motanic, Weathers, Johnson, Wocatsie, Sohappy, Williams, Ives, Charley, Cleveland, Tilloquots, Wallahee, Dick, Saluskin, Derouche, Mancha, Marcellay, Moses, Pakootas, Miller, Scott, Frank, Heath, Suppah, Benson, Squiemphen, Gottfriedson, Marchand, Teton, and many other families would be there. In the first decade of Round-Ups, Gilbert Minthorn, Otis Halfmoon, and James Ghangrow drove teams of four horses in the dangerous stagecoach races, and Gilbert was still a contender in

◀ Bobby Burke, steer roper.
Low Collection.

◀ Vince Williams, calf roper, 1953.
Howdyshell Collection.

▼ Art Motanic competes in the 1962 hide race.
Howdyshell Collection.

The smoke from the Indian tepees makes

a line straight as a pencil against the sky.

—Wallace Smith, 1925

▶ **White (on horseback) with unidentified Indian woman.** *Low Collection.*

▼ **Indian encampment, ca. 1940. At left is the gambling pit where the Indians who gathered at the Round-Up played the stick game, cards, dice, and other games of chance.** *PWM Archive.*

FACING PAGE ▶ **Indian encampment, ca. 1940.** *PWM Archive.*

No. 2382 UMATILLA CHIEF AND SQUAW AT ROUND UP PENDLETON ORE.

LIFE AT THE ROUND-UP

▲ R. C. Bishop greets Mamie and Minnie Patawa in 1923. *PWM Archive.*

▶ From left: Walla Walla headman Poker Jim, R. C. Bishop, and Cap Sumkin, 1920s. *PWM Archive.*

While there are many chiefs in tribal history over the past two hundred years, "chief" is an introduced term meaning "highest rank or leader." Influential tribal men such as village headmen were historically selected from among the sons of former headmen or their kin.

this race in the 1930s. Older local tribal folks will recall Jim White, father of Margaret White and grandfather to 1948 Round-Up queen Virginia Wilkinson and her siblings, Jimmy, Rosalie, Pauline, Anna Jane (Janie), and Leona, who had winning racing teams that traveled to Walla Walla, Yakima, and the Willamette Valley. Today, the number of horses that tribal people bring to Round-Up is a fraction of the number we used to bring when our people filled the arena for the serpentine on horseback. The number of tribal horse owners is on the rise, however, as economics permit and as a resurgence of interest in horses takes hold. Unfortunately, even if we had more horses to bring to town,

Round-Up has very few places to board them now. Instead, pickups and semis park where we used to play stick games and tether horses.

Perhaps one of the great legacies of Round-Up is that one week a year, we have permission to once again be a little fierce. We can even be scary, in some scenes in Happy Canyon and in full-on, ferociously competitive racing and rodeoing. As a child in the Westward Ho! Parade, I can remember non-Indian children being afraid of our tribal men riding through the parade singing tribal songs with hand drums while others were war-whooping and making their horses dance and prance. What most modern parade-goers don't realize is that our people historically had war parades and memorial processions that demonstrated a show of force as well as horsemanship, wealth, and distinction. I joined the Happy Canyon cast at an early age, and I remember all the yelling, war-whooping, and skilled riders on fast horses. It was a unique experience for me since we didn't live that way every day, despite the common stereotypes of the time. I am certain it was just as unique for white onlookers who didn't know Indians in their daily lives or who knew only Indians who didn't act as we did in the raiding scene of the show.

In the early years of the Round-Up, headmen like Gilbert Minthorn, Poker Jim, Cap Sumkin, Uma Sumkin, Allen Patawa, Jim Kanine, Paul Showaway, Jim Badroads, Amos Pond, and Willie Wocatsie knew that being in town for a week without grazing and fishing or hunting would require provisions. Our leaders negotiated for hay, beef rations, potatoes, and watermelons, as well as plenty of room to camp, a pit for cooking, space for dancing, and room for the hundreds of horses that accompanied tribal camps. The liaisons to the tribes were former Indian agent Major Lee Moorhouse and Roy and Chauncey Bishop. The latter two had established tribal relationships through their family's Indian trade blanket design and manufacturing business.

As Pendleton was readying for its first big Round-Up in 1910, it wasn't clear how many tribal people would participate. Bishop family oral history recalls that the employees of the Pendleton Woolen Mill, between the railroad tracks and

◀ From left, tribal singers Clarence Burke, George Spino, and Willie Wocatsie.

Howdyshell Collection.

▲ Allen Patawa, 1936. *Howdyshell Collection.*

Poker Jim 1915

"MAJ. MOORHOUSE LEADING INDIAN PARADE THE ROUND UP"
FOTO BY OGALLEN PENDLETON ORE N036

▲▲ **Indians perform the serpentine in the arena, 1920s.** *By Burns in Low Collection.*

▲ **Major Lee Moorhouse (left) and Poker Jim lead the Westward Ho! Parade, 1915.**

By O. G. Allen in Helm Collection.

the Umatilla River, heard a commotion, saw a cloud of dust, and realized that the enormous cavalcade outside was the tribal response to the invitation to join Round-Up. Then and now, tribal individuals and families decide each year whether they will participate in Round-Up and to what degree.

Multigenerational Indian and non-Indian friendships and partnerships are part of the Round-Up legacy. Old-time directors were ranchers and farmers who leased Indian land and knew the individuals and their families. Back then Indians had cuff accounts at Hamley's and went to market in Pendleton every Saturday. Businesses in town appreciated

our retail trade. The Bishop family worked with local tribal people to provide Pendleton robes and shawls designed to our preferences. In later years, at the end of harvest, Indian and non-Indian men went to town and bought a shave, shower, and haircut, and something cold to drink. Personal relationships between Indians and our neighbors went a long way in making the Round-Up experience work.

New Round-Up traditions were launched. Poker Jim became the first Round-Up chief. After Chauncey Bishop was killed in a hunting accident, Poker Jim introduced the dance contest in 1927 at the Round-Up grounds as a tribal gesture to honor his passing. The Bishop family responded by providing blankets for the contest winners, a tradition that continues today. Poker Jim's friendship with the Bishop family led directly to the tradition of Saturday morning contest dances. One of Poker Jim's sons, Clarence Burke,

LE-LOI-NIN
(WELCOME)

▲ ◀ A traditional welcome sign greets visitors to the Indian Village. *Hall of Fame Collection.*

▲ Jim Kanine, Walla Walla headman. *OHS Collection, CN 011092.*

◀ William Oregon Jones. *OHS Collection, CN 012683.*

WILLIAM O. JONES & JIM KANINE

55

UMATILLAS & ROUND-UP COURT

served as Round-Up chief for more than five decades and continued the family friendship with later generations of the Bishop family, just as his son William Burke did later.

The rodeo queen tradition started at Pendleton, and Pendleton had the first Indian rodeo queen. In 1924, the Indian Beauty Pageant winner was Esther Motanic, and newspapers across the country carried photos of Esther, Minnie Patawa, and Melissa Parr. In 1926, following a lineup of cowgirls and movie stars, Esther Motanic was the first Indian Round-Up queen. Instead of princesses, Esther had two attendants who accompanied her, Minnie Patawa and Louise Martin. Esther wore her regalia in keeping with 1920s style, with her beaded latigo belt low on her hips instead of around her waist.

The gold standard for the women's Indian Beauty Pageant was set by tribal member Melissa Red Hawk Chapman Parr, who won the contest five times (1925, 1926, 1927, 1928, and 1930) and was the second Indian Round-Up

◄ Melissa Parr, ca. 1927. *Howdyshell Collection.*

▲▲ Round-Up court of 1952. From left, Martina Quaempts, Bernice Ryan, queen Leah Conner, Diana McKay, and Audrey Blackhawk. *Howdyshell Collection.*

▲ Chauncey Bishop in the Indian Village with (from left) Melissa Parr, Eliza Bill, Mamie Patawa, and Minnie Patawa, ca. 1925. *Howdyshell Collection.*

queen in 1932, with an all-Indian court of four princesses. In 1948, Virginia Wilkinson was queen with six Indian princesses. Leah Conner, 1952, and Diana McKay, 1953, were Round-Up queens with four Indian princesses. These five women and the princesses who comprised their courts were stunning representatives for what had become the world-famous Pendleton show. Later three tribal members would also serve as princesses on Round-Up courts: Toni Minthorn, Debra Weathers, and Kylie Bronson.

During Round-Up today, visitors will find modern entrepreneurs outfitted as cowboys and tribal administrators camping in teepees. This is not unnatural, as many local folks, Indian and non-Indian, still work livestock, use horses to hunt and to trail ride, and use teepees to camp at

▲ Stephen Williams, winner of the Indian dance contest, 1983. *Howdyshell Collection.*

▶ Round-Up co-chiefs prepare to lead Westward Ho! Parade in 1950. From left, chiefs Clarence Burke and Charlie Johnson of the Walla Walla and chief Andrew Allen of the Cayuse. *OHS Collection, CN 010570.*

The Indians are proud people and like to do a show of who they are. In the early days, that was why you saw them dressed so elegantly, both the men and the women.

—Antone Minthorn, 2008

58

other times of the year in other locations. The Pendleton Round-Up can take credit for the fact that some tribal families, who camp or parade only during Round-Up, continue the annual practice of getting new teepee poles, mending teepees, teaching youngsters how to put up teepees, and readying horses just for Round-Up.

Tribal people are heartened by recent changes respectful of our Indian culture. The announcer for the Indian participants in the arena is now a tribal spokesperson, not the rodeo announcer, and he narrates our perspective, our story, in our voice, occasionally injecting some of our tribal language. The Indians' daily appearance in the arena used to be scheduled after the popular bull riding. The grandstand would empty for bathroom breaks and beer refills as if it were intermission, and little knowledge of our story was imparted. Timing our appearance to follow bull riding continued even after a bull jumped the high bull-pen fence into the midst of hundreds of tribal folks in full regalia who were waiting to enter the arena and largely trapped in the area by locked cyclone fence gates. Then the bull riding was split into two sections, and the tribes took center stage between them. The altered schedule helps to keep an audience for our presentation on the infield and on the track.

The Indian experience of the Round-Up continues to change. While Indian fishermen no longer bring fresh salmon to sell during Round-Up, the resurgence of tribal self-definition is evidenced in the bustling tribal vending area in Roy Raley Park, intended to showcase local Plateau tribal handcrafted works, and the reintroduction of old-style, locally specific tribal dances that occur daily in the same park. Now tribal and non-Indian narrators help Happy Canyon audiences understand the history portrayed in the popular night show instead of relying on silhouettes that theoretically signaled each phase of the pageant's Indian and non-Indian portions.

Behind the scenes, there have been unpleasant truths. Lack of sanitary facilities and poor camping conditions caused tribal people to threaten a boycott in the 1930s. In those days, the horses were all tied and fed along the riverbank, and straw was spread in teepees and all around the horses. Fearing disease-carrying flies, local tribal community leaders enlisted Dr. Louis J. Feves to represent their interests. Dr. Feves had many Indian patients and attended

Indians wore animal hides or robes and blankets of their own manufacture before white settlers arrived in the West. The wool cloth blanket, with its color, traditional designs, and warmth, largely replaced the older robes by the end of the nineteenth century.

◄ **Eddie Bad Eagle of Brockett, Alberta, Canada, at 1981 dance contest.** *PWM Archive.*
▼ **Silk souvenir scarf.** *Hall of Fame Collection.*

to the ill or injured in jail. He knew firsthand the problems the local Indians faced during Round-Up, including police brutality during arrest and incarceration and selective law enforcement against intoxicated Indians.

As public intoxication escalated in the years after World War II, racial prejudice became a routine part of the annual event for many tribal families. Another potential tribal boycott was rumored after the rise of red power in the 1970s and after leading Rodeo Cowboys Association competitors threatened to boycott Round-Up in 1974–1975 unless purses were raised in keeping with those offered by other

PAGEANTRY

The Pendleton Round-Up was always a place of excitement because it was a great rodeo with lots of cowboys and Indians. For the tribal people, I think a big part of the appeal was being a part of the pageantry, of getting ready for the horse parades and the war-dancing in the arena. It was also when kids could earn some spending money for their performances. A big part of the Round-Up was the excitement of the horse races by "Indians camped on the grounds" (echo of the rodeo announcer). Moving to the Round-Up was fun for kids in the old days (the 1940s) because we used to have to ride the horses from the reservation to town. Some of us lived a long way out and it could take most of the day, but we made a big day of it. The excitement also included the Indian Village as it blossomed overnight into a bustling place of business, and the broken hearts when the village vanished, your new friends were gone, and the Round-Up was over. The Happy Canyon Pageant, in the old days, was beautiful and moving. I think this was because the tribal people still retained much of the old culture and regalia, and thereby, the pride.

My mother ensured that her daughters were dressed to perfection when they performed at the Happy Canyon tribal ceremonials; the Indian men likewise.

—Antone Minthorn, Chairman of the Confederated Tribes of the Umatilla Indian Reservation, 2008

▲ **Ethel Jackson, Indian Beauty Contest winner, 1988.** *Howdyshell Collection.*

▲ ▶ **Top right: Detail from border of souvenir scarf.** *Hall of Fame Collection.*

▶ **Right: Lillian Picard in the 2007 Junior Indian Beauty Contest, 2007.** *By Jim Whiting.*

▶ ▶ **Far right: Walla Walla chief Carl Sampson and horse in traditional regalia at the 2007 Round-Up.** *By Jim Whiting.*

shows on the circuit. Neither boycott took place. Facility improvements quelled dissatisfaction enough for tribal families to continue participating, and the Round-Up Association addressed the cowboys' issues.

It is important to recognize that in 1910, we had no tribal government, and the local Indian agent still had more say over our activities than any tribal member wished. During the early years of Round-Up, tribal adults had to pass competency examinations given at the Indian Agency in order to conduct their own farming and ranching business. By 1951, we had adopted our tribal constitution and elected our first Board of Trustees, our tribal governing body. The 1960s civil rights movement was occurring while our historic loss of lands was being argued before the Indian Claims Commission.

◀▼ **Clarence Burke presides over the Junior Indian Beauty Contest, 1982.** *By David Quaempts in Tamástslikt Collection.*

▼ **From left, William Burke, C. M. Bishop III, and Jesse Jones at the 1998 Junior Indian Beauty Contest.** *By Lou Levy in PWM Archive.*

CLOCKWISE FROM TOP LEFT:

▲▲ Senator Barack Obama, campaigning in Pendleton in May 2008, meets Happy Canyon princesses Brittany Cline (left) and Tyera Pete. *Courtesy of the Obama Presidential Campaign.*

▶▲ Mabel Bishop presents a bouquet to Caroline Motanic, Indian Beauty Contest winner, 1952. *Howdyshell Collection.*

▶ Thelma Parr (left), winner of the 1947 Indian Beauty Contest, with her mother, Melissa Parr. *OHS Collection, CN 013363.*

▲ Decorative horse mask, n.d. *Tamástslikt Collection.*

In the 1950s and 1960s Westward Ho! Parades, my grandparents tried to put all of us grandchildren on wagons or horses so that we would not be tempted to pick up the coins that white parade-goers threw at the feet of Indians. In 1985, one young tribal member posted signs on the first wagon full of Indians in the Westward Ho! Parade that read "Please Do Not Throw Money—Respect Indian Parade Participants." He followed the wagon on foot to discourage coin-throwing. In 1993 the sign-maker, Donald Sampson, became Chairman of the Board of Trustees of the Confederated Tribes of Umatilla.

Indians have always been a big part of the draw for Round-Up. Five times in a hundred years, the ambassadors promoting the show were all-Indian rodeo courts. Nine specific traditions of Round-Up and Happy Canyon pay tribute to the dignity, beauty, strength, and pageantry of our tribal culture. The signature aspects that tribal people provide at Round-Up are the teepee encampment; contestants for Junior and Senior Indian Beauty Pageants; applicants to serve as Happy Canyon princesses (since 1955); the daily tribal procession around the arena track; the chiefs near the front of the Westward Ho! Parade; the lone leader in

Happy Canyon who dresses in what we call "slick style," rides bareback throughout the show, and closes the show bearing the United States flag; the organizers, drummers and singers, dancers, whipman and whipwoman (who maintain order in tribal gatherings), and judges for the Saturday dance contest; and the thrilling Indian relay races. The consistent participation of our people in these events at Round-Up symbolizes our commitment to the event. Substantial preparation is necessary for us to camp in town for a week each year and to appear daily in elegant regalia with horses bedecked in magnificent trappings. Most of the bigger rodeos in the Columbia River region, including Lewiston, Ellensburg, Yakima, and Walla Walla, once had substantial Indian participation. Today, the only consistently prominent presence of Indian tribes is at Pendleton. The role of the tribes and the accommodations pursuant to our presence are an on-going negotiation.

Trains used to deliver visitors from throughout the United States to Pendleton's Main Street to attend Round-Up. People still travel from all over the U.S. and abroad to come to the Round-Up, though Pendleton is no longer served by passenger trains. Our tribal people have always been and continue to be hospitable to visitors. The Confederated Tribes built Wildhorse Resort and the Tamástslikt Cultural Institute to be even more welcoming. We are integral to the Round-Up, to Pendleton, and to the region. It is important for us to show anyone attending who we are. We have survived. We have not vanished. Nor have we been permanently banished to the confines of the reservation.

Historically, our people came from a position of wealth, which we maintained through the treaty times. We are only now beginning to recover from the poverty and prejudice that we endured from the 1850s to the 1950s. Our people's community spirit and spiritual beliefs sustained us through it all. Round-Up is part of our lives. Round-Up and the tribes' partnership will continue to evolve.

Round-Up and Happy Canyon are in my blood. My great-grandfather Spokane Jim was a horse trader and gambler. His sister Sisaawipam was a saddle and horsehair rope and cincha maker. My great-grandmother Wyassus loved to camp at Round-Up, visit, and eat cold watermelons in the hot weather. In the 1930s my grandmother Elsie and her sister Vera rode in the arena serpentine with my uncles as

▲◀ Etta Conner presents a Pendleton robe to President Dwight D. Eisenhower. Tom McCall, future Oregon governor, at left. *Howdyshell Collection.*
▲ Melissa Parr's beaded headband with medallion and reverse swastika design, a traditional motif for whirling winds. *Tamástslikt Collection.*
◀ Mariah Watchman, winner of the Indian Beauty Contest, 2007. *By Jim Whiting.*

The men's dances are a profusion of feathers, furs, bells, mirrors, and streaming bustles in intense, driving motion. Some dancers wear traditional costumes, while others experiment with new designs and Day-Glo colors.

▶ Boys' and men's dance contest, all styles, mid 1970s. Dancers include Toby and Zack Patrick, Gene Shippentower, and Roger Amerman. *Howdyshell Collection.*

▶ ▼ Chelsea J. Farrow in the 2007 Junior Indian Beauty Pageant. Contestants are judged on their poise, strength of character, and family regalia. *By Jim Whiting.*

toddlers in front and back of their saddles. My great-uncle William Jones was a Round-Up chief. Grandpa Gilbert performed the Happy Canyon silhouettes for more than two decades. Uncles Cece and Norman and cousins John, James, and Tom depicted the Indian warrior in Happy Canyon who is shot and dies dramatically in the fall over the second-level rocks. My mother was queen in 1952 and my aunt was queen in 1948, and both portrayed the young Indian bride in Happy Canyon, succeeded by six of my cousins and three nieces up through today. Uncle Norman raced horses in the Indian relay, hide, free-for-all, and wild horse races and provided the horse for Mom's queen duty. Many of my cousins have won the American Indian Beauty contests.

Two nieces have been Happy Canyon princesses. Most significantly, my family is only one example of the many multigenerational tribal families faithful to this degree of Round-Up involvement.

In the past fifty-three years, I've missed only a couple of Round-Ups. Like many my age, I began camping with my grandparents at Round-Up. I appreciate fine livestock and enjoy seeing all the tribal relatives who come home for Round-Up. I recognize the economic opportunity visitors bring. Most of all, I welcome the chance to remind our neighbors and visitors that we are still here in our homeland, protecting the gifts from the Creator and taking care of one another.

▼ Louie Dick as the lone leader in the Happy Canyon Pageant, a role he first performed in 1987 and continued through the 1990s.

Courtesy of Louie and Marie Dick.

AT THE BEGINNING

BY MICHAEL BALES

Roy Raley and a group of young businessmen organized

the 1910 frontier extravaganza that grew into the world-famous

Round-Up. From the start, Raley had big ideas of what the

frontier exhibition could do for Pendleton.

▼ **Roy Raley and his grandchildren enjoy a Round-Up parade.** *Howdyshell Collection.*

ROY RALEY

His friends called him "Prince." A banjo-playing attorney, he was known for his dramatic flair, love of celebrations large and small, and gregarious nature. Looking back on Roy Raley's life, it seems fitting that he was born the day Pendleton officially became a city in 1880. No one has done more to make Pendleton synonymous with rodeos and Wild West pageantry.

Raley conceived the ideas for both the Round-Up and the Happy Canyon Pageant and is often called the father of both events. But his penchant

BURRELL

"THE ROUND-UP"
1911.

PRES. ROY RALEY OF THE "ROUND-UP" AND GOV. WEST LEADING THE
GRAND PARADE, GOV. WEST RIDEING THE PRIZE SADDLE

▲ Round-Up president Roy Raley (left) and Oregon governor Oswald West lead the 1911 parade. *By J. B. Burrell in Helm Collection.*

Roy Raley's father arrived via the Oregon Trail in 1862. But Raley knew that for the hundreds of Indians who camped in teepees at the first Round-Ups, the story of the West began much earlier.

for finding and organizing the right people to execute his ideas was his real genius.

Stories conflict about where Raley disclosed his concept for the Round-Up in 1910. One book says it came during an early summer camping trip in the Blue Mountains with Mark Moorhouse, who would become the event's exhibition manager. Another account claims it happened in Portland over a lunch that Raley and Moorhouse had with four other Pendleton men. No matter. After the idea had been refined in subsequent meetings and legal documents drawn up, Raley announced on July 29, 1910, that the Round-Up would be held that fall. Of the 500 shares of stock issued to raise money, he alone sold one share each to 246 people.

Raley was the Round-Up's first president but stepped aside after the second show in 1911. Two years later he developed the concept for Happy Canyon, a popular night show that today tells the story of the West from the perspectives of both white settlers and Native Americans. It debuted in 1913. Raley also organized the American Indian Beauty contest, which is still held during the Round-Up. When the grandstands burned in August 1940, it was Raley who quickly raised money to have them rebuilt in time for that year's show.

In a speech to Portland Rose Festival officials in 1924, Raley said: "When the band starts to play, I start down the street—and I usually find many others doing the same thing. It has been a great pleasure to attempt to analyze the various forms of entertainment . . . to find the elements in them which attract the crowds and then to try to verify my conclusions by using these elements in my own shows."

Born into one of Pendleton's most prominent families, Raley served as city attorney, school board member, and president of the Oregon State Bar. In 1969, he was the first person chosen for the Round-Up's Hall of Fame. Raley also established Pendleton's park system, and Round-Up Park, adjacent to the arena, was renamed in his honor.

It was not unusual for early risers to see Raley on his knees planting flowers and shrubs in Roy Raley Park or Til Taylor Park, named for his successor as Round-Up president. Raley died in 1954 at age seventy-five.

TILLMAN TAYLOR

The dusty history of the West is replete with people whose personas glimmer long after death. In Oregon, few have the enduring luster of Tillman D. Taylor, long-time sheriff of

▶ Til Taylor, Round-Up president, ca. 1915.

By L. Moorhouse in Low Collection.

"Til Taylor"

among them armed robbers and murderers. Descended from an Oregon pioneer family and raised on a wheat farm, he was hired as a deputy sheriff in 1898 and elected sheriff in 1902. In the rest of his eighteen-year tenure, he usually ran unopposed. He helped organize the first Round-Up in 1910 and served as director of livestock. The next year he was named president, and he continued in that role until July 25, 1920, when he was fatally shot as he tried to stop a jailbreak. He was fifty-four.

Taylor's death shocked the region. Nine years later, in a ceremony that drew hundreds of people, a twelve-foot-high bronze statue of Taylor atop his horse was unveiled in a park that still bears Taylor's name. Created by famed sculptor Alexander Phimister Proctor, the sculpture was so large that its head had to be removed to fit through tunnels while en route from Portland, where it had been brought by ship from Europe.

Umatilla County and president of the Round-Up for eight of its formative years. Nicknamed "Til," he looked and lived the part of imposing frontier lawman and charismatic civic leader. All these decades later, it's hard to imagine a man better suited to keep order in a rough-and-tumble place on the prairie and to leverage its cowboy ways into an annual event of international acclaim.

Taylor stood out. A large man with an easy smile, he dressed smartly in western attire, including a wide-brimmed Stetson hat. His erect posture astride a sorrel horse made a striking image as he led the Westward Ho! Parade or circled the Round-Up arena. In a 1970 book about Taylor, writer Ernest L. Crockatt said that while the sheriff's "physical makeup was dominating, there was an inner sureness reflected in his outward appearance." The *East Oregonian* wrote that he had "personal charm and sincerity of manner that won enduring friendships. . . . On countless occasions his skill and daring stood between the peace of this county and the acts of lawless men." (*East Oregonian*, 1929)

Taylor was considered perhaps the shrewdest sheriff in the Northwest, solving many crimes and tracking down through the wilds of eastern Oregon many a lawbreaker,

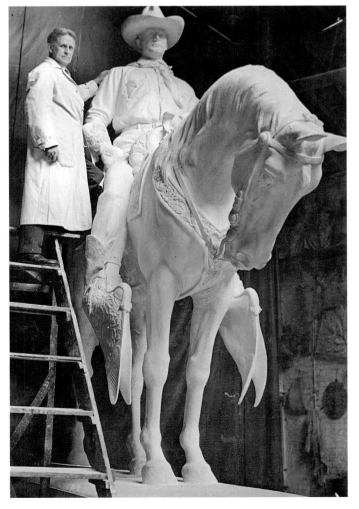

◄▲ President Til Taylor, ca. 1915. *Helm Collection.*

◄ Alexander Phimister Proctor with plaster model of his Til Taylor statue. *By G. Champroux in OHS Collection, bb003692.*

▲ Bronze statue of Til Taylor, Pendleton, 1930s. *OHS Collection, OrHi 93170.*

▼ Beaded gauntlet gloves worn by Til Taylor. *Tamástslikt Collection.*

"Hank" Collins worked closely with R. E. "Chloe" Chloupeck to direct the show's action, setting up the ramrod mechanics of the fastest, best organized rodeo in the world.

—E. N. Boylen,
Episode of the West, 1975

▶ Henry Collins, arena director, ca. 1919.

By L. Moorhouse in Low Collection.

HENRY COLLINS

No one running the Round-Up encountered more highs and lows than Henry W. Collins. His twelve-year tenure as president, the longest in the event's history, began a week after his predecessor, Sheriff Tillman D. Taylor, was murdered in 1920. It ended during the Depression with the Round-Up close to financial ruin. Many of the years in between were among the most dazzling that Pendleton has seen.

During the 1920s, the rest of the country discovered the Round-Up because of unprecedented publicity in newspapers and magazines in the East, much of it centered around cowgirls, and a book and a Hollywood movie, each titled *Let 'er Buck.* Under Collins' direction, events were added, including chariot races and wild cow milking. Attendance swelled to a record fifty-six thousand in 1926.

The Round-Up donated thousands of dollars for civic causes, including parks.

"Henry had a natural administrative ability and was a superb showman, organizer, and director of the course of events," wrote E. N. "Pink" Boylen in his 1975 history of the Round-Up's first fifty years. Boylen, who was events and arena director for many years, described Collins as "a perfectionist and expected others to be the same."

With the rest of the nation, the Round-Up suffered financially after Wall Street crashed in 1929. Collins saw crowds shrink and debts mount, despite budget cuts. Businessmen who had backed the Round-Up financially from its inception were called upon to pay off loans.

For Collins, who had been an integral part of the Round-Up since it began, it was an unhappy ending. He resigned in October 1932 and moved to Portland for

business reasons. Four other key officials also stepped down. The Round-Up's survival looked bleak.

The Round-Up recovered along with the rest of the nation, and Collins attended the show most years until his death in 1970 at age eighty-six. The successful grain business executive was Grand Marshal of the Westward Ho! Parade in 1964. At the time, he said: "The Pendleton Round-Up is the greatest community show on earth. I'll always call Pendleton home. Here I spent the twenty-five happiest years of my life. No wonder I love to come back. Let 'er Buck!"

▲ President Henry Collins (at right) circles the Round-Up arena, ca. 1925. *Low Collection.*

I ▲ **Jesse Stahl rides "Grave Digger."** *By L. Moorhouse in OHS Collection, OrHi 12526.*

THE GREAT BUCKING CONTESTS

BY MICHAEL BALES

Unanswered even now is whether racial bias rather than skill dictated the controversial outcome. In the end, the crowd chose one champion, and the judges chose another.

▼ Jackson Sundown on "Angel," 1916.

By L. Moorhouse in Howdyshell Collection.

1911 BUCKING CONTEST

In an era of stark racial divides, it is remarkable that the Round-Up's most famous contest happened at all. The year was 1911. Segregation was rampant, and memories of Indian wars and slavery lingered. Viewed through the lens of today's world, the story line smacks of something Hollywood might contrive for maximum ratings: three cowboys—one white, one black, and one Nez Perce survivor of U.S. Army bullets—competing to become champion bronc-buster. But the Round-Up had been an open affair from its start a year earlier, and the usually strong grip of prejudice loosened long enough for

Jackson Sundown on "Angel" Pendleton.Ore

©Lee Moorhouse 1916.
Winning the Championship of the World

John Spain, the white contestant,

had won the wild horse race that

year. George Fletcher, the black

cowboy, had learned how to

tame horses from the Umatilla

Indians. The Native American,

Jackson Sundown, had been

wounded by U.S. soldiers in 1877.

the historic competition to take place. Unanswered even now, however, is whether racial bias rather than skill dictated the controversial outcome.

None of the fifteen thousand who crowded into the arena on an autumn Saturday knew they were about to watch a contest that is still the centerpiece of Round-Up lore, or that they collectively would become a key character in the story's dramatic conclusion. In the end, the crowd chose one champion, and the judges chose another.

It was the final day of events, and a ticket line had formed on Main Street before seven in the morning. Prices ranged from $1.50 for box seats to 75 cents for bleachers and 50 cents for anyone viewing from horseback. The skies threatened rain off and on, but this didn't deter the crowd. The 1911 *East Oregonian*, with typical exuberance, described the spectators as "wildly enthusiastic fans of the frontier" who "packed themselves into one mammoth solid mass of humanity."

The crowd had plenty to cheer when twelve bronc riders competed in the semifinals. All but a few made impressive rides, some on notorious horses. The three judges had no easy task determining who should advance to the finals, where $150 and a silver-adorned saddle worth $350 awaited the winner. Apparently the deliberations took longer than usual. Perhaps the judges had trouble choosing the three finalists based on the merits of each performance. Or they might have been reluctant to create a contest that the newspaper later called a "racial struggle . . . for supremacy."

The men they chose were well-known horsemen of abundant skill. John Spain, the white contestant, had supplied horses to the first Round-Up and won the wild horse race that year. His horsemanship was known throughout the Northwest. A day earlier he had won the stagecoach race. George Fletcher, the black cowboy, had learned how to tame horses from members of the Confederated Tribes of Umatilla. His free-form riding style and loose-fitting orange angora chaps gave him a flamboyant air in the saddle. The Native American, Jackson Sundown, had been wounded by U.S. soldiers in 1877 at age fourteen while trying to flee to Canada with his uncle, Chief Joseph, and their band of Nez Perce. Unlike his two competitors, Sundown was lean and reserved. At forty-eight he was the senior citizen of the field, but his skills had not diminished, nor had his reputation for subduing the wildest of horses.

Wearing black angora chaps, Sundown rode first atop "Lightfoot." The small horse whirled and twisted violently at the start. Sundown's sombrero flew off, and his two long black braids, tied beneath his chin, came undone and flapped with the horse's every jolt. "Lightfoot," still whirling in a tight circle, twisted its head sharply to the right and tried to bite Sundown's leg. The horse ran suddenly, brushing against a judge's horse, dislodging one of Sundown's feet from the stirrups. One jump later, Sundown fell off and hit the ground hard, twenty-five seconds after his ride began. He didn't move until two medical attendants with a stretcher reached him. He was carried from the arena sitting upright on the stretcher but was merely stunned.

Spain drew heavy and powerful "Long Tom," a big black horse added to the Round-Up's bucking string after years of pulling a plow and a terror known for delivering a punishing ride. The horse was called a "pitcher" for its habit of throwing itself forward on its front legs while kicking its back legs high in the air. This violent motion often caused the high cantle at the back of the saddle to hit the rider so hard that he lost his breath. Spain rode snugly but didn't "scratch" the horse with his spurs—no one had ever done so and remained on the horse's back. "Long Tom" crashed through the wood fence separating the arena field from the track and raced toward the bleachers. Spain remained in the saddle. Some fans later claimed that he touched the saddle with his free hand and should have been disqualified. The judges said otherwise. In two documentary films, Spain and "Long Tom" are a blurred image seen at too great a distance to determine the truth.

Fletcher rode last. During the semifinals, he had won the crowd's admiration by mastering "Hot Foot," a small black bucker with a long record of sending cowboys airborne. In the finals, he drew "Del." The horse raced around the arena as if fleeing demons but bucked to no one's satisfaction. So the judges ordered Fletcher to ride another mount, "Sweeney," a brute that looks almost white in the colorless old pictures. The horse jumped repeatedly as it raced around the arena, pausing occasionally to lurch almost upright on its back legs. Fletcher spurred the horse's flanks while his torso bobbed forward and back in a long rhythmic arc, all the while waving his cowboy hat in a wide circle and smiling.

The crowd roared loudest for Fletcher. Reports differ on how quickly the judges announced the winner. Some said the decision came immediately, while others said it took several minutes, perhaps indicating disagreement. The announcer, perched in a tower, shouted into a megaphone the victor's name: John Spain.

Although spectators applauded Spain as he rode past the grandstand and bleachers aboard the first-place saddle, they cheered louder and longer for Fletcher. In the 1998 award-winning documentary *American Cowboys*, narrator William Hurt says the audience declared the black cowboy the "people's champion." Sheriff Tillman Taylor, a Round-Up director at the time, cut Fletcher's hat into small pieces and sold them to the crowd, raising enough money for Fletcher to buy a $350 saddle like the one awarded to Spain.

Newspaper accounts said the judges chose Spain because he rode a tougher horse in more traditional buckaroo style, while Fletcher rode sloppy and loose.

The next day, friends of Fletcher's and Spain's continued to argue about who deserved to win. Fletcher said that he could master "Long Tom" if given a chance, and the two sides put up $250 each. The bet fell apart when Round-Up officials refused to make the horse available.

Spain told the *Live Wire*, a weekly Pendleton newspaper, that he had won the championship fairly. "The judges said so, at least, and their word must go. Fletcher made a good ride all the way though. If he made a better ride than I, the judges should have given him the saddle. There is no trouble or argument between George Fletcher and me." Fletcher was also interviewed. He said "the drawing of the color line" decided the outcome and that Spain had "pulled leather" when "Long Tom" broke through the fence. He also said he could ride any animal at the Round-Up if given the chance.

The debate was just beginning.

JOHN SPAIN

Ask anyone familiar with Round-Up history, and there's a good chance they can describe John Spain's disputed victory in the 1911 saddle bronc–riding contest as if they had witnessed it from the grandstands. Did Spain "pull leather," touching the saddle with his free hand and therefore requiring his disqualification? Or did he outride George Fletcher,

In the 1998 award-winning documentary *American Cowboys*, narrator William Hurt says the audience declared the black cowboy the "people's champion."

◄ John Spain rides "Long Tom," 1911.

By W. S. Bowman in Low Collection.

No [cowboy] is more typical than Johnny Spain. He's that strapping buckaroo there with silver cuffs to his leather chapps and heavy silver-studded trimmings and fringe on his pocket covers.

His right arm is gone below the wrist—"burnt off"—got caught in a hitch in his rope—with the horse on one end and the steer on the other pulling different ways.

—Charles Wellington Furlong,
Let 'er Buck, 1921

▼ John Spain trick roping.

By L. Moorhouse in OHS Collection, bb003686.

FACING PAGE ▶ George Fletcher.

Howdyshell Collection.

whom the crowd's roar anointed the true winner? We'll never know. What's clear is that such controversies long burn bright, illuminating a single event for generations but relegating to shadows other worthy stories, including the broader one of John Spain's life and career.

John's story is intertwined with that of his older brother Fred, another star in the Round-Up's early days. These cowboys spent their best years together on horseback and on the range, leading a windy and dusty existence as vestiges of a nearly extinct way of life. They were big, rugged men, as if they had walked off the screen of a western movie—"the real article," as Fred's son King recalled. Colorless photographs and films show John making his famous ride astride "Long Tom." Tall and thick bodied, he seems unmovable, a force heavier than gravity. Judging from his scant hairline, his youth is fading, but his face is all determination. It was Fred, however, who was judged "most typical cowboy" three times at the Round-Up.

As boys they saw Buffalo Bill's Wild West show, which inspired them to stage their own shows in cities across the Northwest as early as 1903, when John was twenty-two, until 1915. One stop included what used to be Hawthorne Park in southeast Portland, Oregon, now a commercial area ten blocks from the Willamette River. The earliest performances were informal and modest. Called the Spain Brothers' Wilde West, the show initially consisted of the two cowboys and a few friends riding bucking horses for small crowds and then passing a hat for donations.

The brothers lived in Union, Oregon, sixty-seven miles southeast of Pendleton. It was wild horse country, a time before fences broke up the range. According to King Spain, the brothers chased, caught, and broke the mounts, then often sold them to the cavalry. In 1902, with two other men they herded six hundred horses from south of Hell's Canyon almost to Canada. The Spain brothers also provided a string of bucking horses for the first Round-Up in 1910 and led the inaugural Westward Ho! Parade.

Like many of the early Round-Up competitors, they tried their hand in several events and sometimes won or placed high in the wild horse, cow pony relay, and stagecoach races. In one race, John was hanging from the side of a stagecoach, and it toppled over on him. The crowd gasped, thinking he'd been killed. His nephew, King, said

that after the dust cleared, John appeared and waved his hat to signal he was unhurt. John continued to compete in the Round-Up and other rodeos long after a roping accident involving a steer cost him his right hand in 1912.

Charles Furlong, a writer who chronicled the early Round-Up years in his 1921 *Let 'er Buck,* described John Spain's "happy smile and his ever-genial 'that's right' reply— no matter if you tell him it's a pleasant day when it's raining."

King Spain wasn't happy about Ken Kesey's 1994 fictionalized account of John Spain's famous competition with George Fletcher, an African-American, and the Nez Perce horseman Jackson Sundown, or with plans for a movie version. The novel portrays John as a profane racist from Tennessee (he was born in Cottage Grove, Oregon). In an interview with western writers Doug and Cathy Jory, King said John wasn't bigoted and called him a "fine man. The worst language he or my dad ever used was 'dod donnit.' He was nothin' like they tried to make him out to be. An' they wanted to cast Willie Nelson as John Spain. I said no! No to the movie. Can you imagine Willie Nelson as John Spain?" (Jory, 2002)

GEORGE FLETCHER

When George Fletcher traveled the Oregon Trail as a boy around 1900, it was not the ordeal of deprivation and danger that so many thousands faced in earlier decades. For him, a more trying odyssey began when he arrived in Pendleton from Missouri with his mother and stepfather. About ten at the time, Fletcher must have been wide-eyed upon beholding his new world: the Wild West hadn't yet faded into history at this bustling frontier outpost. Cowboys and native people abounded, as did saloons and brothels. Black faces like his were rare, and Oregon had earned its reputation for discouraging African-American families like the Fletchers from settling in the state.

Information about the legendary horseman's boyhood is fragmentary, but the assembled pieces create a mosaic of travails and triumphs. A winning personality, good looks, athletic prowess, and extraordinary help from diverse people were critical aids to Fletcher as he overcame hardships, including a less than stable home life and racial prejudice. Surprisingly, some people who remember him fondly and marvel at his rodeo exploits still refer to him by his commonly used nickname, "Nigger" George, as if his achievements cleansed the word of insult. Even if Fletcher felt no disrespect after hearing the name so many times, it must have been a ceaseless reminder of second-class citizenship and the long road of hurdles he faced.

As a boy, Fletcher lived near the train station in a one-room wooden shack that the Pendleton Hotel provided to his family. His stepfather worked for the hotel as a train porter, and his mother cleaned homes and businesses. In his teens Fletcher was self-employed; saloons and prostitutes paid him to deliver liquor to patrons of the brothels. This earned Fletcher good money and the condemnation of a Presbyterian minister, who decided to take the boy in. For several years thereafter, Fletcher lived and worked at the preacher's church, which was on the reservation of the Cayuse, Umatilla, and Walla Walla tribes. The minister also taught him reading, writing, and math.

The lessons that one day would elevate Fletcher to fame came at the hands of the Indians, with whom he eventually lived. They taught him how to catch and train wild horses. In the documentary *American Cowboys*, the narrator, actor William Hurt, says: "The old chiefs trained Fletcher how to break horses without killing the spirit of the animal. He learned how to become one with the horse by feeling the movements of the muscles and the direction of the horse's head and ears."

Cedric and Tania Wildbill wrote, directed, and produced *American Cowboys*. As a child growing up on the Umatilla Indian Reservation, Cedric became friends with Fletcher, by then an old cowhand. The documentary provides new insight into Fletcher's early life and includes rare footage of his most famous competition, the controversial world bronc riding championship at the 1911 Round-Up. Fletcher was the first black man to compete in the event. Although he placed second, many fans believed he should have won and accused the judges of racism.

He continued to compete at the Round-Up and other rodeos, although he was barred from some shows because cowboys refused to ride against him. Fletcher found a niche in exhibition stunt rides. At the 1914 Round-Up, he and another accomplished black rider, Jesse Stahl, rode a bucking bronco at the same time, facing different directions.

For much of the remainder of his life, he worked as a ranch hand. Fletcher was also a movie fan. John Matlock of Pendleton, who owned the Rivoli theater, said the "old timer" always sat in the back of the section reserved for whites. "He used to come to the theater in the afternoon, and he'd stop and talk to us. He was a wonderful guy, he really was. . . . At the time we could have been arrested for not segregating." (Jory, 2002)

Fletcher died in 1973, four years after his induction into the Pendleton Round-Up and Happy Canyon Hall of Fame. He was eighty-three. Since his death, he also has been inducted into the National Cowboy Hall of Fame and Cowboys of Color National Hall of Fame.

JACKSON SUNDOWN

Images of Jackson Sundown adorn books, films, and museums. His pictures sell on eBay and other Web sites. Together they help perpetuate the Nez Perce horseman's lofty place in rodeo and Native American history. His graceful daring, quiet aura of confidence, striking physical features, and dashing cowboy garb made him a natural for the camera lens.

Consider, for example, the photograph he posed for after winning the world bronc riding championship in 1916. The rare close-up, taken against a white background, conveys a formality befitting the occasion. Yet Sundown's erect posture also connotes a wellspring of coiled energy, as if without warning he might dash from view and leap atop a wild horse. His attire—beaded gauntlets extending halfway up his forearms, ornate and oversized silver belt buckle at his narrow waist, trademark feathery chaps covering his legs—might appear gaudy on someone else. But on Sundown they look as natural as skin. His expression is stoic and inscrutable, but his eyes appear pensive, even wistful. His gaze, focused away from the camera, suggests he's staring at something not just far away, but vanished.

Jackson Sundown was fifty-three at the time, more than twice as old as either of the men he defeated for the title. His story, like those of many competitors in the early Round-Ups, tells a slice of the epic tale that defines the transformation of the West.

At the 5th Annual RoundUp Pendleton (Moorhouse)

▲▲ **George Fletcher rides in 1914.**

By L. Moorhouse in OHS Collection, OrHi 12527.

▲ **Fletcher (at left) enjoys the Round-Up with two old-timers, ca. 1964.**

Howdyshell Collection.

They each received $10. A photograph from the 1916 Round-Up shows a broadly smiling Fletcher astride a buffalo he apparently has ridden to exhaustion. The animal is prone, and its tongue is hanging out.

The cowboy found other work. Umatilla County sheriff Til Taylor, the long-time Round-Up president, hired him as an unofficial deputy to help track down criminals.

When the United States entered World War I, Fletcher enlisted in the army, as did many men from the Pendleton area, and served in the infantry in Europe. In Paris, he rode a bucking horse in an exhibition and earned 400 francs. His performance made him a celebrity, judging from the crowd's cries of "*Viva, viva!*" Later in the war, Fletcher was injured—either wounded in action or hurt while breaking horses for the army—leaving him with a limp and ending his rodeo career.

Ray F. Bishop

Jackson Sundown
Nez Perce

▲ **Roy Bishop (at left) with Jackson Sundown in the Indian encampment, 1910.**

OHS Collection, OrHi 59805.

▶ **Jackson Sundown.** *Howdyshell Collection.*

▲ Sundown at the Round-Up in Indian attire. *Low Collection.*

Jackson Sundown is a full-blooded Nez Perce. . . . Not only his remarkable riding, but his splendid quality of mind and character have made him a prime favorite with all. Physically he is a sight for the gods with his erect carriage and lithe, agile body, which still bears the scars of three bullet wounds in fights against the whites in the long ago.

—Charles Wellington Furlong, *Let 'er Buck,* 1921

No photographic images depict Sundown's childhood, a period most remembered for his people's struggle to stem the accelerating loss of traditional Nez Perce lands to white settlers, a struggle that led to war. But the few details handed down about his early life make it easy to visualize Sundown the boy in both bucolic and bloody scenes across the Northwest's hilled grasslands, river valleys, and mountain ranges.

Although a member of the Wallowa band of Nez Perce from eastern Oregon, Sundown was born in Montana in 1863. According to one account, his people were on a horse-raiding mission in Flathead Indian territory. Another account says his mother was a Flathead, and he was born on her reservation. A nephew of Chief Joseph, he was called Waaya-Tonah-Toesits-Kahn—"Earth Left by the Setting Sun." (When he began performing at rodeos around age forty, he used the name Buffalo Jackson; later he changed to the more evocative Jackson Sundown.) He formed a strong early bond with horses, striking even in a culture best known among all tribes for breeding and training the animals. Such was his harmony with horses that his father gave him a pony when he was five years old.

Nine years later, at fourteen, Sundown was among eight hundred Nez Perce who defied the federal government's order to move to a reservation in Idaho. War broke out, and the U.S. Army Cavalry pursed the Nez Perce on what became a fourteen-hundred-mile quest for freedom in Canada.

Too young to be a warrior, Sundown helped keep watch over the horses at night and herded them in the morning. After several battles, the Indians crossed Lolo Pass in the Bitter Root Mountains in Montana and camped at a place called Big Hole. Before dawn on August 9, 1877, army troops launched a surprise attack. Eyewitnesses said the fusillade of bullets sounded like rain pelting the teepees. Inside one, Sundown held a younger brother to protect him, but the boy was killed in his arms. The teepee was set on fire. Sundown may have scrambled to safety, or a soldier may have wrapped him in a blanket and carried him out of danger. (Some troops were sympathetic toward the Nez Perce cause, especially the plight of their women and children.)

The Nez Perce fought off the soldiers and escaped, but as many as ninety were killed. In early October, Sundown was with the band when it reached the Bear Paw Mountains, just forty miles from the Canadian border. They had been on the move since June. The weather had turned bitterly cold, and many lacked blankets or shelter. Snow was falling when they camped along Snake Creek. Another attack came, this time from high ground on either side of the camp. Sundown used all his horse skills to escape the ensuing carnage. Wounded and without moccasins, he concealed himself by clinging to the side of a horse. He traversed the rugged terrain to Canada with about one hundred and fifty members of his tribe.

After a five-day siege at Bear Paw, Chief Joseph surrendered. Sundown spent two years in Canada encamped with Sitting Bull and the Sioux. In the United States, he was a wanted man with a bounty on his head. But he slipped back into the country with several other Nez Perce, avoiding soldiers and bounty hunters. He stayed at the Colville Indian Reservation in Washington State before traveling to Montana.

Sundown honed his horse skills. Eventually he was given land on the Flathead Reservation, where he married and had two daughters. He raised and trained horses to make a living.

Rodeos were springing up in towns across the region, and Sundown started riding wild horses and bulls for prize money. Now white people paid him to do what he loved most, while a few decades earlier they had taken his tribe's lands, hunted and tried to kill him, and slaughtered thousands of Nez Perce horses to deprive the Indians of mobility and their most prized possessions. If Sundown ever spoke of this irony, it was not recorded for posterity.

As Sundown's reputation grew, his name began to appear in newspapers. In Pendleton in 1911, he made the finals of the bronc riding championship and won many fans. The next year he was the sensation of a rodeo in Grangeville, Idaho. Frank Gillett, a member of the Grangeville Cowboy Band, recalled the bull riding event:

On the first day a local cowboy tried to ride a big red bull. The bull made a whip-popper of that cowboy. He went to the hospital and was there for six months. On the second day Sundown rode that bull. At times he was clear over on one side and then the other side. A bull's hide rolls with the saddle and you can't cinch the saddle tight enough. The bull bucked all the way across the arena with Sundown. . . . [H]e finally stopped bucking. (Alcorn, 1983)

The ride broke the bull—it never bucked again. But Sundown wasn't done wowing the crowd. When a white man refused to ride the horse he drew in the bucking contest because the animal was so fierce, Sundown stepped in and climbed aboard "Cyclone." Fifty jumps later, the tall and lithe Indian was still firmly in the saddle. Then the horse used the desperate trick all bronc-busters feared: "Cyclone" reared up and fell over backward. The crowd cried out in horror. But Sundown jumped to his feet and bowed to the cheering spectators.

The Nez Perce believed that Sundown's spiritual power, or *weyekin*, was his ability to be one with horses, to understand them and meld with their rhythms. One historian suggested that this power was represented by a horsefly. The only way a bucking horse can dislodge a horsefly is to fall over on its back, and Sundown was said to keep one of the insects behind his ear in a tiny buckskin bag woven into his braided hair.

Sundown had moved to Idaho in 1910 after separating from his wife. In 1912 he married a Nez Perce widow. A mother of two sons, Cecilia Wapshela had a ranch near Jacques Spur, Idaho, and the family lived there. Wapshela often accompanied Sundown to rodeos, where she and her husband sometimes performed in ceremonial dances.

At the 1914 Pendleton Round-Up, Sundown caught the eye of sculptor Alexander Phimister Proctor, whose western-themed works had received wide attention. Proctor saw the Indian horseman as the ideal model for a project he had started. The next year, he returned to sketch and measure Sundown before the Round-Up began and to arrange for intensive modeling sessions in 1916.

That summer, Proctor, his wife Margaret, and their seven children camped on Sundown's ranch for six weeks in a teepee beneath a stand of cottonwoods next to a stream. "Every day Sundown rode back and forth in front of me or posed quietly while I modeled details," Proctor wrote in his 1971 autobiography, *Sculptor in Buckskin*, published twenty-one years after he died. "Sundown worked patiently all summer. Occasionally his wife would entice him away to visit relatives, and I would take the day off to go fishing."

In 1923 Proctor's daughter Hester described the sessions more vividly to the *Idaho County Free Press* in Grangeville: "[Sundown] wore only a breach [sic] cloth and

Jackson Sundown may ride again—on the big screen. Pendleton filmmakers Cedric and Tania Wildbill are producing a fictionalized film about Sundown in time for the Round-Up's centennial in 2010. "We're almost there," Wildbill said in 2008.

▲ Silk souvenir scarf. *Hall of Fame Collection.*

▼ Jackson Sundown with prize Hamley saddle, 1916. *Helm Collection.*

moccasins. He rode bareback with an Indian-style halter. He would come at full gallop directly at Dad, and I would hold my breath wondering if he would stop in time or turn."

From these sessions Proctor completed two works that were later cast in bronze. *Buffalo Hunt* depicts an Indian astride a galloping horse and spearing a fleeing buffalo. When Margaret Proctor asked Sundown how he liked the statue, he didn't comment on the quality but said he might not have posed had he known how long the work would take. In the other work, titled *Sundown: Nez Perce Chief*, Proctor chose to embellish Sundown's achievements by making him a tribal leader, sculpting a bust of him wearing an elegant headdress of eagle feathers and an uncharacteristically grim expression. The bust was later exhibited in Europe.

Sundown had decided not to compete in the 1916 Round-Up, but Proctor persuaded him to appear at Pendleton one more time. When he won the bronc riding championship, the wave of publicity also drew attention to Proctor's work, which received stellar reviews in New York and added to Sundown's already lofty reputation.

The collaboration of the sculptor and the Indian cowboy didn't end there. In 1918, while working in Los Altos, California, Proctor hired Sundown to model for another equestrian sculpture. With the permission of the superintendent of the Nez Perce Indian Reservation, Sundown, his wife, and son Willy moved from Idaho to a cottage in Los Altos. They spent several months there, though Proctor complained in his autobiography that Sundown's participation in rodeos interfered with his modeling. Progress was slow, and Sundown and his family grew restive and finally returned home, leaving Proctor to find another model for *On the War Path*. A factor Proctor didn't mention in his book was Sundown's friendship with "Foghorn" Murphy, a well-known figure in San Francisco and Oakland who rode around downtown streets on a big white horse announcing baseball news through a megaphone. (Murphy later became a millionaire in real estate, liquor, and horse-racing businesses.) According to newspaper reports, Murphy and Sundown were seen roaming the bars and back streets of San Francisco, an image that's difficult to reconcile with

▲ Happy Canyon princesses Rosalie Alexander Samuels (left) and Darlene Terry (right) present Mrs. Adeline Sundown Adams, Jackson Sundown's daughter, with a plaque commemorating Sundown's induction into the Pendleton Hall of Fame in 1972. *Howdyshell Collection.*

▶ Sundown by a touring car, his long braids tied under his chin. *Low Collection.*

Sundown's quiet and reserved character. Murphy's example and the enticements of the big city may have proved too much to resist.

Sundown spent his final years working on his ranch and as a horse trainer for hire. Still the camera sought him out. Several months before he died at age sixty, victim of a waning influenza epidemic that claimed millions of lives worldwide, an unannounced visitor arrived at his ranch. Will E. Hudson, the first newsreel cameraman in the Northwest, stopped by hoping to persuade Sundown to put on an impromptu riding exhibition. Sundown's nephew, a student at the University of Idaho, told Hudson that his uncle wouldn't come to the door because he had a headache, apparently because the Cadillac he had bought recently to replace his Model T wouldn't start. Hudson fiddled with the engine and soon had the motor running. Sundown, pleased at this turn of events, greeted the photographer then thanked him by putting on an hour-long demonstration with three horses.

Sundown concluded his one-man rodeo atop an old but tough horse named "Lightning," while Hudson filmed everything. As Hudson later remarked,

This was without saddle or bridle or even a rope around his neck. The rider controlled the horse by holding his hat over first one of the horse's eyes then the other eye all the while riding at top speed. Finally, with no signal, the horse stopped near the camera and Jackson Sundown slipped gracefully to the ground. . . . Sundown walked over to the camera and tripod position and held out his hand for a shake, then with a sunny smile he quietly said, "That should be plenty." He turned and walked over to his new car, climbed in and started the engine. In a roar he was gone. (Webber and Webber, 1999)

Theaters around the country showed the film in a weekly newsreel then re-released it after Sundown's death on December 18, 1923.

Jackson Sundown was buried in an unmarked grave in the Slickpoo Mission Cemetery near Jacques Spur. More than fifty years after his death, a stone monument was erected over his grave. Adeline Adams, his daughter, unveiled it in a ceremony that included members of the Nez Perce, Umatilla, Yakama, and Colville tribes. An Indian appaloosa was tethered at the head of the grave, saddled but restless.

1916 BUCKING CONTEST

Dust from pounding horse hoofs rose in the afternoon light, casting everything in a yellow glow. The spectators waited, their cheers muted for the moment into a drone of anticipation. They had selected the winner with their voices. Some wanted perceived wrongs of the past made right. But the decision rested with the judges and their secret deliberations. Whether they weighed factors other than a horseman's ride had long been debated but denied. This time, would the judges select an Indian over two white cowboys for the title of world champion bucking-bronc rider?

It was 1916, and Jackson Sundown of the Nez Perce tribe was reliving his past. He had ridden magnificently again yet had reason to believe that victory might prove elusive. In 1915, at age fifty-two, he had conquered the rough and quick "Culdesac" but was voted third. In the 1911 finals, Sundown was mastering the small but cunning "Lightfoot" when a collision with a judge's horse led to a fall. Some fans argued he deserved a remount, but the judges disqualified him.

After the 1915 Round-Up, Sundown said he was retiring. But sculptor Alexander Proctor, for whom he was modeling, persuaded him not to give up. Proctor even paid Sundown's entry fee. Once again he showed why he was widely considered the region's most skilled horseman. Sundown swung into the saddle atop "Angel" from the right side, the traditional Indian way. He rode through two initial pivots then weathered a series of long, high jumps. At one point the trim bay gelding seemed to bend nearly in half. Thousands of spectators stood and yelled: "Sundown! Sundown! Ride 'em Sundown!" Goading "Angel" to greater violence, Sundown used his spurs, first on the horse's shoulders then on its flanks. The jolts he endured were measured in the bounces of his long-haired, black-spotted orange chaps. "Angel" tried one more time to throw him, but Sundown fanned the horse with his sombrero as if telling it, "Why bother?" A gunshot signaled the end of the ride.

▲ Mrs. Adeline Sundown Adams with Annette Blackeagle Pinkham Burke, Nez Perce, in 1972. *Howdyshell Collection.*

dark-bronzed face. He tossed his hat into the air, a sign to the crowd that the judges had agreed with their choice. Rollen placed second and Hall third. A Native American had never won this, the most prestigious, Round-Up event.

The *East Oregonian* described what happened next: "Sundown was led to the front of the grandstand and there placed on the horse of Guy Wyrick. At an easy gallop he circled the quarter-mile track, and the ovation that was given him might have made the breast of a king of landed empires swell with pride. The crowd got to its feet, yelling like a frenzied mob, waving hats and hands and cheering with an enthusiasm that was wild beyond all restraint."

When Sundown was awarded the $500 silver-trimmed saddle, he was asked what name he wanted engraved on it. "You put my wife's name," he said. (Furlong 1921) Cecelia Wapshela had watched her husband's triumph, as did two hundred Nez Perce who traveled from Idaho to Pendleton to join the Umatilla, Cayuse, and Walla Wallas at the Round-Up. Sundown was also awarded the title of best all-around cowboy.

LEE CALDWELL

▲ Sundown, Hall, and Rollen, 1916.

By W. S. Bowman in Low Collection.

FACING PAGE ▶ Lee Caldwell.

Howdyshell Collection.

The other two finalists stayed astride their horses, too. Bronco Bob Hall of Pocatello, Idaho, drew "Speedball," a lean black plunger with a penchant for high, long bounds. The horse lived up to its reputation yet couldn't dislodge Hall, but the cowboy never used his spurs. Rufus Rollen of Claremore, Oklahoma, rode last. Known as one of the best riders in the country, he had recently won in Kansas City, Chicago, and New York. His horse was "Long Tom," the large sorrel with a long neck that the judges respected. Winners of the event in 1911, 1913, and 1915 had all ridden this horse. Rollen took all that "Long Tom" gave but didn't "scratch" the brute until the horse's energy had waned.

As the crowd waited for the judges' decision, spectators began yelling Sundown's name. Soon it rang throughout the arena. A few rowdy fans pulled up pieces of wood from the grandstands. There were fears that a riot might break out if Sundown wasn't declared the winner.

Just before the winner was announced, cowboys rushed up to Sundown and began shaking his hand. They knew the outcome. A rare smile spread across Sundown's

If rodeo enjoyed the popularity of baseball, the name Lee Caldwell might carry the cachet of the name Babe Ruth. Not that Ruth overcame obstacles equal to those the Pendleton cowboy faced during the bronc riding finale in 1915. Few athletes in any sport have persevered through as many challenges as Caldwell did that Saturday afternoon.

A day earlier in the wild horse race, Caldwell had severely sprained his right wrist. The same injury to the other wrist would have knocked him out of the bucking competition because he held the halter rope with his left hand. He used his right hand to thrust his hat high in the air and swing it in a wide circle. Still, pain was inevitable with the violent and unpredictable jolts of the horse.

Only twenty-two and with a boyish face that made him look younger, Caldwell didn't need the acclaim of the bucking championship. No one in the country was riding better, judging from the titles he had won across the West. In 1914, he had finished first in six events and second three times, including in Pendleton against Red Parker. In 1915, he had already claimed three titles. Caldwell was known for his determination and fiery temperament. In 1910, he competed in the bucking contest after suffering a twisted ankle in a famous pile-up of cowboys and horses in the cow pony race at the first Round-Up. The next year, a few days before the Round-Up, he sprained his shoulder in a riding accident, but still he saddled up for the bucking contest. Despite a spectacular ride, he didn't make the finals.

Even as a boy, Caldwell displayed spunk. When he was eight, he climbed on one of his father's horses and rode from Pendleton through the Blue Mountains in the winter to the family's first home in Joseph, Oregon, where he was born. Later he had many chances to ride untamed horses at his father's large farming operations on the Umatilla Indian Reservation near Pendleton. He was only sixteen when he won his first bucking contest in nearby Athena in 1909.

In 1915, Caldwell wanted badly to win in his hometown, where the *East Oregonian* boasted "real 'honest-to-God' champions are made." But his Pendleton roots made the challenge all the greater. A Round-Up official had warned him that he would have to win decisively because the judges feared any appearance of favoritism. No one from Pendleton had won the bucking contest in the Round-Up's first five years. Even without the wrist injury and the bias he faced as a hometown rider, Caldwell knew he was in for stiff competition. Two formidable and popular stars, Yakima Canutt and Jackson Sundown, also had made the finals. Earlier in the day, the trio had defeated twelve other riders in the semifinals. Now, with the crowd watching, each man stood in the arena, took a turn reaching into a sombrero held by one of the judges, and pulled out a small piece of wadded paper. Each read the name of the horse he must ride: "Culdesac" for Sundown, "Speedball" for Canutt, and the much-feared "Long Tom" for Caldwell.

Sundown and Canutt made dazzling rides. Sundown was so focused that he failed to hear the timer's gun announcing he had conquered "Culdesac" and rode for another minute until the gun was fired again.

Caldwell knew that to win he'd have to ride aggressively. As wranglers pulled the blindfold from "Long Tom" and turned him loose, Caldwell did what no previous rider had dared try: he raked the horse's flanks with his spurs. "Long Tom" responded with a high kick of his legs and a low plunge of his head. Caldwell was thrown forward against

the saddle horn with such force that the blow broke his breastbone. Sick with pain, he kept spurring "Long Tom" as the horse thrashed across the arena. The jumps caused Caldwell to loosen his grip on the halter rope. Fearing that the slack would doom his ride, he momentarily held the rope in his teeth to tighten the grip.

When the ride was finished, the eighteen thousand spectators cheered wildly. They had just seen one of the greatest rides in the Round-Up's six-year history. But the judges weren't satisfied and ordered Caldwell to make another ride, this time on "Spitfire." Caldwell rode the horse easily. To everyone's surprise, Caldwell wasn't announced the winner but was asked to ride yet again. In late afternoon, he climbed atop "P. D. Nutt," the fourth horse he had mounted in forty-five minutes, starting with the animal he rode in the semifinals.

The *East Oregonian* described what happened next: "With a broken breastbone, a sprained wrist, his wind gone and his strength spent, Caldwell . . . rode him on his nerve alone. He threw the steel into the mount with utter disdain of consequences and, so conclusive was this demonstration of his ability, that the crowd took up the yell of 'Caldwell' and the judges could not but give him the victory."

The next year, in 1916, Caldwell won several state championships, the Southwest bucking title, and the Canadian championship. Despite his success, he was already considering a new career in the movies, partly because of the toll rodeo had taken on his body. He portrayed himself in the silent movie *The Cowpuncher*, the first feature film shot in Idaho, and he was weighing more offers, though with reluctance. "I don't like the moving picture game. I played in one film and felt like a four flusher posing before the camera," he told the Pendleton newspaper. "But if they are willing to pay me the money, I reckon I'd better try them out."

At the time, Caldwell didn't know that within a year the United States would enter World War I, and in his next career he would lead men into battle.

After the war, Caldwell trained thoroughbred race horses. He died in Stockton, California, in 1952. He was inducted into the National Cowboy Hall of Fame in 1966, and he was among the ten cowboys inducted into the Pendleton Round-Up and Happy Canyon Hall of Fame when it opened in 1969.

DWELL CHAMPION BRO
OF THE WORL

NO 28-B, LUCIELE MULHALL WORLDS CHAMPION, COWGIRL ROPER

W.S.BOWMAN PHOTO

| ▲ **Lucille Mulhall, 1914.** *By W. S. Bowman in Low Collection.*

OLD-TIME COWGIRLS

BY ANN TERRY HILL

They had pluck and grit, putting on the most glamorous and

dangerous display with as much derring-do as their male

counterparts, and with true class and grace.

—Wills and Artho, *Cowgirl Legends*, 1955

▼ Lucille Mulhall, 1914.

By L. Moorhouse in Low Collection.

T he word "cowgirl" had been used throughout the West. Theodore Roosevelt, the twenty-sixth President of the United States, added it to the national vernacular in the early 1900s when he saw Lucille Mulhall perform during a roping exhibition in Oklahoma City. Will Rogers had already used the term when he saw Lucille in her first public appearance in her father's Roping and Riding Contest in 1899 in St. Louis. Lucille toured the rodeo circuit and competed in roping in Pendleton in 1914. Records are unclear as to whether she took home any prize money.

From the turn of the nineteenth century through the 1940s, the cowgirls were revered and feted, their dramatic exhibitions and showy costumes copied. Across the United States, in Europe, and in East Asia, crowds turned out to watch them perform and, if they were lucky, to entertain the cowgirls in their homes when the women were not busy attending their horses or in the arena.

They were charming, tough, colorful, and true sportswomen—the precursors of American movie stars. In fact, many worked in Hollywood as stuntwomen and extras when they weren't on the rodeo circuit. During their glory years they did much to enhance the rodeo world and add to the kaleidoscopic history of the West. Truth is often hard to separate from myth, but their legendary successes and the hardships they endured make the yellowback dime-novels they inspired read like nursery rhymes.

The women who ride . . . are skilled in the lore of the race and the horse no less than the men of the range. They not only put their horses to the utmost, but ride with consummate knowledge displayed in every form of generalship in the race.

—Charles Wellington Furlong, *Let 'er Buck*, 1921

The emancipation of women may have begun not with the vote, nor in the cities where women marched and carried signs and protested, but rather when they mounted a good cowhorse and realized how different and fine the view. . . . From the back of a horse, the world looked wider.

—Joyce Gibson Roach,
The Cowgirls, 1990

◄ **Mabel Strickland.** *Low Collection.*

FOX HASTINGS

FOX HASTINGS
ONLY LADY BULLDOGGER
© 1924 R.R. DOUBLEDAY

The 1925 Pendleton Round-Up program lists Fox Hastings as the world's only woman bulldogger. She competed in Pendleton for years. Her career was rigorous, and she overcame many injuries. During a ride in Kansas City, the bronc she was riding fell on her. Twice the horse tried to get up; both times it fell back on her. Hastings was carried from the arena, and everyone thought she was dead. Fifteen minutes later she reappeared and asked for a re-ride. She got one and rode successfully—even managing to dismount and bow to the crowd. This was a display of sheer nerve, for afterwards she went behind the chutes and collapsed. Unfortunately, for all her fame and verve, she lost a contest with private demons and took her own life in a hotel in Phoenix in 1948.

FOX HASTINGS

◀◀ **Fox Hastings, 1924.** *By R. Doubleday in Low Collection.*

◀ **Fox Hastings, 1928.** *By R. Doubleday in Low Collection.*

▲ **Fox Hastings and Hoot Gibson at Round-Up, ca. 1934.** *Howdyshell Collection.*

Official Photo

| ▲ **Cowgirls greet the train from Portland in 1911. Round-Up queen Laura McKee is at center.** *Helm Collection.*

▲ Early cowgirls. Fox Hastings is second from left; Mabel Strickland is third from right. *By R. Doubleday in Low Collection.*

▼ Mabel Strickland, 1923. *Low Collection.*

MABEL DELONG STRICKLAND

Mabel Delong Strickland was queen of the 1927 Round-Up and a Round-Up and Happy Canyon Hall of Fame inductee in 1971. Originally from Walla Walla, Washington, she was known as the "Cowboys' Sweetheart." Not only beautiful and feminine, she excelled in trick riding, relay racing, steer roping, and Roman riding. She was a natural athlete and bested most of the men. She could usually be spotted wearing her favorite boots, which had the four suits of a deck of cards cut out and stitched on the chimney top. Fred Hill, Round-Up president in 1961–1962, recalled his memories of the old-time cowgirls in a 1996 interview. He said about Strickland: "I remember one time she took her horse out in the center of the arena and jumped it over a touring car. She just flew over it. Those were exciting days."

Mabel Strickland went on to become a Hollywood stuntwoman and actress. She was a 1981 inductee of the Rodeo Hall of Fame, National Cowboy and Western Museum in Oklahoma City, Oklahoma, and the 1992 Cowgirl Honoree at the National Cowgirl Museum and Hall of Fame in Fort Worth, Texas. She is the only woman ever featured on the cover of a Cheyenne Frontier Days program.

▶ Mabel Strickland, champion roper.
By R. Doubleday in Low Collection.

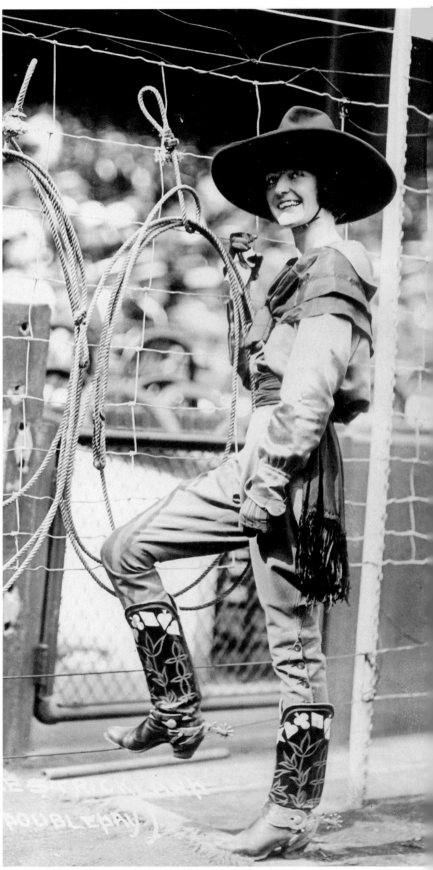

Hugo Strickland, Mabel's husband, with prize saddle, 1926. *Low Collection.*

Red, white, and blue horsehair bridle presented to Mabel Strickland by the VFW of Walla Walla. *Hall of Fame Collection.*

By R. Doubleday in Low Collection.

Howdyshell Collection.

MABEL STRICKLAND

Strickland Steer Roping in Record Time of 18 sec.

STRICKLAND ROPING PENDLETON ROU

Strickland's graceful victory gesture. *Low Collection.*

Round-Up president Bob Hales inducts Mabel Strickland into the Pendleton Hall of Fame, 1971. *Howdyshell Collection.*

MABEL STRICKLAND

91

KITTY CANUTT

Kitty Canutt, once married to popular cowboy and movie star Yakima Canutt, is a legend in rodeo lore. Famous as the Pendleton Round-Up champion lady bronc rider in 1916, Kitty is even better known for the diamond studs she wore in a front tooth. It is said that when times were hard and she needed entry fees, she would pawn the diamonds, later retrieving them with her winnings. Tad Lucas, another cowgirl rodeo star who often competed against Kitty, is said to have commented in later life, "She was the meanest woman I ever knew. I don't know how many times she took a shot at that husband [Yakima] of hers."

▲ Kitty (Wilkes) Canutt after winning first place in the cowgirls' bucking contest, 1916. *Low Collection.*

FACING PAGE

► Kitty Canutt rides "Billy Buck." *By L. Moorhouse in OHS Collection, OrHi 92617.*

▲▲ **Early cowgirls.** *By R. Doubleday in Low Collection.*

▲ **Yakima and Kitty Canutt, 1919.** *By L. Moorhouse in OHS Collection, bb003679.*

► **From left, Kitty Canutt, Prairie Rose, and Ruth Roach.** *By R. Doubleday in Low Collection.*

Kitty's 1916 marriage to Yakima Canutt was a disaster. The couple's blowups and breakups set tongues wagging, and they divorced in 1919.

Katy Wilkes Canutt on "Billy Buck"
Round-UP Pendleton Ore   Moorhouse

© W. S. BOWMAN VERA McGINNIS IN THE DRUNKEN RIDE.
No 15-C.

Two photographers captured McGinnis in an exhibition ride. Bowman, a professional photographer by trade, and Moorhouse, a prolific amateur who used professional equipment, were both sons of Oregon Trail pioneers who migrated west from Iowa.

◀ Vera McGinnis performs the "drunken ride." *By W. S. Bowman in Low Collection.*
▼ McGinnis performs the "drunken ride." *By L. Moorhouse in Low Collection.*

Since it was September and Pendleton Roundup time, my feet began to itch, but I didn't say anything. I knew if we [Vera and her husband Earl] were ever going to settle down, as we had decided to do, I'd just have to ignore my longings. But Old Dame Rodeo was whispering to Earl behind my back.

Finally he came out with it. "Baby, it's Roundup time. We could run up there and make a little dough, quick like."

"Yeah! I've been thinking about that," I confessed sheepishly. "But we don't have our winter's wood in. What if the snow comes early?"

"Heck. We won't be gone over ten days. We've got plenty of time."

So when the famous Pendleton Cowboy Band played "The Star Spangled Banner" and the bomb burst in the air unfurling an American flag, which a weighted parachute brought swaying back to earth, the Roundup was on, and we were there.

—Vera McGinnis, *Rodeo Road,* 1974

"Moorhouse" Vera McGinnis Trick Riding Round Up Pendleton Oregon

94

VERA McGINNIS

VERA McGINNIS

Known as the cowgirl who was the toughest and dared to ride the fastest and the wildest, Vera McGinnis often competed in Pendleton. "Old Dame Rodeo," as she called the love and lure of the sport, got in her blood when she placed third in a relay race in Salt Lake City, Utah, in 1913. Coincidentally, the relay string she rode was provided by Barney Sherry of Pendleton. Letting her ride his stable of ten or twelve horses was the magic key to the beginning of her rodeo career. In 1914 she won the Roman standing race at Pendleton. Her career took her all over the world and to Hollywood, but rodeo always called her back. McGinnis is usually credited with inventing the "flying change" during the relay, after the rules changed and riders didn't have to saddle each horse but could leap from one already saddled horse to the next.

An accident during a relay race in 1934 left McGinnis with a collapsed lung, broken ribs, crushed vertebrae, and a broken hip and neck. She was given little chance to live. But Vera was ever the champion. She underwent multiple operations, and six months later she was able to ride her horse "Tiny" again. Her 1974 memoir *Rodeo Road: My Life as a Pioneer Cowgirl* chronicles her adventures and is now a collector's item.

VERA McGINNIS PENDLETON ROUND-UP (DOUBLEDAY)

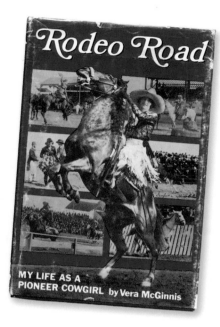

◄ **Vera McGinnis.** *By R. Doubleday in Low Collection.*

▼◄ **Early cowgirls. From left, Prairie Rose, Vera McGinnis, Donna Glover, Mabel Strickland, and Bonnie McCarroll.** *Low Collection.*

▼ **McGinnis, relay racer, with her relay string.** *Low Collection.*

PRAIRIE ROSE   BONNIE McCARROLL
VERA McGINNIS DONNA GLOVER MABLE STRICKLAND

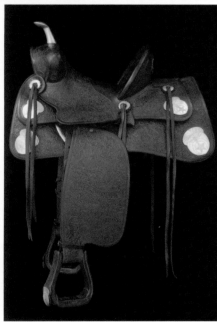

▲▲ Lorena Trickey. *Low Collection.*

▲ Hamley saddle won by Lorena Trickey in 1923 for first place in the women's relay race. This was the last ladies' trophy saddle awarded at Pendleton. *National Cowboy & Western Heritage Museum, Oklahoma City, OK. R.256.2.*

LORENA TRICKEY

Oregon cowgirl Lorena Trickey was one of the stars in the Pendleton arena who went on to Hollywood. She was a stand-in for silent-screen actress Mary Pickford in *Through the Back Door* (1921), riding a horse through the back door of a house. The same year, she drove a chariot in the Tom Mix movie *Queen of Sheba.*

Lorena's father took her to the first Pendleton Roundup in 1910, where she saw her first relay race. She quickly made a name for herself riding relay strings, and in 1919 she won her first national championship at Pendleton, becoming the "World Champion All-Around Horsewoman."

Trickey used the dangerous "Let 'er Fly" technique of jumping from one galloping horse to another in the relay race, where contestants switched horses three times. Earlier riders stopped one horse, jumped off, then jumped on the next. The airborne saddle-to-saddle exchange cut precious time. At the 1929 Pendleton Round-Up, Trickey over-leaped the saddle, and her pants caught on the horn and ripped, exposing her white bloomers. Not only did she lose the race, but she was escorted out of the arena by a gallant cowboy who took his sweater off to cover her exposed derrière.

Soon Trickey was again in the headlines, this time for stabbing her boyfriend J. P. "Smiling Slim" Harris to death with her pocketknife. At the 1927 trial, she pled guilty but claimed self-defense. A stock contractor attending the trial testified he had seen her lover attacking her with a wrench. It took only seventy-five minutes for the jury to find Trickey innocent.

After that fateful event, she never seriously rodeoed again. Eventually she married a man she had met in Hollywood, and she lived peacefully for the remainder of her life. Trickey died in Nevada in 1961. It is said she was buried in her favorite cowgirl outfit. She was admitted to the Rodeo Hall of Fame in Oklahoma City in 2000, and in 2008 she was a nominee for the Cowgirl Hall of Fame in Fort Worth, Texas.

Competing against men, Lorena Trickey won at least two Roman races, standing atop two horses with one foot on the back of each.

◄ Thelma Thompson, queen of the 1922 Round-Up, with Lorena Trickey, women's champion rider. *By R. Doubleday in Low Collection.*
► Lorena Trickey. *Low Collection.*

BERTHA BLANCETT

In his 1921 book *Let 'er Buck,* Charles Wellington Furlong referred to Bertha Blancett as "The Queen of Reinland." Blancett was a fearless competitor, not only in bronc riding, where she rode "slick" (not hobbled), but also in the relay and flat races. Recognized as the first female bronc rider, she won the bucking championship in Pendleton in 1911, 1912, and 1914. In 1914 she came within twelve points of winning the all-around championship of the Round-Up, for which the women's and men's points were tallied together. Cowboys considered this too close for comfort, and the rules were subsequently changed, separating tallies from women's and men's events.

Bertha Blancett was married to champion bulldogger Dell Blancett, and the couple traveled the world doing exhibitions. Hollywood also called. One of Bertha's movies, *Cowboy Sports and Pastimes,* featured a new face—that of Ed "Hoot" Gibson, another longtime star at the Round-Up.

It takes the best woman rider living to outclass Bertha Blancett and none have so far found it possible.

—Charles Wellington Furlong, *Let 'er Buck,* 1921

▲▲ Bertha Blancett in the arena. *Howdyshell Collection.*

▲ Blancett standing on the back of her horse. *Low Collection.*

◀ Bertha and Dell Blancett, ca. 1914. *OHS Collection, CN 000173.*

▶ Blancett, cowgirl champion. *By W. S. Bowman in Low Collection.*

Bertha Blancett

BONNIE McCARROLL

Bonnie McCarroll, a colorful bronc and steer rider, reportedly told her husband Frank at the 1929 Round-Up, "I want to ride in Pendleton one last time." These words were prophetic. McCarroll, "hobbled" in the saddle bronc contest, drew the rank horse "Black Cat." Accounts vary, but no one in the arena that day will ever forget her violent ride. Knocked unconscious in the saddle and hung up in the stirrups, McCarroll bounced back and forth like a rag doll before she was finally thrown to the ground, fatally injured.

This was the beginning of the end for women broncriders. Pendleton said "no more," and other rodeos gradually followed suit. The danger of the event—coupled with the Great Depression, when purses were thin and most of the prize money went to the cowboys—contributed to the demise of this competition. The last female bucking contest was held at Madison Square Garden in 1941.

Bonnie McCarroll was inducted into the National Cowgirl Hall of Fame in 2006.

Women were allowed hobbles on their broncs: that is, a piece of leather tied under the horse's belly from one stirrup to another. This prevented the women from spurring, but it helped them stay in the saddle.... The horse was given a score for how well he bucked, and the rider was given a score for how well she stayed on.

—Joyce Gibson Roach, *The Cowgirls,* 1990

▲ **Bonnie McCarroll, fearless cowgirl of Round-Up's early years.** *Howdyshell Collection.*

ELLA LAZINKA

A 1912 story from the *East Oregonian* shows the pioneer pluck and spirit of Ella Lazinka, daughter of well-known cattle rancher Henry Lazinka. A lady who remained a cowgirl all her life, Ella Lazinka was honored as Pendleton Round-Up Grand Marshal in 1963 and inducted into the Pendleton Round-Up and Happy Canyon Hall of Fame in 1987.

Miss Lazinka is out of the race for the championship of the world. An injury on the upper turn as she was riding the second horse of the string tore open her left leg that took 13 stitches to close it. Suffering the pain of the wound, however, Miss Lazinka finished the race, making two other changes of horses and won the race against the other contestants.

The young woman is a local favorite, a student in the high school. Miss Lazinka rode horses in Barney Sherry's string. Her first mount was Pinto and with this animal she got a good lead on the rest of the field. On the change Mrs. Bertha Blancett succeeded in getting saddled and away before Miss Lazinka, but before the course was finished Miss Lazinka was ahead. It was on this run the young woman was injured. "The fence at the turn had been scraped leaving several large pieces of wood sticking out." Determined to overtake Mrs. Blancett, Miss Lazinka started off at a rapid pace, the horse hugged the rail at the turn and the splinters from the fence tore into her flesh. "I felt the pain," Miss Lazinka said, "but I thought no more of it. I was determined to overtake Mrs. Blancett and show her I could win. I wanted that race and I made up my mind to take it." Miss Lazinka made two more changes despite the wound and won the event that day.

Doctors kept her from competing in the final race the next day.

▲ Ella Lazinka in 1912. *Courtesy of the Lazinka family.*

▼ Winners of the women's relay race, 1910. At right are Ella Lazinka and Henry Lazinka Sr., who holds his racehorses. *By O. G. Allen, courtesy of the Lazinka family.*

WORLD WAR I

BY MICHAEL BALES

In 1918, the Round-Up raised $5,099 for the Red Cross. Support for the war came from stars such as Yakima Canutt, who was on leave from the U.S. Navy but wore his sailor hat and uniform while competing.

▼ Yakima Canutt bulldogs a steer in his U.S. Navy uniform, 1918. *Howdyshell Collection.*

The civic spirit that made the Round-Up a success in its earliest years re-emerged in 1917 with a fervor befitting a loftier goal: to help the country succeed in World War I.

Fierce patriotism triggered an outpouring of emotions, as did unfounded fears that isolated eastern Oregon faced attacks from Germany and its allies, collectively referred to in newspaper headlines as the "Huns." Soon after the United States entered the war on April 6, 1917, boys from Pendleton High School were hired to guard railroad bridges and tunnels from sabotage. Managers from the *East*

LET'ER BUCK THE ROUND UP PENDLETON OR. 1918 (BURNS)

▶ Mollie Minthorn on horse with a travois in the 1918 Westward Ho! Parade. *By Jim Whiting; original by Burns, at St. Anthony Hospital, Pendleton.*

Oregonian marched in formation along city streets in the evenings, as if to underscore the newspaper's extensive war coverage. Nearly everyone in Pendleton and Umatilla County bought war bonds. The total eventually topped $700,000, and those who didn't buy were labeled "slackers."

Henry Collins, a member of the Round-Up board at the time, offered to let the federal government take over his grain business to aid its wartime food programs. Roy Ritner resigned as Round-Up vice-president and business manager to work in France for the American Red Cross.

Pendleton's greatest source of pride was a cavalry of cowboys who volunteered for battlefield duty. Dell Blancett, a Round-Up favorite and winner of the steer roping contest in 1912, proposed creating what came to be called Troop D, but he failed his physical and enlisted instead in the Canadian army. Lee Caldwell, the champion bronc-rider and winner of the all-around championship in 1915, was second to volunteer and was unanimously elected troop captain. The bulldogging champion from that year, Frank Cable, also signed up.

The troop of one hundred and eight men billeted at the Happy Canyon pavilion. Some cowboys developed blisters from the initial drills, because they were accustomed to riding on horseback instead of marching. Before shipping out, the troop was honored at a community celebration. An honor guard of local girls tied a silk souvenir Round-Up scarf around the neck of each troop member. The crowd donated $700 for the troop's mess fund, which would help to feed them when supplies were scarce.

A troop corporal, "Rattlesnake Pete" Inman, wrote a letter to Germany's ruler, Kaiser Wilhelm II, addressing him as "Bill." The letter, published in the newspaper, warned him that the war bond sales and other patriotic activities in Pendleton represented residents' desire "to give you a punch in the jaw."

When the troop departed before dawn on August 11, 1917, an event that was supposed to be secret, more than five hundred people assembled at the train station. The *East Oregonian* described the scene: "The arrival of the train and its departure with the troops was the signal for wild cheering that woke up nearly all the sleepers in the city. Until the train pulled from view the troopers were waving their goodbyes."

The next month, the Round-Up attracted a smaller crowd than usual, and American flags were draped everywhere. A telegram from Caldwell on the newspaper's front page said Troop D's squadron was commanding a horse remount station in North Carolina. "Yell three times for us and 'Let 'er Buck,'" Caldwell wrote. By January of the next year, the troop had arrived in France as part of a field artillery unit.

In February 1918, Dell Blancett left England for the front in France with a Canadian cavalry regiment. Before leaving, he sent a riding crop and spurs to Round-Up director Roy Raley. During a battle on March 30 at Picardy, a German sniper fatally shot Blancett. His battalion commander told Raley in a letter that as Blancett lay dying, he said to his fellow soldiers: "Those German bullets sure hit hard—well, boys, there's a little change in my jeans which you better divide between you." He died a few minutes later, "quite cheerfully and without suffering." With his wife Bertha Blancett, Dell had made Pendleton his headquarters as he won trophy after trophy and staged frontier shows. His death brought the war close to home.

The war had reached a critical stage, and Allied forces mounted a broad offensive across Europe. Before moving into action in July, Pendleton's cowboys emblazoned artillery guns, tractors, and wagons with the Round-Up's symbol of a cowboy on a bucking bronc along with the slogan "Let 'er Buck." A week before the 1918 Round-Up began, the troop fought at the historic battle of St. Mihiel, France, and participated in what was called "the greatest artillery concentration in history."

At the front, Caldwell found time to write a fellow star at the Round-Up, Fred Spain. Interviewed by Doug and Cathy Jory for their 2002 book *From Pendleton to Calgary: An Oral History of Rodeo*, Spain's son King said Caldwell described "hittin' a shell hole just like he was bulldoggin' a steer. Somebody was after him in an airplane. He sent Dad a piece of fuselage off a German plane that had been shot down."

In 1918, the Round-Up raised $5,099 for the Red Cross. Support for the war came from stars such as Yakima Canutt, who was on leave from the U.S. Navy but wore his sailor hat and uniform while competing. No queens or princesses were chosen that year or the following two. The crowd

flocked to four railroad cars that displayed German war booty, and the Kaiser was hanged in effigy at the arena. Blancett's widow, Bertha, herself a Round-Up champion, wore a black armband decorated with a gold star while taking part in the Happy Canyon show.

During the war, more than a thousand men from Umatilla County volunteered for military service or were drafted. They included forty-six Indians from the Umatilla Reservation and the flamboyant black cowboy George Fletcher, whose rodeo career was ended by war injuries. Some soldiers returned to Pendleton with stories about the clout of imitation ten-dollar bills used at the Happy Canyon shows, which had been sent to them in Europe as reminders of home. The bills had a high exchange value as souvenirs,

passed as collateral in crap games, and were accepted as real currency during a respite at a German village on the Rhine.

After the armistice in November 1918, celebrations took many forms. In his 1921 book *Let 'er Buck*, Charles Furlong described Indian tribes at the 1919 Round-Up staging a unique victory dance during the Happy Canyon evening program. Elaborately dressed and painted in war-victory symbols, the tribal people turned out in larger numbers than usual and included the old and infirm. Some carried sticks decorated with human scalps—long rumored to still be in their possession but never before displayed in the presence of whites. Furlong said that when an Indian representing the dead enemy was brought into the ceremony, the old women yelled loudest of all.

FACING PAGE ◄ Captain Lee Caldwell, Troop D. *By W. S. Bowman in Low Collection.*

▲ **World War I—era parade.** *By Jim Whiting; original at St. Anthony Hospital, Pendleton.*

THE GLORY YEARS

BY MICHAEL BALES

"Pendleton treated me right when I was flat," Gibson told the *East Oregonian* when he returned to Pendleton in 1924 to film *Let 'er Buck*. "It never forgets the cowboys that helped put the Round-Up over when it was young, and I wanted to show that the boys never forget Pendleton either."

THE HOLLYWOOD CONNECTION

In the early 1920s, movies and the Round-Up forged a symbiotic bond. The Round-Up provided movie-makers with a ready-made set filled with unscripted action and a large cast of colorful characters. Added attractions were Umatilla County's wealth of sunny days and its countryside of illuminated wheat fields, forests, and mountains. In return, the movies provided the Round-Up with a powerful tool for promoting itself nationwide.

At the time, the motion picture industry was growing rapidly, churning out several hundred

▼ Winners at the 1917 Round-Up:
Yakima Canutt (center) took first prize in
the bucking contest, Bob Hall (right) took
second, and Dave White (left) took third.

By L. Moorhouse in Low Collection.

104

YAKIMA CANUTT
CHAMPION
1917.

W.S. BOWMAN
PHOTO.

BULLS EYE FILM CORP.
PRESENTS
"LET'ER BUCK"
1919
PENDLETON, OREGON
ROUND-UP

In 1917 Yakima Canutt met
cowboy film star Tom Mix,
who recruited him as a
stuntman. Canutt had a knack
for daredevil antics—wild
pursuits, horse spills, leaps
onto runaway horse teams,
wagon wrecks and rescues.
He quickly became one of
Hollywood's leading fall guys.

◄ Yakima Canutt in 1917.
By W. S. Bowman in Low Collection.
▲ Poster for 1924 film *Let 'er Buck.*
Courtesy of Mervin Swearingen.

▲ Leah Conner, 1952 Round-Up queen, with Hollywood stars Lyle Bettger (left) and Jeff Chandler during the filming of *The Great Sioux Uprising*. *Howdyshell Collection.*

films a year for viewing at thousands of movie houses across the country. America's love for the new medium seemed boundless, and westerns were the most popular genre. The Pendleton area had the requisite components for western flicks—cowboys, cowgirls, Indians, horses and cattle, and a business community eager to attract and accommodate film crews. Movie productions might take only a few weeks, but they brought excitement, a brush with glamour, and a chance for locals to earn extra money.

Movie cameras weren't new to the Round-Up in the 1920s. Grainy highlights of its earliest years were staples of newsreels shown at theaters nationwide. In 1919, the documentary *Romance of Pendleton* was made in the area. Leland J. Burrud, who specialized in filming interviews with celebrities and newsmakers (including the Mexican revolution leader Pancho Villa) shot rodeo competition that September as well as footage of Indians worshipping at the nearby Tutuilla Protestant Mission.

From 1924 to 1933, eight silent movies were filmed in Umatilla County; four of them incorporated footage shot at the Round-Up. The movies might have been made elsewhere if Edmund "Hoot" Gibson hadn't fondly remembered Pendleton. After spending part of his youth working as a farm hand in the Umatilla County hamlet of Echo, he entered the 1912 Round-Up. Barely able to pay the entrance fees and wearing torn dungarees, Gibson came away with the all-around championship and cash in his pocket. During the next twelve years he appeared in 133 movies and became one of the country's best-known stars. His star power apparently allowed him to influence his studio, Universal Pictures, on movie location decisions. Gibson returned to Pendleton in 1924 as part of a cast and crew of forty to make *Let 'er Buck*, a $50,000 venture and the first feature film with a story built around the Round-Up.

"Pendleton treated me right when I was flat," Gibson told the *East Oregonian* when he arrived for the start of filming. "It never forgets the cowboys that helped put the Round-Up over when it was young, and I wanted to show that the boys never forget Pendleton either."

With the exception of scenes filmed at a grandstand reproduction at Universal City in Hollywood, the one-hour movie was shot entirely in Pendleton and the surrounding countryside. As part of the contract, Round-Up officials stipulated that filming not interfere with any contests and that actors must enter the competitions to appear on camera. Action shots of Gibson included him driving a team of four palominos to victory twice in the Round-Up's first chariot races. Another Round-Up champion, Yakima Canutt, in the early stage of a long and storied movie career, also competed that year. He would direct the famed chariot races in the 1959 version of *Ben-Hur*, and he received an honorary Oscar in 1966.

Let 'er Buck was one of three films shot in Umatilla County in 1924. All featured Gibson and were directed by Edward Sedgwick. *Let 'er Buck* received a favorable review in the *New York Morning Telegraph*. The movie also starred Josie Sedgwick, the director's sister. At Gibson's suggestion, the Round-Up board of directors named her queen of the 1924 rodeo, a move that attracted more publicity to the event. The value of this marketing synergy was not lost on the Round-Up board and its president Henry Collins, who had a small part in *Let 'er Buck*. Champion cowgirl Mabel Strickland, in the midst of a modest career as a stuntwoman and actress, was named queen in 1927. The next year, stage and screen star Mary Duncan was selected queen as part of an arrangement for Movietone Films to produce *Our Daily Bread* in and around Pendleton with her in the starring role. (Unfortunately, the movie was a flop.)

Edward Sedgwick directed two more movies in the Pendleton area in 1925, *Under Western Skies* and *The Last Frontier*. Once again the city developed movie fever. Businesses closed for an hour so townspeople could greet the train carrying the production crew. A horse-mounted cowboy band, a drum corps, and residents dressed in cowboy attire turned out. Speaking for the Umatilla Tribes, Chief Poker Jim welcomed the crew.

Golden Harvest, filmed in Umatilla County's sprawling wheat fields in 1933, earned extras seven dollars a day. An actor with a small part received three Oscars later in his career and became a television icon in the long-running series *The Real McCoys*—Walter Brennan.

Movie crews returned to Pendleton in 1952 to make three films, but with less emphasis on the Round-Up or no mention at all. Tribal people, many of them active participants in the Round-Up, benefited most from these films, cast in supporting roles that through no fault of theirs sometimes lacked authenticity. *Bronco Buster* used the Round-Up Indian Village in the film but wrongly identified the tribal people as members of the Lakota nation. *The Lusty Men* starred Robert Mitchum and Susan Hayward and included scenes from the Round-Up and its Indian Village.

Jeff Chandler was the marquee name in the most ambitious and successful film made in Umatilla County, which featured many members of the Umatilla and Nez Perce Tribes but was called *The Great Sioux Uprising*. Cayuse tribal member Leah Conner, Round-Up queen in 1952, was among dozens of Indians who appeared in the movie or contributed to its production. Among them were four Indian women who also had bit parts in *The Flaming Frontier*, one of Gibson's films in the 1920s—Susie Williams, Margaret Naneges, Eliza Bill, and Susie Burke.

On the first day of filming in the rugged Blue Mountains, director Lloyd Bacon ordered young men from the Umatilla Reservation to race through a movie-set Indian village with loud war whoops as if they were entering battle. The riders found their roles so much fun that they couldn't stop smiling. It took them eight takes to portray the dramatic tension Bacon wanted, and the riders became known on the set as the "Laughing Umatillas."

Even before World War I, some early Round-Up stars and regulars besides Gibson and Canutt parlayed their rodeo skills, charisma, and good looks into roles for movies filmed elsewhere in the West. Dell Blancett appeared with 1915 all-around champion Lee Caldwell in *The Cowpuncher*, filmed in Idaho in 1915. Both Tommy Grimes, three-time winner of the Round-Up's steer roping contest, and "Skeeter" Bill Robbins, an accomplished steer roper who late in his life managed Gibson's ranch in California, acted in thirteen movies. Vera McGinnis appeared in two movies until her rodeo and acting careers were cut short when a horse somersaulted and fell on her in 1934, breaking her back in five places and causing several other fractures. (A testimony to her toughness: she lived to be ninety-eight.) Strickland performed in eleven movies, mostly doing stunts and serving as a double, though she had a cameo role in the 1936 Bing Crosby film *Rhythm on the Range*. Art Acord, the Round-Up's bulldogging champion in 1912, appeared in more than a hundred films over a twenty-year period, mostly in credited roles. Acord's career suffered from chronic heavy

Wallace Smith observed how the presence of movie cameras influenced rodeo participants. Many were so eager to be discovered by Hollywood that they began dressing the way cowboy stars dressed and spoke in subtitles. They were getting their styles from the Hollywood wardrobe rooms and their manners from the actors who were, in turn, getting their Western traditions from the director's megaphone.

▲ Art Acord wrestles a steer to the ground and bites its lip to keep it down, 1912. *Howdyshell Collection.*

drinking, which intensified when he couldn't land film roles in the "talkies" because of his high-pitched voice. Despondent and penniless, he went to Mexico, where he worked briefly for a mining company. He died there in 1931. Although police declared his death a suicide from ingesting cyanide, friends maintained he was murdered.

Art Artego may have set an unofficial record for bit parts, appearing in 217 films from 1912 to 1955. Often without screen credit, he portrayed nameless characters such as the barfly, town cowboy, circus Indian, or henchman.

HOOT GIBSON

No competitor at the Round-Up amassed the fame or fortune of Edmund "Hoot" Gibson, winner of the all-around championship in 1912 at age twenty. In the 1920s and '30s, kids across the country packed movie houses for Saturday matinées to watch the cowboy-turned-actor ride to the rescue atop his loyal steed "Goldie." Sometimes they stamped their feet and chanted "Hoot! Hoot! Hoot!" until he arrived and set things right. In the heyday of westerns, few actors were more popular. But like so many who found movie stardom, Gibson saw his popularity and wealth fade then

vanish, partly because of personal excesses as predictable in Hollywood lifestyles as the plots of his movies.

Typical of Round-Up stars in the making, Gibson learned to ride horses as a young child on a ranch. His family's ranch was fifteen hundred miles from Pendleton in eastern Nebraska, just west of the Missouri River in Tekamah, an Omaha Indian word meaning "big cottonwoods." Born there in 1892, Gibson had his own pony when he was two and a half years old. He may have earned his nickname in Tekamah because of his skills hunting owls in caves. Or it may have been later, after his family moved to the Los Angeles area, when as a young teen he delivered packages for the Owl Drug Company. In interviews over the years, Gibson gave both accounts. No matter the genesis of "Hoot," the name stuck.

While still in his teens, Gibson began working on a ranch, where he honed his skills as a rider and roper. He also entered small rodeos. As his prowess grew, so did his yearning to roam the vanishing western range with the brotherhood of cowboys he later immortalized in 275 films as a stuntman and actor with many leading roles. Tired of school, Gibson ran away to join a circus, worked as a cowboy in Wyoming and Colorado, then worked in Oklahoma for the famous Miller Brothers' 101 Ranch, where he got to know other wranglers destined for stardom. They included Tom Mix, Buck Jones, and Ken Maynard, who with Gibson became known as Hollywood's Big Four cowboy movie stars. Starting in 1907, Gibson spent four years showing off his cowboy skills for audiences across the United States and Australia as part of a Wild West show called the Congress of Rough Riders.

In 1910, Gibson and five other cowboys herded one hundred wild horses from Nevada to California's San Fernando Valley and sold them to ranchers. Flush with cash for a change, he was eating a steak at a restaurant when he heard about a movie crew needing stunt riders. So began his fifty-year movie career, with a job that paid $20 a week plus an extra $2.50 for portraying an Indian, getting shot, or falling off a horse.

Gibson took on many daredevil stunts along with acting parts. He was considered fearless, and not just on horseback. He once drove a speeding motorcycle off a raised drawbridge. When a director asked him to consider a spectacular fall from a horse for an extra $5, he said, "Make it ten bucks and I'll let him kick me to death." (*New York Times*, 1962) Within ten years, Gibson was making $14,500 a week for starring roles and was on his way to total earnings of $6 million—many millions more in today's dollars when adjusted for inflation.

Despite his riding skills and impeccable cowboy credentials, Gibson wasn't the prototypical leading man. He was neither physically imposing nor classically handsome. Yet he smiled easily, exuded a genuine charm, and brought a natural comedic bent to some roles. He was an original who didn't wear a holster but stuck his six-shooter in his belt or his boot. Somehow he connected with audiences.

His first film, *Pride of the Range* of 1910, starred Tom Mix and included Art Acord, another alumnus of the 101 Ranch who was later a Round-Up champion. Gibson and Acord also appeared in the 1910 *Two Brothers*, directed by D. W. Griffith, who five years later directed the epic *Birth of a Nation*.

For several years, Gibson spent the summers competing in rodeos and performing in Wild West shows and the winters building his film career. His reputation received a boost in 1912 when he won the Round-Up's overall championship as well as the Calgary Stampede's fancy roping championship.

Gibson made a dramatic return to the Round-Up in 1924 with a film crew to star in *Let 'er Buck*, which included scenes shot during competitions. Gibson won both chariot races, which the Round-Up staged for the first time that year. Round-Up officials presented him with an unusual gift—"No Name," the horse that had thrown him in the 1913 bucking competition, when he competed with an injured arm in a sling.

At the 1911 Round-Up, Gibson fell in love with stunt and rodeo rider Helen August Wegner. Whether they married is open to question, though Helen adopted Gibson's name. She apparently made most of the couple's income until they split up in 1920 as Gibson's movie career began to take off. Helen became Hollywood's first professional stuntwoman and starred in more than half the 119 episodes of *The Hazards of Helen*, the movie industry's longest-running serial. At seventy, she had her last movie role—driving a team of horses in *The Man Who Shot Liberty Valance*, for $35. She died in Roseburg, Oregon, in 1977 at eighty-five.

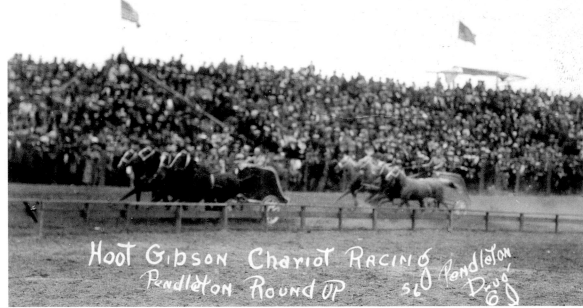

▲▲ Hoot Gibson (left) with Paddy Ryan, 1924 winner of the Roosevelt Trophy. *Low Collection.*

▲ Hoot Gibson wins the 1924 chariot race.

Low Collection.

Today's tabloids would have screamed with salacious headlines about Gibson's personal life. He married singer Helen Johnson, with whom he had a daughter; she divorced him several years later, claiming infidelity and abandonment. He later married the flamboyant actress Sally Eilers, who like Gibson was known for living on the wild side. In 1933, when Gibson was forty, he crashed one of his four airplanes while racing against friend and fellow actor Ken Maynard at the National Air Races in Los Angeles. While recuperating in the hospital from three fractured vertebrae, broken ribs, and a leg injury that left him with a permanent limp, Gibson announced that he and Eilers planned to divorce. At his side was June Gale, a twenty-one-year-old actress, who agreed with Gibson's statement that they were "madly in love."

Gibson's tumultuous love life hurt his finances, as did the Wall Street crash, bad investments, and spending on airplanes, race horses, cars, a Beverly Hills mansion, and other real estate. His career faltered in the mid 1930s, when he was unable to compete with the sudden popularity of singing cowboys such as Gene Autry and Roy Rogers. He left film work for several years and returned to the circus and western show circuit, where he still drew large crowds.

In 1942, a month before his fiftieth birthday, Gibson married a twenty-two-year-old yodeler in his show, Dorothy Dunstan. The marriage lasted until his death in 1962 and endured Gibson's declining health and finances. In 1953, Gibson starred in *The Marshal's Daughter*, his last leading role. While battling cancer during his last years of life, he worked as a greeter for the Last Frontier hotel and casino in Las Vegas.

Famed director John Ford, who roomed briefly with Gibson in the earliest days of their careers and directed Gibson in his first starring role in the 1921 film *Action*, sought out the aged and infirm star in 1959. Gibson agreed to play an army sergeant in Ford's *The Horse Soldiers*, starring John Wayne, if someone would hoist him upon a horse.

While in the hospital in 1960, Hoot expressed no bitterness or regrets. In an interview he said, "I don't cry. I guess we'll eat." (*New York Times*, 1962)

Gibson has a star on the Hollywood Walk of Fame and was inducted into the Western Performers Hall of Fame at the National Cowboy and Western Heritage Museum in Oklahoma City.

YAKIMA CANUTT

Yakima Canutt, one of the Round-Up's greatest champions and Hollywood's most renowned stuntman, was eleven when he first rode a bucking bronco, and he rode out of revenge.

The story line could have come from one of the more than three hundred western films Canutt played a part in or directed. But it was a real-life drama set in a potato patch at his family's farm on Penawawa Creek in the Snake River Hills of eastern Washington. His older brother Alex had recently bought a horse and named him "Buck." While trying to tame Buck, Alex was thrown and dragged, fracturing his skull.

During Alex's long convalescence, Canutt watched the horse getting fat and wild. It was 1906. "Every day I went out to the pasture and studied Buck. Knowing what he had done, I just couldn't stand by and let him enjoy that green grass," Canutt wrote in his 1979 autobiography, *Stunt Man*. Before his brother's injury, he had wanted to try his luck breaking a horse, knowing that in the Northwest "a man who was a good bronc rider was a bit of an idol—much like an astronaut today."

Buck "bawled like a bear in a trap" as he tried to throw the boy, who spurred him again and again. As the subdued

MAJOR MOORHOUSE

Yakima Canutt "U.S. Navy" on The Fighting Top of Monkey-Wrench Pendleton Oregon

◄ **Canutt of the U.S. Navy rides "Monkey Wrench" in 1918.** *By L. Moorhouse in OHS Collection, OrHi 4042.*

▼ **Canutt rides "Bill McAdoo" in the early years.** *Howdyshell Collection.*

Even some Indians thought Yakima Canutt was one of their people, including a well-educated man named White Cloud. Canutt described the conversation in his 1979 autobiography:

"Yakima, what tribe are you from?"

"I'm not Indian," I replied.

"You ashamed of it?" he asked, with a scowl.

"If I was Indian I would be very proud of it, but I have traced my ancestry as far back as possible, only to learn that I am Scotch and Irish on my mother's side and Dutch and German on my father's side."

White Cloud . . . gave me a sympathetic look, shook his head and walked away.

FACING PAGE ▶ Charlton Heston and Yakima Canutt, stunt director for *Ben-Hur* (1959), on the movie set outside Rome. *Courtesy MPTV.net.*

horse started to slow, Canutt's parents ran from their house to investigate the commotion. "I just wanted to give him a lesson," he told his angry father.

Canutt knew then that he wanted to become a cowboy and set out to achieve his boyhood dream: winning the bronc riding contest at the annual rodeo in nearby Colfax, Washington. His first chance almost came in 1911 when he was fifteen. As he started to mount the fearsome bucker "Hotfoot" in a qualifying round, "two big hands grabbed me from behind. I knew the feel of those powerful hands—it was Dad. He had one hand on my collar, the other on my britches at the belt line. He took me kicking to the fence and boosted me over. I was humiliated." Over the next several months he secretly rode several wild broncs and then an especially tough one with his father observing. At sixteen, Canutt had permission to enter the competition at the Colfax Fair. He won.

During the next decade, he proved to be one of the nation's most successful rodeo riders, specializing in saddle bronc riding and bulldogging steers. At Pendleton, he won the all-around championship four times—in 1917, 1919, 1920, and 1923. Only two other cowboys equaled this feat: Bob Crosby later in the 1920s and Shoat Webster from 1949 through 1952. Canutt also won his lasting place in rodeo lore by mastering horses so wild that no one had been able to ride them. They included the legendary bucker "Tipperary." By one account, "Tipperary" had thrown eighty-two men before Canutt rode him to a stop in 1920 at the Black Hills' Tri-State Roundup in Belle Fourche, South Dakota, a feat he repeated there the next year. Both horse and rider were inducted into the National Cowboy Hall of Fame in 1976.

The hard-living Canutt was less successful in his marriage to another Round-Up star, Kitty Wilkes Canutt. In 1916, they had finished competing in Kalispell, Montana, where Yakima had won two events, and they planned to marry the next day. Canutt's friends threw a bachelor's party at a bar, the party became a drinking contest, and the contest ended with the groom-to-be badly losing a fistfight. Try as he did to hide his hangover at the wedding ceremony, Canutt couldn't hide his battered face. When the newlyweds were finally alone, Kitty expressed her displeasure regarding "just what kind of no good character a man is," Yakima wrote in

his autobiography. "It didn't take long for me to figure out we should have been saying 'I won't' instead of 'I do.'" They divorced three years later.

Canutt's real first name was Enos. No one called him Yakima until 1914, a few days before he competed in the Round-Up for the first time. He and two friends from Yakima, Washington, decided to try out some of the rodeo's notorious bucking horses. To settle their nerves before they rode, they quickly emptied a bottle of Old Crow. "I never realized how much of a wallop that Old Crow really had," Canutt wrote. "From my point of view, looking down over the front of my saddle, that bronc had two very fuzzy heads. They quickly transposed to four or five spurred boots with my feet in them and nothing but the blue sky on beyond. The little bronc was gone. I hit the ground with a painful thud, to the joy of the spectators who were in hysterics."

Pendleton photographer Walter Bowman took a picture of Canutt airborne and upside down above the horse. In a 1917 story about the nickname's genesis, the *East Oregonian* said that when Bowman asked the identity of the thrown rider, a cowboy replied, "Oh, that's Canutt of Yakima." Bowman captioned the photograph: "Yakima Canutt leaving the deck of a Pendleton bronc."

The nickname, often shortened to Yak, led some people to assume that Canutt was Indian, perhaps a member of the Yakama nation. The newspaper, using a pejorative common in that era, said Canutt is not a "redskin" and has "black hair and eyes but his skin is just as white as any man's." In his book, Canutt wrote that after rodeo parties, people would try to guess what tribe he was from, and he would play along, at various times saying he was a Sioux, Umatilla, or Nez Perce.

Like many early rodeo stars, Canutt was attracted to the growing film industry and the prospect of movie work as a cowboy, especially during the winters. In 1919, at a Los Angeles rodeo, he met the actor Douglas Fairbanks. Soon afterward, Canutt's friend Tommy Grimes, a Round-Up steer roping champion turned actor, took him to Fox Studio, where he met the western movie star Tom Mix. With little effort, Mix persuaded Canutt to portray an outlaw in a movie he was making. Canutt kept showing up on the set clean-shaven, though the role called for a rough-looking, disheveled man. "I didn't want to run around with whiskers, so I never went back," he wrote in his book. He appeared in two other movies that winter, as a deputy sheriff in *The Girl Who Dared* and as a fist-fighting cowboy in *Lightning Bryce*.

The movies marked the start of a film career that spanned more than half a century. Canutt worked as an actor, stuntman, writer, director, and producer in 350 movies. Without the athleticism, cowboy skills, and daring that helped make him Hollywood's foremost stuntman, Canutt's movie career might have ended in the late 1920s when the silent film era began to give way to "talkies." He explained: "I had the flu in 1918, while in the Navy, and my vocal chords were permanently damaged." When he heard his voice for the first time on a soundtrack, he said it sounded "like a hillbilly in a well."

Canutt performed some of his best-known stunts in two 1939 films. In *Gone with the Wind*, it's not Clark Gable playing Rhett Butler who rescues Vivian Leigh's Scarlett O'Hara, but Yakima Canutt furiously driving a one-horse buggy through the flaming ruins of Atlanta. In *Stagecoach*, Canutt plays an Indian who leaps from a horse onto the lead horse in a rampaging team pulling a coach driven by John Wayne. Canutt falls between the horses and lets the stagecoach pass over him. Then, doubling for Wayne, he leaps from the stagecoach onto the runaway horses and brings them under control.

Decades of rodeos and movie stunt work took a toll on Canutt's body. He broke both ankles while portraying Roy Rogers in the 1943 film *Idaho* and decided to turn to directing stunts and live-action sequences. Canutt developed and directed some of Hollywood's most memorable action scenes, including the chariot race in *Ben-Hur* and battle scenes in *El Cid* and *Spartacus*. In the climactic massacre in *Khartoum*, filmed in Egypt, he choreographed five thousand foot soldiers, seven hundred fifty camel riders, and hundreds of horsemen. He also directed stunt work in *Swiss Family Robinson*, *Old Yeller*, and *Cat Ballou*.

In 1967, actor Charlton Heston presented Canutt with an honorary Academy Award for creating the profession of stuntman and developing its safety devices. Canutt trained Heston to drive a chariot in *Ben-Hur*. Two years later Canutt was among the first group inducted into the Round-Up and Happy Canyon Hall of Fame. He was ninety years old when he died in North Hollywood in 1986.

MONTIE MONTANA

MONTIE MONTANA

No Round-Up performer did more with a rope and a smile than Montie Montana. He made his first appearance at the rodeo in 1927 at age seventeen and dazzled the crowd with his display of trick roping. He made his last in 1997 at age eighty-seven, when he rode in the Westward Ho! Parade, performed at the Happy Canyon show to a standing ovation, and judged the Indian Beauty Pageant, lassoing the winners.

Throwing his rope around people was Montana's trademark gesture. In 1953 it earned him headlines nationwide when he snagged Dwight D. Eisenhower during the President's inaugural parade—a stunt that was approved in advance but rattled the Secret Service all the same. Another trademark was Montana's frequent and broad grin, and he was often called the "smiling cowboy."

Montana, whose long career included appearances in some thirty movies and television shows, had a way of making others smile, too. When he was inducted into the Round-Up and Happy Canyon Hall of Fame in 1980, he rode his horse into what is now the Doubletree Hotel and spoke to the audience assembled for the ceremony from atop the horse. To the people seated behind him on the dais, who had a close-up view of the horse's rear end, Montana said: "Please excuse the Democrat end of my Republican horse." (*East Oregonian*, 1998)

Montana, whose real name was Owen Harlan Mickel, was born in Wolf Point, Montana, in 1910 and grew up there on his parents' ranch. He began performing with his mother and father at rodeos and Wild West shows when he was fourteen. The family billed themselves as the Montana Cowboys. In 1929, an announcer at a Buck Jones Wild West show couldn't remember his name and called him "Montie from Montana," and his nickname was born.

Two years earlier he had to audition at 6 a.m. to win his first spot in the Round-Up. The audition committee included Round-Up president Henry Collins. "I just did a few tricks, and they said, 'You're all right. We'll hire you,'" he recalled. (*East Oregonian*, 1975) Montana, who could lasso ten running horses with a single loop of his rope, was a regular at the Round-Up in the 1930s and 1940s. He returned to Pendleton in 1975 to serve as Grand Marshal of the Westward Ho! Parade.

Like many rodeo stars, Montana used his talents in western films. He was an accomplished trick rider whose acting and stunt credits included *The Man Who Shot Liberty Valance* (1962), starring John Wayne and Jimmy Stewart, as well as episodes of TV's *Gunsmoke* and *The Rifleman*. His biggest role came in *Circle of Death* (1935), in which he starred as a young white man who was raised by Indians from infancy and returned to the tribe to aid a rancher. (Round-Up champion Yakima Canutt played an Indian

▲ Montie Montana's custom-made boots, red leather with white butterfly design and double M double bar brand.
Hall of Fame Collection.

▼ Montie Montana performs the seven-horse catch, 1949. *By DeVere in Low Collection.*

115

brave in the film.) Montana also performed rope tricks in Broadway's award-winning *Oklahoma!* in 1979 and 1980. He and his pinto "Rex" (at least eight horses named "Rex" graced Montana's career) performed on the roof of the Empire State Building in the late 1980s.

Besides acting and making frequent rodeo appearances around the country, Montana taught roping to other actors and entertainers, including Steve Martin and Steve Allen, and to thousands of schoolchildren in a twenty-year public relations role for a Los Angeles–area bread company. Among his friends were Slim Pickens, Tom Mix, Roy Rogers, and Will Rogers. He considered Will Rogers to be the greatest of all trick ropers. In a 1975 interview with United Press International, Montana called trick roping a "lost art" because "no young people are taking it up. Roping takes too much time and practice and it doesn't pay off big anymore."

Montana, who appeared in every major rodeo in the United States and Canada, was a fixture in the New Year's Day Tournament of Roses Parade in Pasadena, riding in more than sixty consecutive parades and occasionally lassoing children in the audience. He was inducted into the National Cowboy Hall of Fame before his death in 1998.

A series of strokes debilitated Montana in the months before he died. One of his longtime Pendleton friends, Bill Shaw (who originated the falling horse skit in the Happy Canyon show), recalled speaking to Montana on the phone. "He couldn't talk, but he could laugh," Shaw told the *East Oregonian* in 1998. "I'd talk to him and he'd just laugh and laugh. Then we'd hang up and I'd just sit in the bunk house and cry."

CHARLES WELLINGTON FURLONG

Someone among the Round-Up's countless enthusiasts may have lived a more diverse life and built a richer litany of achievements than Charles Furlong. But they would be hard pressed to match his résumé: jungle and desert explorer, scientist, ethnographer, military spy, emissary to foreign kings and generals, aide to President Woodrow Wilson, New Englander at home on the western range, celebrated artist and writer. And that's the condensed version.

Certainly no one wrote more prolifically or fondly about the Round-Up and Pendleton, or with greater effect.

While Furlong mostly observed the Round-Up up close as a magazine correspondent given unprecedented access to the competitions, he also rode bulls three times—once with spectacular results. In doing so, he may have set a standard for participatory journalism, injecting himself in a story to improve its telling—and selling. Whether contrived or serendipitous, the result was extraordinary publicity for the Round-Up in its early years that reached far beyond the Northwest.

Born in Cambridge, Massachusetts, Furlong studied art in Boston and Paris. When he first visited Pendleton in 1913 on assignment for *The World's Work* magazine, he was thirty-eight. He had already taught drawing and painting and chaired the art department at Cornell University in Ithaca, New York, and completed expeditions to North Africa and South America.

In 1904, he became the first American to explore the Sahara Desert in what is now Libya. He caravanned with Arab bandits and found the century-old wreckage of the U.S. frigate *Philadelphia*, which burned and sank in Tripoli during the Barbary Coast Wars. The trip also produced his first book, *Gateway to the Sahara*, published in 1909 and reissued in 2002, and articles for several magazines, including five for *Harper's*, all ripe with sensory detail and lavishly illustrated with his paintings of an exotic land and its peoples.

Furlong's most important scientific findings came in 1907 and 1908 on a *Harper's*-financed expedition to Tierra del Fuego, "Land of Fire," the archipelago at the southern tip of South America. There he catalogued plants, mapped the area, took hundreds of photographs, and lived among native tribes. He hauled along an Edison phonograph and wax recording cylinders weighing forty pounds that captured the now-extinct languages of two tribes. The recordings are housed at Dartmouth College and the Library of Congress. Eleven of Furlong's paintings from the trip are at the Smithsonian American Art Museum.

In a second South American expedition in 1910 and 1911, Furlong trekked across Dutch Guinea and became the first American to travel down the treacherous Oronoco River in Venezuela. The trip debilitated him. Like his friend Teddy Roosevelt, he went to the West to recuperate—not by resting, but by working on ranches in Montana and

▲ Furlong's hat, last worn when he was Grand Marshal of the Westward Ho! Parade in 1966. *Hall of Fame Collection.*
◄ Charles Wellington Furlong (left) with Jackson Sundown, 1916 all-around champion.
By W. S. Bowman in Helm Collection.

Oregon. It marked the start of a love affair with the land, the people, and the rapidly changing way of life.

Despite his worldliness, Furlong fit in. He made friends easily and was a veteran horseman who dressed the part. "I would like people to know those chaps are mine: I did not borrow them," he told the *East Oregonian* in 1913. That year he rode the fearsome bull "Henry Vogt" twice, and the newspaper said he "made a very respectable showing though he did not get his feet in the stirrups."

Furlong returned the next year as a writer for *Harper's*. The Round-Up board made him an arena and track assistant, giving him the best possible vantage point. The *East*

Oregonian also retained him to write a story published each day of the Round-Up. Though his reporting lacked the precision and detail of his magazine work, and the overwrought prose meandered, Furlong's celebrity must have been a marketing boon for the newspaper.

Before the Round-Up, he delivered a lecture in Pendleton about his South American travels, complete with his photographs, which the newspaper said "proved a revelation for his audience." But the real revelation came when he, like so many before him, tried to ride the infamous bull "Sharkey."

Anyone could earn five dollars for merely climbing aboard the beast. One hundred dollars awaited riders who

► From left, Charles Wellington Furlong, Jackson Sundown, and A. Phimister Proctor at the 1916 Round-Up. *By W. S. Bowman in OHS Collection, bb003687.*

stayed on the bull's back for ten seconds or longer, money that had never been paid. During three days in Salinas, California, "Sharkey" threw thirty-six riders within a few seconds each. On the Round-Up's last day in 1914, Furlong accepted a challenge to try his luck.

"The colossal proportions of that ton-and-a-half black brute looked even larger to me as I watched Happy Jack tighten up the [saddle] cinch with a smile," Furlong wrote in his 1921 book *Let'er Buck: A Story of the Passing of the Old West.* "Well, Jack could afford to smile—he wasn't going to ride him." A bone-jarring twelve-and-a-half seconds later, Furlong was sprawled in the dust with a broken wrist and a permanent place in Round-Up lore.

Published with fifty of Furlong's photographs, the book became a huge best-seller. Reissued in September 2007 after being out of print for eighty years, it ranked as the twelfth-highest-selling rodeo book on Amazon.com four months later.

The book celebrated the West and its vanishing ways; it ignored mistreatment of native people. There have been whispers that embellishments crept into Furlong's reporting—not unusual for that era. For example, only in

Let'er Buck is Lee Caldwell described as riding bucking broncos on his way to the championship in 1915 with a plaster cast on his injured wrist and getting pain-killing injections through a hole in the cast. No cast is visible in photographs or mentioned in newspaper articles.

Furlong continued his expeditions and writing about them, traveling to Africa and the Middle East, though the treks began to serve another purpose: political and military intelligence for the U.S. government as World War I broke out. He created the Geographic Military Intelligence Division and later served on the U.S. delegation to the Paris Peace Conference as an aide to President Wilson.

His later assignments included diplomatic work as an emissary to Saudi King Faisal and other missions in the Middle East, where he met T. E. Lawrence ("Lawrence of Arabia") and became an expert on Turkey after extensive travel there. His writings about ethnic conflicts in Turkey resurfaced in 2007 during U.S. congressional debates about genocide among Turks and Armenians.

In 1929 and 1930, Furlong explored Central and East Africa, where he found artifacts of the Sir Henry Stanley expedition and lived among pygmies. Film he shot during the expedition, along with footage from the Round-Up, was discovered at Dartmouth College and sold at auction in 2007. A meticulous record keeper, Furlong spent his later years organizing his papers and collections and distributing them among a dozen universities, museums, and other institutions, including the University of Oregon and the Round-Up and Happy Canyon Hall of Fame in Pendleton, which displays some of his cowboy attire and a saddle.

A highly religious man who embraced conservative politics, Furlong died at the age of ninety-two in 1967 in Hanover, New Hampshire, home of Dartmouth.

Genealogical message boards on the Internet include robust correspondence among the colonel's friends and relatives. A former student assistant who helped him in the early 1960s wrote that Furlong was "very much a gentleman, with a strong sense of *noblesse oblige* in the best sense of the term. He was not an elitist . . . did not wear his accomplishments on his sleeve or make any effort to garner attention. . . . He had a resolute sense of 'right and wrong,' and 'how you play the game.'"

In a 2008 email exchange, Furlong's great-grandson, Chuck Furlong of Austin, Texas, wrote that the colonel—called "Big Dad" by family members—was "very concerned with the preservation of cultures. He spent his whole life studying various cultures and trying to understand them."

A year before his death, Col. Charles Wellington Furlong returned to Pendleton for the last time in 1966 as Grand Marshal of the Westward Ho! Parade. He and his second wife, Edith, rode in a horse-drawn carriage at the head of the parade. They watched the bull riding with special interest, and in an interview Furlong noted that safety reforms had reduced the action in the arena.

Throughout his four days in town, Furlong found himself shaking hands with the children and grandchildren of his friends from the old days, friends who had all passed away.

ALEXANDER PHIMISTER PROCTOR

For a sculptor in search of dramatic subjects symbolizing the vanishing West, Pendleton and the Round-Up's cavalcade of cowboys, Indians, and wild horses must have seemed like nirvana. When Alexander Phimister Proctor, born in 1860 in a rural township of Ontario, Canada, arrived for the 1914 Round-Up, he found subjects galore, as well as a way of life that imbued his work with energy, emotion, and beauty.

Pendleton embraced Proctor, who was already known as the country's foremost sculptor of life-size large animals. Proctor reveled in his good fortune and quickly asked his wife Margaret and their children to move from New York to Umatilla County for a months-long stay.

"Within two weeks [Margaret] had given up the big house in New Rochelle, stored the furniture, and sublet my New York studio," Proctor wrote in his autobiography, *Sculptor in Buckskin*. "When Margaret and our seven children arrived, people outdid themselves to help us."

His arrival created a stir. Proctor was already well known in Portland's robust art scene, where in 1911 a major exhibition had featured his sculptures. His bronze piece *The Indian Warrior* was the first original work of sculpture purchased by the Portland Art Museum.

"Since sculptors were then quite a novelty in eastern Oregon, I was almost considered an exhibit myself," Proctor wrote in his autobiography. Officials gave him run of the Round-Up grounds to sketch potential sculpture subjects but were wary of letting him enter the arena during competitions. Assuming he was from the East, they feared he might endanger himself. When they learned he had grown up an avid outdoorsman in Colorado and hunted wild game across the United States and Canada, they loaned him a horse because, as he said, "having a mount somehow lessened the danger of having me around. I couldn't sketch too easily on horseback, however, and continued to go about on foot with pad and pencil in hand."

During the Round-Up's bucking contest, Proctor stood inside the arena fences making action sketches. Once, when a wild horse was set loose with a cowboy aboard, the animal zeroed in on Proctor, bucking while chasing him no matter how he tried to dodge it. Only a last-second sideways leap saved the sculptor from the horse's front hooves as they crashed down from a high buck. It wouldn't be his last brush with danger.

Proctor converted a Round-Up building into a sixteen-by fourteen-foot studio, intent on sculpting a cowboy on horseback there. For models he bought an Indian-bred cayuse—"a wall-eyed brute, a direct offspring of the

The Pendleton Round-Up is the Wild West unadulterated: there the most famous daredevils gather each year to ride the most famous bucking broncs. . . . It is a regular Wild West Coney Island. It is the kind of thing which is the breath of life to an adventurous spirit.

—T. R. Ybarra, *New York Times*, June 1921

▲ John Mulligan (right), 1969 Round-Up president, inducts George Fletcher into the Pendleton Hall of Fame.

Howdyshell Collection.

FLETCHER SAVED!

George Fletcher survived bucking horses galore and army service in World War I. But before enlisting he almost didn't survive a serious gunshot wound and a twenty-five-mile trip to the hospital over a rough mountain road.

A firsthand account of the shooting and the harrowing trip appears in Alexander Phimister Proctor's autobiography, *Sculptor in Buckskin*. The book was edited by Proctor's daughter Hester and published in 1971, though it was written decades earlier. Proctor had taken his automobile to an informal rodeo on McKay Creek. He witnessed an attack by a drunk cowboy, who shot Fletcher in the stomach. Driving as fast as he dared, Proctor took the bleeding cowboy to the hospital in Pendleton.

"The next day the doctor told me that five minutes more and George would have cashed in his chips," Proctor wrote of the incident, which reads like a scene in a Wild West movie.

The book identifies the cowboy merely as "George" and "one of the best riders in the outfit"—a group of cowboys Proctor recognized at the rodeo. But a typewritten draft of Proctor's manuscript, among his papers at the Oregon Historical Society, identifies the wounded man as "Nigger George" and "one of the best riders around."

There can be no doubt that Proctor was referring to Fletcher, one of the few black residents in sparsely populated Pendleton and Umatilla County. Fletcher was outgoing, friendly, and a superb rider. Folks in the area liked him. Yet even his friends used the nickname, as did the *East Oregonian* on occasion. Such were the customs of the times.

One can only presume that Hester Proctor deleted the racial epithet, which by 1971 had become incendiary. It's also likely that she wouldn't have known of Fletcher's prominent place in Round-Up history.

The shooting occurred in 1915 or 1916—Proctor isn't specific. "All the boys knew I was studying buckers, and the roundup boss called out, 'Who's goin' to ride that buckskin SOB for Proctor?'"

"I'll ride the bastard for him," Fletcher said in another deleted passage.

The drunk cowboy, Charley Runyan, boasted he was the only one who could ride the horse, then took offense when a grinning Fletcher referred to him as a sheepherder.

From atop his horse and without warning, the cowboy pulled a six-shooter, shot Fletcher in the stomach, and galloped away. Proctor wrote, "I rushed over to George, who was rolling about with hands on his stomach. 'Shoot me, shoot me—for God's sake, kill me!'"

Proctor's 1915 Cadillac was the only car at the rodeo. Fletcher was loaded on the floor with his feet sticking out the open door. Not only was the terrain rough— "George cried out every time I hit a rough spot in the road"—but the engine nearly quit when the car plowed through water at a river crossing.

Ten days later, Fletcher was out of the hospital with nearly sixty years ahead of him.

GEORGE FLETCHER

devil"—and hired a popular cowboy, Bill "Slim" Ridings. When Ridings posed atop the horse in the tight quarters, chaos erupted. "Stovepipe, splinters, boxes, table, and high profanity flew around for a time," until Slim brought the horse under control, Proctor wrote in his autobiography. (The sculptor calls his model "Red" in the book. However, news reports at the time detailed Proctor's work with "Slim" Ridings, and a draft of the autobiography in Proctor's papers at the Oregon Historical Society identifies the model as "Bill 'Slim' Ridings.")

In July 1915, the result of months of work was shown in Seattle and then Portland: a small plaster casting of the *Buckaroo*. It depicted a cowboy modeled after Ridings leaning far back to stay astride the horse as its hind legs kicked high in the air and its head nearly touched the ground. The *East Oregonian* reported that the horse most resembled the well-known bucker "Angel" and that Proctor relied on a photograph of Lew Minor's 1912 championship ride aboard the animal. Other accounts suggest that "Long Tom" most influenced the work.

That same month, the *Morning Oregonian*'s art critic, Lillian Tingle, wrote that the statuette was "full of verve and action, both horse and man typically American, typically Western." Even when the sculptor is "primarily concerned with the expression of action," she continued, "he never loses the rare sense of decorative beauty which is characteristic of his more monumental works."

Later that month, Proctor showed the plaster casting at the Frazier Book Store. The *East Oregonian* set Pendleton abuzz when it reported that Proctor wanted to make a monument-size bronze casting of the *Buckaroo* for Pendleton for $10,000, much less than his normal fee. Private fundraising began in Portland and Pendleton.

The excitement proved premature. The purchase never materialized, apparently because of news that Ridings had run afoul of the law, and not for the first time. Featuring a horse thief in Pendleton's symbol of cowboy and rodeo would have invited controversy.

From jail Ridings wrote Proctor and asked for $800 in bail money, pending his trial. Well-known Harney County cattle rancher William Hanley, one of Proctor's patrons, believed Ridings was innocent and put up the bail. A jury disagreed and sent Ridings to prison.

During his career, Proctor had ten small bronze castings of the *Buckaroo* made, including one that Pendleton citizens acquired and later donated to C. S. Jackson, publisher of Portland's *Oregon Journal* and a tireless Round-Up promoter. Before acquiring the *Oregon Journal* in 1902, Jackson had been publisher of the *East Oregonian*, and he retained a substantial ownership share until 1913. The Jackson family bequeathed the bronze to the Oregon Historical Society in 1958.

A wealthy Denver man commissioned Proctor to make the heroic-size bronze for $15,000. *Broncho Buster* was erected in 1920 in Denver's Civic Center Park, where it stands to this day.

Proctor also sculpted a bust of Ridings that the art critic Tingle described as recording "for future generations the typical cowboy of story and tradition." The bust was bequeathed to the Oregon Historical Society in 1982 by Charlotte Corbett.

While in Pendleton, Proctor hired champion bronc rider Jackson Sundown as a model. Proctor worked with him during the summer of 1916 at Sundown's ranch in Jacques Spur, Idaho, and again in 1918, when Proctor opened a studio in Los Altos, California, near Palo Alto. Their collaboration produced at least three bronze sculptures.

From his first days in Pendleton, Proctor was friendly with Umatilla County sheriff and Round-Up president Tillman D. Taylor. After Taylor's murder in 1920, the sculptor proposed memorializing the sheriff in a statue. Carved and cast in Europe and viewed there by the king and queen of Italy, the statue was dedicated in Pendleton in 1929. It remains a pride of the city.

Proctor produced other notable sculptures that are on permanent public display in Oregon and across the country. Among his Oregon works are *Rough Rider* in Portland's South Park blocks, depicting President Theodore Roosevelt on horseback; *Circuit Rider* outside the state capitol building in Salem; and *Pioneer Mother* on the University of Oregon campus.

Proctor continued sculpting until his death at age eighty-nine in 1950. He wrote that he had been "eternally obsessed with two deep desires—one, to spend as much time as possible in the wilderness, and the other, to accomplish something worthwhile in art."

Proctor had studied at the National Academy of Design in New York City and at the Académies Julien and Colarossi in Paris. His academic training made him as comfortable in international art circles as he was hunting grizzlies in the Rocky Mountains.

▼ Proctor statue in Pendleton's Til Taylor Park, 2007. *By Jim Whiting.*

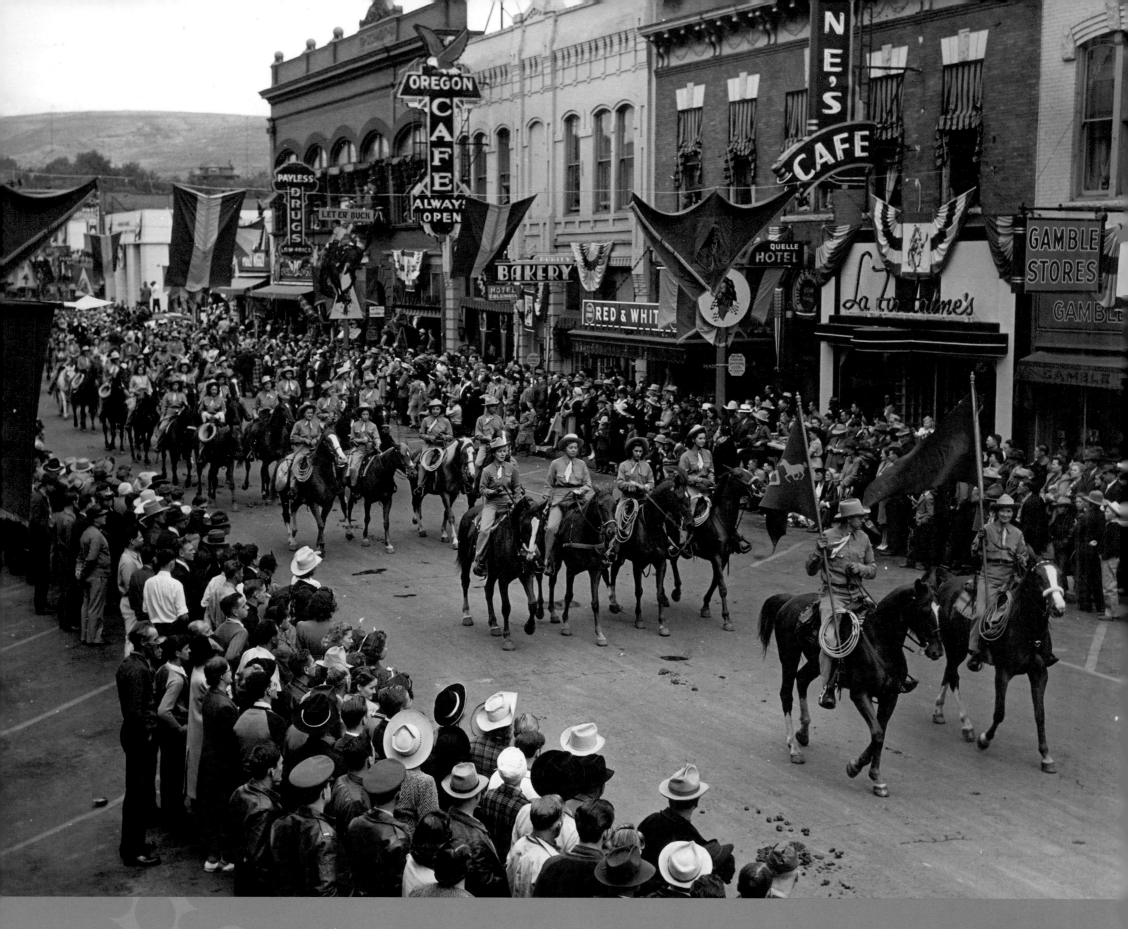

Westward Ho! Parade in the 1940s. *Howdyshell Collection.*

WORLD WAR II

BY MICHAEL BALES

When the thirty-second Round-Up began in September, military police patrolled Pendleton's streets. A headline in the *East Oregonian* proclaimed, "1941 Western Classic to Be Staged in New Setting—One Colored With the Khaki of American Troops."

▼ Pendleton field, home of the 17th bombardment group, 19th air base group, and 89th reconnaissance squadron, 1941.
By Bus Howdyshell in OHS Collection, OrHi 71475.

Staging the Round-Up during World War I had long been a source of civic pride, a show of the can-do spirit underpinning the event since its inception. In 1941, that spirit was equally evident. The show went on despite frenzied activity throughout Umatilla County that portended the United States' entry into World War II a few months later.

Early that year, as the war engulfed Europe and much of Asia, work began on two sprawling military installations. Construction of a twenty-four-square-mile ammunition and supply depot in the county's northwest corner turned Hermiston

In 1942 Fritz Truan loaned out his cowboy gear and enlisted in the U.S. Marine Corps. He was at the height of his rodeo career. In uniform, he continued to compete, winning the bronc-riding championship of Hawaii in 1944. He was killed on Iwo Jima on February 28, 1945. Headlines read, "Sergeant Fritz Truan, Once King of Cowboys, Killed in Iwo Action."

into an overnight boomtown, jammed with traffic and thousands of construction workers. Pendleton's small airport and surrounding wheat fields were transformed into an Army Air Corps base with two runways, each nearly a mile long; more than a hundred and thirty buildings, most of them barracks for several thousand army personnel; and squadrons of B-25 bombers and reconnaissance aircraft.

When the thirty-second Round-Up began in September, military police patrolled Pendleton's streets. A headline in the *East Oregonian* proclaimed, "1941 Western Classic to Be Staged in New Setting—One Colored With the Khaki of American Troops."

The show attracted large crowds and earned a $6,000 profit. More importantly, it was a respite from the fast-spreading gloom of war. National rodeo champion Fritz Truan of Salinas, California, won the all-around title and the Sam Jackson Trophy on the strength of his bulldogging and bronc riding. He edged out Everett Bowman by only five points. Bowman had won the title twice before and would have taken permanent possession of the trophy had he triumphed.

For the rodeo world, Truan came to personify the sacrifice and tragedy of war. Within three months, Japan bombed Pearl Harbor, and Germany declared war on the United States. A year later, Truan enlisted in the Marines.

Government-imposed rationing of many foods and other items and imposition of security measures transformed daily life in the United States. In March 1942, for example, twenty-three passenger car tires were allotted for the entire county. Many people deemed low priority for gasoline purchases stopped driving because they could buy only three gallons a week, a ration later cut to two gallons. Labor was also in short supply.

Two questions prevailed that summer. Should Pendleton cancel the Round-Up for the first time since it began in 1910? If not, could the city marshal the resources needed to stage the elaborate show?

The board voted unanimously, and the *East Oregonian* announced the outcome: "Western Classic Steps Aside for Greater Round-Up of the Axis." The event that had been both a grand annual celebration and a dependable infusion of commerce for more than three decades became a casualty of war.

With shortages even more severe in 1943, the board asked the Round-Up's stockholders whether the show should resume. The answer was "No," although sentiments ran strong to hold the rodeo for military personnel in the county. Pendleton Field had grown still more and was training thousands of people for the aerial war effort. Locals were especially proud that the base had been the training ground for the seventy-nine men General Jimmy Doolittle led on the first U.S. bombing of Japan.

Umatilla County, bustling with an unprecedented business boom, found new ways to demonstrate civic pride. In each of seven campaigns to buy war bonds, the county far exceeded its quota. During one drive, Umatilla had the highest per-person bond sales in Oregon, and the state had the highest rate nationwide. By the end of the war, the official county tally topped $13 million.

The generosity of Pendleton and Umatilla County was rewarded. In 1944, a B-17 bomber was named the "Spirit of Umatilla." The next year, a cargo ship built in Portland was christened the S.S. *Pendleton*. Melissa Parr, the second Indian Round-Up queen, did the honors.

The weapons depot and air base pumped millions of dollars into the county's economy; construction alone totaled $20 million. Allied forces around the world ate peas grown and canned in the area and bread made from its bountiful wheat harvests. So severe was the labor shortage that nearly a thousand German prisoners of war were brought in to work in the canneries.

In March 1944, the prospect of an Allied victory appeared strong, and Round-Up stockholders voted to resume the rodeo to boost morale at home, further promote war bond sales, and entertain military personnel and war workers.

As the show began in September, the *East Oregonian* identified another reason to stage the show before the war ended. "The men at the front want the Round-Up to go on—it's one of the things they are fighting for and one of the things they want to see again when they get home from a nasty job well done."

In 1945 the war finally ended, and Pendleton hosted its second "Victory Round-Up," twenty-six years after the first one celebrated the end of World War I. Many familiar cowboys were missing from the arena, including the 1940 all-around champion Clay Carr, who had joined the Marines, and rodeo clown Monk Carden, who was with the navy and stationed in Texas. Fritz Truan had been killed in combat at Iwo Jima seven months earlier. A tribute to Truan was read to the crowd.

More than three thousand men and women, including a hundred and twenty members of the Confederated Tribes of the Umatilla, served in the military—about ten percent of the county's population. One hundred and seventeen were killed or declared missing in action, a loss the *East Oregonian* described on the Round-Up's first day as "a frightful toll, but a necessary sacrifice to the gods of war, and a sacrifice not in vain."

FRITZ TRUAN

Fritz Truan rode atop the rodeo world when the United States entered World War II. His ascent began in 1939 when he was judged the nation's premier bronc rider. In 1940, he again won the title and was crowned king of the cowboys, winning the all-around championship of the Rodeo Association of America. A year later he won the Round-Up's all-around title and its $5,000 prize on the strength of his steer-wrestling mastery.

During this span Truan won rodeo events across the country, including at New York's Madison Square Garden. He conquered fierce horses others avoided, among them "Hell's Angel," voted by cowboys the greatest bucking horse in the country. Truan's wife, Norma, traveled everywhere with him, putting on trick-riding exhibitions that delighted fans. Life was good for the slender part-time boxer known for his easy smile, toughness, and wild side.

In the 2007 book *Man, Beast, Dust: The Story of Rodeo*, Clifford P. Westermeier wrote that the California cowboy "did everything in a most spectacular way," including "poker-playing, driving a car or getting tight."

In 1942, on the one-year anniversary of the Japanese attack on Pearl Harbor, Truan enlisted in the U.S. Marines at the age of twenty-seven. In doing so, he followed a trail other Round-Up stars had blazed in World War I, setting aside family and career for duty to country.

Details of Truan's time in the U.S. Marine Corps are sketchy except for his final day, but much has been written about his division. Known as the Fighting Fourth, it fought

◄ Fritz Truan, 1941 all-around champion.

Howdyshell Collection.

in the war's most violent battles in the Pacific, including island assaults on Roi-Namur, Saipan, Tinian, and Iwo Jima.

Truan rose to the rank of sergeant. While on furlough in 1944, he competed in a few rodeos, winning the saddle bronc title in Honolulu. Westermeier, who chatted with Truan at one show, said he was "quiet and reticent, and seemed much changed. From his conversation, one knew he had seen plenty of action and was anxious for the war to be over."

On February 28, 1945, while leading an assault platoon during the Fourth Division's attack on Hill 382 on Iwo Jima, Truan was killed in a burst of gunfire. He was twenty-nine years old. Inside his pockets was found the National Rodeo Association's newsletter.

Later that year, during a night-time ceremony at the Hawaiian rodeo, the lights were dimmed and the six thousand fans stood in silence. The horse that Truan had ridden to victory in 1944 was led riderless around the arena. A Marine private who had been with Truan on Hill 382 played "Taps."

"Fritz was a square shooter and a keen competitor," said E. N. "Pink" Boylen, arena director of the Round-Up at the time. "Rodeo lost a real champ when Fritz went west." (Boylen, 1975)

In 1955, Truan was inducted into the Rodeo Performers Hall of Fame at the National Cowboy and Western Heritage Museum in Oklahoma City. Forty years later, he was inducted into the Pro Rodeo Hall of Fame in Colorado Springs, Colorado, joining the horse "Hell's Angel."

THE ARENA

BY MICHAEL BALES

"Are your clothes burning?"one man in the grandstand asked another man. "No," the man answered, but a moment later he shouted that his back was on fire and began scrambling over seats in a dash toward the playing field.

GRANDSTAND FIRE

On August 15, 1940, the thirtieth Round-Up was less than a month away. Germany's newly launched aerial assault of Great Britain had made "blitzkrieg" and "conflagration" familiar words in the newspaper, though the horror of Europe's growing war remained a distant abstraction. The talk of Pendleton was softball.

That night fifteen hundred people made their way to the Round-Up grandstand to watch the hometown Elks take on the Colored Ghosts of Sioux City, Iowa. The Elks were champions of eastern Oregon, but the Ghosts were the big attraction. Fast-pitch softball's equivalent of the Harlem Globetrotters, the all-black Ghosts had toured the West, Midwest, and parts of Canada and Mexico. Their combination of dazzling skill and comedic antics was helping to pave the way for the integration of professional baseball.

Only a few innings had been played when a night watchman, observing the game from the east side of the grandstand during his rounds, smelled smoke, as did some spectators. He told them not to

| ▲ **Fire destroyed the old wooden grandstand in 1940.** *Howdyshell Collection.*

| ▲ **Stagecoach race, 1928.** By R. Doubleday in Low Collection.

ROUND-UP EVENTS

BY MICHAEL BALES

At one time the Round-Up included as many as twenty-eight different events. Anyone perusing old programs risks feeling a nostalgic yearning to see many of these events staged again. Who wouldn't want to watch a galloping parade of five hundred cowboys and cowgirls?

▼ Trick riding in 1925.

By R. Doubleday in Low Collection.

EARLY EVENTS

Long before rodeo became the dominion of professional cowboys competing in standardized events, the Round-Up featured an array of contests and exhibitions ranging from the sublime to the silly. Together they helped the Round-Up appeal to a broad audience and created chances for more people to participate.

Every year organizers brainstormed to find new ways to keep the crowds entertained and growing, and their marketing savvy showed in their annual program adjustments. This was especially true in the Round-Up's first two decades.

HANK DURNELL TRICK RIDING PENDLETON
(DOUBLEDAY) ROUND-UP 1925

FACING PAGE ◄ Cowboy race, 1937. *OHS Collection, CN 000615.* ▼ Indian war bonnet race, 1925. *OHS Collection, CN 000358.*

◄ Roman riding exhibition, 1911. *By Marcell in Low Collection.*

◄▼ Princess Red Bird in the Indian women's baton relay race. At right, a mounted judge surveys the action. *By L. Moorhouse in OHS Collection, OrHi 56224.*

and women—not to mention a wide assortment of trick riding, fancy roping, and spectacular stunts that only can be called oddities.

The wild horse race was intended as the rousing, chaotic conclusion to the Round-Up. Twenty unsaddled bucking broncs were released into the arena. Cowboys had

For a time, black and white cowboys tried their luck riding alone on bucking buffaloes, steers, and an especially fearsome bull, "Sharkey." In 1913, the Round-Up bought "Sharkey" and offered $100 to any comer who could endure ten seconds of bucking. No one lasted more than a second or two until the next year, when writer and explorer Charles Wellington Furlong astounded the crowd with a ride of twelve-and-a-half seconds.

Cowgirl Bonnie McCarroll's death from injuries in the 1929 saddle bronc contest led to the elimination of most events for women. But women's relay races continued through the next decade. In a 1930 exhibition, cowgirls tried to ride zebus, long-legged cousins of brahma cattle with the same signature hump. The animals looked awkward, and the event was dropped.

Financial challenges of the Great Depression forced curtailment or elimination of many events. Some made cameo returns, such as the popular chariot races, revived in 1960 for the fiftieth anniversary of the Round-Up. But the racers with their two-horse teams didn't match the grandeur of rodeo and movie star Hoot Gibson driving a team of four-abreast palominos to victory, not once but twice in 1924. In addition, it was difficult to compete visually with the epic chariot races portrayed in the blockbuster movie *Ben-Hur*, released a year earlier in 1959.

Several horse races remained on the program at the end of the twentieth century: a baton relay race, a free-for-all Indian race, Indian relay races, and the wild horse race. The latter had been controversial, partly because of danger to the horses and cowboys alike.

▲ Bell awarded to "Sharkey," Pendleton's famous bucking bull, in 1978 on his induction into the Pendleton Hall of Fame. *Hall of Fame Collection.*

▶ Eldon Harvey, John Hodgen, and Bill Severe compete in the 1961 chariot race. *Howdyshell Collection.*

FACING PAGE ▶ "Sharkey" unloads Tuck Reynolds in 1913. *By R. Doubleday in Low Collection.*

At this time of year, [Sharkey] is probably the most anxious beast that roams the fields or eats grass off a back lot. Everybody who knows about the Round-Up knows about Sharkey—for Sharkey has unmade more reputations than any other animal of like sex in the annals of history.

—*East Oregonian*, September 1915

"SHARKEY" THE BULL

When the cowboy signals with a head nod that he's ready, a gatekeeper opens the chute, and the frenzy begins.

How strong is the bull, and how rough the ride? Analogies abound: eight professional football linebackers in one body, the force astronauts experience at liftoff, a violent move every half second.

How does a cowboy remain aboard for the required eternity of eight seconds? Tactics include staying centered on the bull's back and leaning slightly forward, keeping eyes focused on its massive neck, and digging in with spurs to increase leg grip. But security is an illusion: the bull might fling its head back or to the side to hook the rider with horns or spin hard and fast to throw him to the side.

"You're continually having to put your body in a position that counteracts the bull's movement," Ty Murray, a former star bull rider and past PBR tour president, told the *New York Times* in 2007.

A rider must never touch the bull with his non-grip hand; doing so is automatic disqualification. He scores higher if he appears to never lose control.

The dismount can be as dangerous as the ride. The cowboy uses his free hand to release the grip hand, slings a leg over the bull's shoulders, tries to land on both feet, and heads for the arena fence while rodeo clowns try to distract the animal.

But even then he isn't safe. In 1989 at the Cheyenne Frontier Days in Wyoming, a rider familiar to Pendleton was killed when a bull gored him in the back. Lane Frost had been thrown clear of the bull and was walking away. The bull turned and rammed him. Frost, of Quanah, Texas, won the Round-Up bull riding title in 1985 and 1987. He was twenty-five years old when he died.

PBR members sign a liability waiver that mentions death five times. Fans often describe bull riders as crazy because of the risks they take. While many of the cowboys say they ride for the adrenaline rush, money is a big lure.

◀▲ **Harley May rides, 1957.** *Howdyshell Collection.*

◀ **Dell Machau on "Bobo" in 1976.**

Howdyshell Collection.

FACING PAGE ▶ Atop a high bucker, 1970s.

Howdyshell Collection.

BUCKING BULL

DICK McCALL

The point system and the Professional Bull Riders' aggressive marketing of the bulls' menacing stature and demeanor explain why the toughest animals are sometimes better known than the cowboys who ride them.

◄ Chuck Shelton hits the dirt, 1958.
Howdyshell Collection.

◄▼ A bull rider takes a fall, 1950s.
Howdyshell Collection.

The PBR broke from the Professional Rodeo Cowboys Association in 1995 and started its own circuit of events. Since then, revenue from television and corporate sponsorships has soared. Purses far exceed those of any other rodeo event. Justin McBride, top all-time money winner as of June 2008, had earned nearly five million dollars.

▶ **PAGES 146 AND 147. Bull riders take big risks for big money.** *Howdyshell Collection.*

FACING PAGE, FAR RIGHT ▶

▲ **Red Cross workers lend aid, 1912.** *By L. Moorhouse in OHS Collection, bb003680.*

▶ **Stretcher-bearers carry a cowboy from the arena.** *Howdyshell Collection.*

▼ **Red Cross workers at the ready.** *Low Collection.*

Crazy or not, they're a tough breed.

The PBR show, which debuted in Pendleton in 1999, is held in the Happy Canyon arena before the Round-Up begins. Many of the same cowboys also appear in the Round-Up bull riding competitions.

Long before the PBR, there was Jim Shoulders. Like most in his profession, the legendary rodeo cowboy endured many fractures, including twenty-seven to bones in his face. He was featured in a *Life* magazine article head-lined "Mister Broken Bones." In those days, bull riders

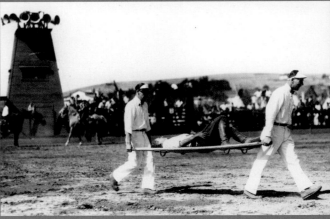

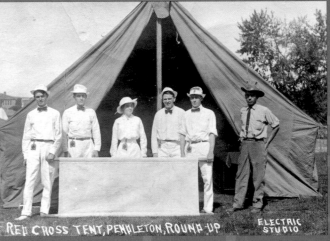

RED CROSS IN ACTION
R&B ROUND-UP 1912
PHIL MOORHOUSE

RED CROSS TENT, PENDLETON, ROUND-UP   ELECTRIC STUDIO

A rider must never touch the bull with his non-grip hand; doing so is automatic disqualification. He scores higher if he appears to never lose control.

The philosophy then of bull riding is simply—hang on—convince yourself you're not coming apart, you only feel that way—just hang on.

—Charles Wellington Furlong, *Let 'er Buck,* 1921

▶ Bull and rider burst from the chute in 1963. *Howdyshell Collection.*

A cross between a she bear
and a bad four wheel drive

With the fury of an eagle when
it makes a power dive

A snake who's lost its caution
or a badger gone berserk

He's a screamin', stompin', clawin',
rabid, mad dog piece o' work.

—From "Legacy of the Rodeo Man,"
by Baxter Black

Copyright 1996; reprinted with permission
from Baxter Black, www.baxterblack.com

◄ A flimsy fence separates the bulls from
photographers and arena personnel, 2007.
By Jim Whiting.

didn't wear modern safety equipment, such as a protective vest, mouthpiece, and in some cases headgear with a face cage.

Between 1949 and 1959, Shoulders won eleven world titles—seven in bull riding (Round-Up, 1958) and four in bareback riding (Round-Up, 1958 and 1959)—and five all-around world championships (Round-Up, 1958). Shoulders, of Henryetta, Oklahoma, never earned more than fifty thousand dollars annually. He was inducted into the Round-

Up Hall of Fame in 1999 and died in 2007 at age seventy-nine.

Several months before his death, Shoulders talked of bull riding's inherent danger and popularity. "When we go to a car race, if you don't see a wreck, you are a little disappointed," he told the *Daily Oklahoman* in Oklahoma City. "If you go to a rodeo and don't see some wrecks, you are disappointed. The American people don't want to see somebody get killed, but if somebody gets killed, we don't want to miss it."

149

the cowboy climbed into the saddle. The event began when the blindfold was pulled off. If riders weren't thrown, judges decided when to signal the rides had ended. Often cowboys rode until their horse stopped bucking—in some cases a full minute—and might be required to ride a second horse.

Riders have always received higher scores if they aggressively used spurs during the horse's leaps and turns. In modern-day rodeo, they are required to start with both feet over the bronc's shoulders and rake the spurs all the way to its flanks at its first jump. A key to high scores is continuing this motion in rhythm with the horse's jumps: feet back at the apex of jumps and extended forward just before the horse's front legs touch the ground.

Other scoring factors take into account how hard the animals buck, how high they kick, and how much they change direction. Skilled riders will take this bone-jarring delivery of violence in a smooth and effortless way. Rides that look rough are scored lower.

A hornless saddle and thick bridle rope are used. Riders hold on with one hand and must never touch the horse, the saddle, or their own body with their free hand.

Bareback riding debuted at the Round-Up in 1948, although it had been introduced at other rodeos many years earlier. While saddle bronc horses are stocky, durable, and strong, their bareback counterparts are smaller, faster, and wilder. The equipment, too, is different from that used in saddle bronc riding. Instead of a bridle attached to a halter, bareback riders hold on to a leather handle affixed to a wide band that fits around the horse's belly like a girdle. This gives the riders less control and requires far more strength.

▲ Silver spur that belonged to Mose Kruger, Indian bronc rider. *Hall of Fame Collection.*

▶ Pickup man Bryce Baker rushes to pick Mose Kruger off his horse after the eight-second whistle. *Howdyshell Collection.*

◀ Pete Knight, 1929. *Low Collection.*

As in the saddle bronc event, riders hold on with one hand and must not touch the horse, the saddle, or their own body with their free hand.

Judges favor a higher, more aggressive spurring technique and horses that display the most wildness. In both events, cowboys with scores in the eighties are considered contenders.

The winners of the first saddle bronc and bareback riding events at the Round-Up had markedly different careers. Bert Kelly, the saddle bronc champion in 1910, is memorialized wearing white shirt, tie, and woolly chaps in a grainy black and white photograph. He died of consumption four years later. Bob Maynard, the bareback winner in 1948, remained in rodeo for two decades, achieving more success as a bull rider and steer wrestler. He won the bull riding championship at Madison Square Garden in 1950.

Seventeen years later in Long Beach, California, he wrestled a steer in a remarkable 4.3 seconds.

Only two cowboys have won Round-Up titles in both saddle and bareback bronc riding: Bud Linderman in 1949, and the renowned Casey Tibbs, who tied for first in bareback riding with Jim Hailey in 1950, won it outright the next year, and claimed the saddle bronc crown in 1959.

Pete Knight, a Canadian cowboy, won the saddle bronc contest in Pendleton an unprecedented five times, from 1929 to 1936. Aware of the risks associated with both sports, Knight donated thousands of dollars to injured and destitute rodeo riders during the Great Depression. In 1937, he was thrown from a horse and trampled at a rodeo in Hayward, California. "Duster" came down with the full force of his body on the fallen cowboy's chest. Knight died in an ambulance en route to the hospital.

STEER ROPING

▼ **Shoat Webster lifts steer off its feet, 1959.**

Howdyshell Collection.

▼ ▼ **Bob Crosby ropes a steer in 1927.**

By R. Doubleday in Low Collection.

▶ **Roper poised to go down the slope a**

moment after the steer, 2007. *By Jim Whiting.*

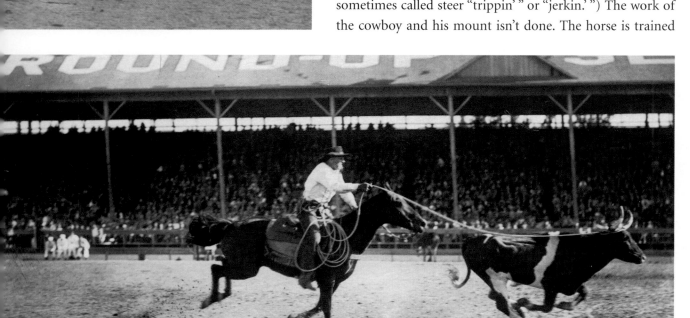

Block out the crowd, forget about the clock, and you see the steer-roping rodeo rider not racing across the arena but charging back into time. For a few seconds he enters the distant past, just another rough-and-tumble cowboy lassoing a doggie to the ground.

No other rodeo event emulates so closely the work of cowhands on the range: a man with horse and lariat pursuing a runaway steer. But the best in the business make more money than their predecessors on the cattle drives. Trevor Brazile of Decatur, Texas, a familiar star at the Round-Up, earned a record $425,115 in the 2007 rodeo season for his world title steer roping and performances in other events.

Despite its simple appearance, steer roping is intricate and dangerous. The steer is in one chute and the cowboy atop his horse in another, with a barrier string stretched across his gate to the arena. The steer runs down the hill to the grass. When it has the specified head start, an electric eye breaks the roper's barrier. The cowboy is penalized if he gives chase prematurely.

He lassoes the steer around the horns, flips the slack over the animal's right hip, and turns his horse sharply to the left. This motion, combined with the steer's momentum, trips or jerks the doggie to the dirt. (The sport is sometimes called steer "trippin'" or "jerkin.") The work of the cowboy and his mount isn't done. The horse is trained to pull the rope tight, pressure that keeps the steer from scrambling to its feet while the cowboy jumps off and uses a "pigging string" to tie any three legs. The steer must stay tied for six seconds.

Winning times, recorded from when the cowboy begins the chase until the legs are tied, often range from ten to fifteen seconds. The record is 8.1 seconds.

Typically used are large horses that can hold their ground against steers weighing upwards of 750 pounds. Accidents involving the horses pose the biggest risk to steer ropers. In 1999, a highly ranked cowboy, Colby Goodwin, was fatally injured at the national finals in Guthrie, Oklahoma. After Goodwin lassoed a steer, his horse tripped on his slack rope and fell on him.

Because the event is considered the most dangerous to rodeo animals, some states have outlawed it.

While steer roping hasn't changed much from the days of the Wild West, cowboy lingo has. "It's awesome," Brazile said of his accomplishment.

PENDLETON ROUND-U

2   3   4   5   6

ROPING

CLOCKWISE FROM TOP LEFT

▲ ◄ **Sea of saddles at Pendleton's slack, 2007.** *By Jim Whiting.*

▲ ▲ **Ropers awaiting their turn in the qualifying rounds, 2007.** *By Jim Whiting.*

▲ **Hugo Strickland's roping saddle.**
Hall of Fame Collection.

◄ **Ropers compete in 1949.**
Courtesy of Mervin Swearingen.

TEAM ROPING

Some jobs take two cowboys, such as snagging a big, ornery steer. From this reality of ranch life sprang team roping, the only tandem event in professional rodeo and one requiring a close working relationship—so close that some cowboys joke about being married to each other, which leads to more jokes.

Joking aside, success depends on much-practiced communication and coordination to execute precisely timed maneuvers. The loss of a few hundredths of a second might mean the difference between finishing in or out of the money. Success also depends on how well the two cowboys—one a "header," the other a "heeler"—work with their horses in capturing and subduing a runaway steer.

The cowboys flank the steer in separate stalls next to a chute, the header on the left, heeler on the right. When the steer is released and reaches a designated head-start point, the header takes off in the arena first.

As quickly as possible, the header lassoes the steer. The rope must loop around one horn and the head, both horns, or the neck. Otherwise the header is disqualified.

How fast this lead rider catches and ropes the steer is paramount, said the aptly named header Speed Williams. "If he does his job well, it makes it easy for the heeler to do his job." (Groves, 2006)

The header's next move involves a word that means the opposite of its usual sense outside the arena—"dally." In

▲ Ropers' specialized gear, slack 2007.

By Jim Whiting.

▶ Ike Rude with championship saddle, 1953.

Howdyshell Collection.

▶▲ Down the slope to the grass, 2007.

By Jim Whiting.

rodeo's colorful lexicon, "dally" derives from the Spanish *dar la vuelta*—to take a turn, as in to quickly turn the rope twice around the saddle horn. By dallying and turning left, the header hopes to cause the steer's hind legs to rise. In this moment the heeler has a chance to lasso the legs. If on target, he too "dallies up," tightening the loop and preventing the steer's escape.

When both ropes are taut, header and heeler turn their horses to face each other, their prey roped on both ends and brought to a standstill. Time is called. What is a winning time? Charly Crawford of Prineville, Oregon, and Cody Hintz of Spring Creek, Nevada, won the Round-Up's 2007 team roping title, averaging slightly more than six seconds for each of three rounds.

Team roping, though known for costing cowboys fingers and thumbs caught between saddle and rope, is less demanding physically than other events, enabling some cowboys to compete past most men's retirement age.

One of rodeo's most honored cowboys, Ike Rude of Oklahoma, competed in team roping in his seventies. He died before the event began in Pendleton in 1991. Rude won the Round-Up's steer wrestling title in 1953 at age fifty-nine. He was inducted into the Hall of Fame in 1981, three years before his death at ninety.

The most fruitful team roping "marriage" in rodeo history began at the Round-Up in 1997. That year header Speed Williams and heeler Rich Skelton, both Texans, won the championship, the first of eight consecutive years of winning world titles in the event.

WILD COW MILKING

Chaos with few rules. That is one way to describe wild cow milking, an event not sanctioned by the Professional Rodeo Cowboys Association but a mainstay at the Round-Up since 1922.

Unlike other events in which competitors take turns in the arena with all eyes only upon them, wild cow milking features an everyone-at-once free-for-all: ten one-thousand-pound beef cows, ten horses, and twenty cowboys. Instead of the finesse and precision timing of an event like team roping that begins and ends in mere seconds, the milking event features men and animals careening around like pinballs for up to two minutes.

The cows are released en masse into the arena, a stampede of swinging udders. The teams of two cowboys each, one on horseback and the other on foot, give chase. One cowboy ropes a cow, and the other tries to subdue it. The rider dismounts. Depending on the circumstances, he joins the fray or immediately tries to squeeze milk from an angry moving target into a bottle.

The object is simple: be the first to deliver any measurable amount of milk to the judges.

Weighing much more than the steers used in other events and with no horns to grab for leverage, the cows are nearly impossible to wrestle down. Some cowboys try but end up exhausted on the ground. It is not unusual to see a cowboy head-butted, trampled, or dragged by the rope, or the cowboy with the bottle running alongside a perturbed cow as he gropes under her belly.

During all this, the announcer delivers commentary, including advice and encouragement to the cowboys. When a cowboy finally gets milk, he sprints to the judges.

The event isn't as prestigious as those on the rodeo circuit—non-professionals can enter—but it has its stars. In 2005, Ron Hudson of Pendleton was inducted into the Round-Up and Happy Canyon Hall of Fame, in part for winning three titles in twenty years of wild cow milking. Hudson also bulldogged steers, took part in the wild horse race, and served as president of the Round-Up in 1989–1990 and as a board member from 1981 to 1990.

▲ **The contest begins.** *Howdyshell Collection.*

◄ **Wild cow milking, 2007.** *By Jim Whiting.*

BARREL RACING

By Ann Terry Hill

The headlines read: BIG ROUND-UP NEWS: PENDLE-TON BRINGS BACK WOMEN COMPETITORS IN 2000! After the death of Bonnie McCarroll in 1929, women were barred from competition at Pendleton until 2000, when barrel racing became an event sanctioned by the Professional Rodeo Cowboys Association and was added to the list of official Round-Up events. This did not happen overnight, as the board had obstacles to overcome before the PRCA racers would agree to ride in Pendleton. The success of the negotiations was largely due to the groundwork of Steve Corey and his brother Doug. Helping out on the committee were Mark Rosenberg, Butch Thurman, Jack Purchase, Bill Capplinger, and Jade Robinson.

The grass arena posed a major problem, yet PRCA and the barrel racers were putting pressure on the Round-Up board to find some way for them to compete in Pendleton and share in the large purses the men were winning. Parking the racers' big horse trailers was a practical problem to be solved. To remain in good standing with the PRCA, the Round-Up had to find a way to make it work.

Many feared that making the fast, close turns around the barrels on the grass infield would hurt the horses. The board laid out a pattern that extended the usual 120 feet between barrels to 288 feet, thus allowing racers to make the turns on the dirt track in front of the north and south grandstands and the east gate. Execution time went from the usual twelve to fifteen seconds to twenty-eight seconds or more.

Before the women agreed to tackle the Pendleton course, they required a veterinarian's assurance that racing across the grass would not harm the horses. Doug Corey, a PRCA vet and extremely good horse doctor, was convinced that if the horses were in shape for the shorter pattern, they would be in shape for the longer one. Grass is not particularly good to run on, but statistics have shown that no more accidents occur on the grass than on the dirt. A special grass from Canada was seeded. All competitors were advised that their horses should be conditioned like racehorses and should have no skeletal or respiratory problems. The barrel racers agreed to a trial in the 2000 show. Nine out of the ten PRCA racers were in Pendleton the first year, and barrel racing has grown each year since, becoming one of the most popular events of the rodeo.

Barrel racer Gloria Freeman, from Georgia, riding her great horse "Bull," won the first year. When interviewed by telephone in 2007, she was still raving about the uniqueness of the event and Pendleton in general. "Pendleton is just the best," she said. "A lot of rodeos seem commercial—almost packaged. When I got to Pendleton, I realized this is what a rodeo was like a hundred years ago."

"That barrel race is so scary," she confided. "You just run so far, so fast. It's the biggest thrill I've ever had in running barrels. The pattern is so big, a lot of the girls are a little intimidated by it.

"I couldn't have picked a better horse to run in Pendleton. 'Bull' loved it too. After the run he let out a big squeal, and I said, 'I know, "Bull," I want to squeal too!' I tell everybody, 'You've got to run in Pendleton. It's the most fun you'll have in your life.'"

In 2001, Kelli Currin, who married Tony (one of the famed Currin brothers from Heppner, Oregon), held up the family's reputation by winning in Pendleton. She recalled her win in a 2007 telephone interview. "It was exhilarating to compete in Pendleton—the large surface, the grass. It really makes your heart beat fast. There's a lot of money at stake, and there is a family history of wins in Pendleton. It was really special. It's so prestigious. I won a Severe saddle and a lot of money!"

Other past winners include Charmayne James, National Finals Rodeo champion, in 2002 and 2003; Jolee Lautaret in 2004; Maegan Reichert in 2005; and Linzie Walker in 2006, 2007, and 2008.

Former queens Joan Barnett Rugg and her daughter Julie Rugg Williams (herself a barrel racer) provide the championship saddle for the event, and former queen Marilyn Foster Corfield donates the champion belt buckle to the winner.

SPECIALTY ACTS

Along with barrel clowns and bullfighters, specialty acts are a part of each year's Round-Up entertainment. The performers display a spectacular range of talents, from trick and fancy roping and riding to whip-cracking, gun-juggling, and sky-diving. Rodeo crowds may be treated to a ten-year-old Roman rider racing at breakneck speed atop two horses with one foot on each; to riders and their specially trained mounts leaping over automobiles and through rings of fire; to expert marksmen shooting holes in tossed-up coins or drawing pictures with bullet holes. With their assorted dogs, monkeys, longhorns, ponies, horses, and all the props needed to put on a carefully rehearsed show, acts with names such as "The Moore Family with Beeswax the Mule" travel from rodeo to rodeo along with other professionals in the business. Some are families who have honed their skills across generations; others are champion cowboys and cowgirls who prefer exhibition to competition.

CLOCKWISE FROM TOP MIDDLE

▲◀ Brandi Phillips of the Riata Ranch Cowboy Girls performs in 2007. *By Jim Whiting.*

▲ Tillie Baldwin stunt riding in the Round-Up's early years. *Howdyshell Collection.*

◀ Sherman Crane parades with burro and monkey in 1955. *Hamley Archive.*

◀◀ Clown Don Green parachutes into the arena, 1983. *Howdyshell Collection.*

167

"PINK" DAY

In 2006, Pendleton Round-Up added to its long list of traditions by introducing "Tough Enough to Wear Pink" Day on Thursday of Round-Up week. Funds raised by the event help Pendleton-area patients during and after treatment for breast cancer. "Pink" Day has been a tremendous success, as cowgirls, cowboys, fans, merchants, and the general public have joined forces to support the fight against breast cancer.

"Tough Enough to Wear Pink" Day came about when breast cancer survivor Terry Wheatley, mother of professional

[The clown's refuge] is just a reinforced barrel with padding. You take a good pounding when a bull knocks it around.

—Flint Rasmussen, 2006

roper Wade Wheatley, asked her son if he would wear a pink shirt to help raise awareness of the deadly disease at the National Finals Rodeo in Las Vegas in 2005. Wheatley enlisted the support of his colleagues, and all but two cowboys competing that year wore pastel pink shirts. Now rodeos all over the country feature "Tough Enough to Wear Pink" events.

At the Round-Up, the royal court sports pink outfits on Thursday. All the directors wear pink shirts, as well as most of the cowboys, the rodeo clown (even his barrel is wrapped in pink), and many of the fans. Pink souvenirs are available for purchase, and all proceeds go to the cause.

As bareback rider Silas Richards put it to the *East Oregonian* in 2007, "It's a great cause. We cowboys are pretty tough, but there are people out there that go through a lot tougher things."

CHILDREN'S RODEO

On Wednesday of each Round-Up, just before the first day's rodeo action begins, forty to forty-five children ages five through nine have a chance to be cowboys and cowgirls in the famous arena. The children have disabilities ranging from autism and Down syndrome to cerebral palsy and visual and hearing impairments. They delight in the opportunity to participate in activities such as barrel racing (with a stick horse), steer roping (lassoing a make-believe

steer), bull riding (riding a hand-rocked bull), riding in a horse-drawn buggy, and riding a real horse with a genuine cowboy or a member of the Round-Up court. Each participant receives a shirt, hat, and scarf, a lariat, a trophy, and an autographed picture taken with a cowboy. The events are non-competitive, and the children look forward to coming back from year to year, as long as their age is appropriate.

◄◄ Exceptional rodeo in its early years, ca. 1985. *Howdyshell Collection.*

◄ Six-year-old Braden Linnell of Heppner, Oregon, ropes a steer with the help of John Trumbo, Umatilla County sheriff, 2007. *EO Archive.*

169

W.S.BOWMAN
to 29-C.

BONNIE McCARROL THROWN FROM SILVER

"Silver" throws Bonnie McCarroll at the 1915 Round-Up. *By W. S. Bowman in Howdyshell Collection.*

THE RISKS

BY MICHAEL BALES

Bonnie McCarroll's spill from the horse "Silver," captured by W. S. Bowman, is among the most dramatic of rodeo history's iconic images. That she landed unhurt seems miraculous, yet the photograph presages McCarroll's fate in the same arena fourteen years later.

▼ Bonnie McCarroll performs in 1921.
Low Collection.

BONNIE McCARROLL'S LAST RIDE

One last rodeo, Bonnie McCarroll said.

It was 1929, the first day of the Round-Up. For fifteen years McCarroll had lived the cowgirl's dream, and she was retiring at thirty-two. She had conquered bucking broncos and won championships throughout the United States, including at Madison Square Garden and Yankee Stadium in New York, and in England.

Her first big show was the 1915 Round-Up, and the diminutive, blue-eyed rider won a first place.

"BONNIE McCARROLL, TRICK RIDING."
59 PHOTO: BY ROUND-UP ASS'N.
PENDLETON, ORE., 1921

171

Moorhouse

Bonnie McCarroll on Happy Canyon's "Bull"

Her spill from the horse "Silver," captured by W. S. Bowman, is among the most dramatic of rodeo history's iconic images. That she landed unhurt seems miraculous, yet the photograph presages McCarroll's fate in the same arena fourteen years later.

Most cowgirls of that period preferred to ride with stirrups tied under the horse's belly. McCarroll, however, told a writer that cowgirls who "like the game well enough to play should play it just like the cowboys do. Why, I'd feel insulted . . . if I was told to tie my stirrups down!"

But the Round-Up required women to ride "hobbled." Would it have made a difference if McCarroll had ridden "slick" as the men did? Soon after her mount, "Black Cat," began bucking, it stumbled and somersaulted. The horse leaped to its feet with McCarroll, unconscious, hanging head down, her foot caught in the left stirrup. "Black Cat" jumped six more times, and each time McCarroll's head hit the ground. Finally, her boot came off, and she was left sprawled in the dirt.

Suffering from spinal injuries and pneumonia, McCarroll died eleven days later. At her hospital bedside was her husband, Frank McCarroll, a champion steer bulldogger with whom she had toured all those years. He had recently finished building a new home for them in Boise, Idaho, near the cattle ranch where Bonnie was raised.

DEATHS AT THE ROUND-UP

In the century of Round-Up events involving thousands of people, three people besides Bonnie McCarroll died as the result of injuries in the arena.

A bizarre, unauthorized stunt in 1918 led to the first fatality. During an intermission, Jack C. Jenkins doused his clothes with gasoline, climbed aboard his horse, and set himself afire. He was immediately engulfed in flames, and the horse whirled in a tight circle, knocking him off.

While his wife and five-year-old child looked on, Jenkins ran along the arena track until guards tackled him.

◄▲ **Bonnie and Frank McCarroll, ca. 1927.**
By Paul Strayer. National Cowboy & Western Heritage Museum, Oklahoma City, OK. RC2006.076.650.

▲ **Ladies' bronc riding saddle, ca. 1925, owned by Bonnie McCarroll. Ring stirrups were easily secured under the horse's belly.**
National Cowboy & Western Heritage Museum, Oklahoma City, OK. 83.5.4.

FACING PAGE ◄ McCarroll rides Happy Canyon's bull, 1920s. *By L. Moorhouse in Low Collection.*

Before they could smother the flames with a blanket, he broke away and ran again. They finally caught him and doused the blaze with a fire extinguisher. He died the next day.

Two years later, Winnemucca Jack was killed during the wild horse race while working as a ground assistant. The Bannock Indian was helping to bring a horse under control as its rider slowed down the animal. When Winnemucca Jack prepared to blindfold the horse, it lunged suddenly and struck him in the forehead with a hoof, splitting his skull.

The fifty-two-year-old wrangler had a reputation as a skilled horseman and stood out in his black-spotted angora chaps. He had played drums in the Happy Canyon Pageant.

The only fatality in the following sixty-six years occurred in 1995. Mike Boothe, a twenty-five-year-old professional team roper, died of complications a day after breaking his left leg in four places when his horse fell on him. Boothe, of Bishop, California, appeared to be doing fine in the hospital but suffered an embolism when fatty tissue lodged in a lung.

▲ First Aid room beneath south grandstand, 2007. *By Jim Whiting.*

▶ Rare postcard showing Jack Jenkins' fatal ride in 1918. *Low Collection.*

JENKINS' LAST RIDE

The *East Oregonian* reported that Jenkins, who worked hauling wheat, had approached Round-Up officials with his idea for a "daredevil fire ride" but was turned down. He apparently believed that his three layers of clothing—two pairs of overalls beneath a corduroy suit—would protect him while the wind from his galloping horse would put out the fire.

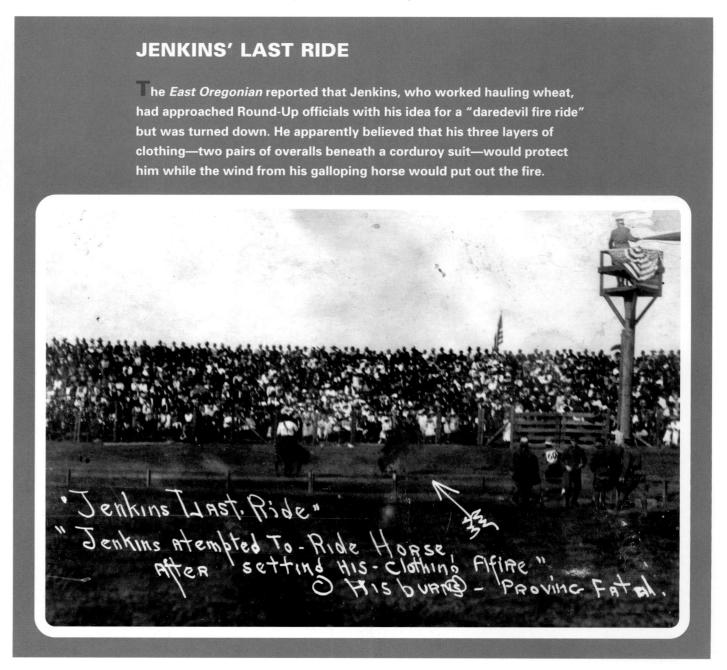

"Jenkins Last Ride"
"Jenkins Atempted To Ride Horse,
After setting His Clothing Afire"
His burns — Proving Fatal.

◄ Two of the three men who murdered Til Taylor in 1920. At left is Neil Hart, who pulled the fatal trigger; beside him is Jim Owens. Sheriff "Jinks" Taylor stands at right.

Low Collection.

"JINKS" TAYLOR

Death also struck outside the arena at the Round-Up. In 1925, the Pendleton police chief, W. R. "Jinks" Taylor, was thrown from his horse and killed as he tried to chase down runaway steers during preparations for the rodeo. Taylor was the brother of Tillman D. Taylor, the Umatilla County sheriff and Round-Up president who had been murdered in 1920.

"Jinks" Taylor was moving roping steers from the arena to nearby barns. The animals bolted free through a gate someone had mistakenly left open and bounded over the railroad tracks. As Taylor gave chase, his black horse "King" stumbled and somersaulted, throwing him to his death.

Both Taylor and his horse were familiar sights at the start of each Round-Up, leading the opening parade and carrying the American flag. But "Jinks" Taylor's biggest contribution to Pendleton might have been what he prevented from happening.

"Jinks" was appointed acting sheriff after his brother Til was killed by three prisoners escaping from the county jail. When two of the three suspects were captured, Taylor brought them from LaGrande to Pendleton. He tried to keep their arrival quiet because people were angry about the murder and threatening to dispense with a trial and lynch the prisoners. Word leaked out, and angry citizens flocked to the courthouse lawn and demanded custody of the pair. Taylor soothed the mob by invoking his dead brother's view of justice: "Boys, Til believed in the law. He fought for it and he died for it. If he were here he would ask you to go home and let the law take its course."

Taylor and the law prevailed. The three prisoners were later convicted in court and eventually hanged as Taylor watched.

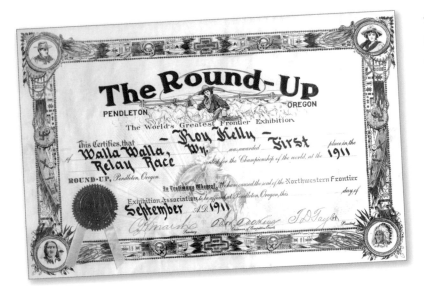

totaling $80. Jim Clark of John Day, Oregon, won $5 as the fifth-place winner of the wild horse race, enough to buy twenty meals at The Quelle restaurant on Pendleton's Main Street.

No prizes were given in six events that were considered exhibitions or ceremonial, such as the "Indian War Parade" or "Spectacular Galloping Parade" by five hundred cowboys and cowgirls. But that would change. As the Round-Up grew, it gave more recognition to people who participated in tangential events that made the show as much a celebration of western life as a spectacular sporting event. For example, Bobby Bond won $2.50 in 1927 for best children's costume in the inaugural Dress-Up Parade, which attracted eight hundred boys and men.

Beginning with the first Round-Up, competitions for native people were part of the rodeo program. In 1910, the half-mile Indian race was open to all who participated in the war dance and parade. The three top finishers split a purse of $15. Indian men's and women's horse relay races remained popular in 2007, when each team member received an embroidered jacket and a blanket from Pendleton Woolen Mills.

In 1915, the best-decorated native woman and man were singled out, winning a $2 silk muffler and a $2.50 bridle bit, respectively. More recently, the Indian deemed the best-dressed in the Westward Ho! Parade received fifty silver dollars. In 2007 the most generous award among six non-rodeo events for tribal members went to the winner of the American Indian Beauty Pageant—$600 and a Harding shawl (named for a specially designed Pendleton Woolen Mills blanket tribal chiefs gave to Florence Harding, wife of President Warren G. Harding, at a highway dedication in Meacham, Oregon, in 1923).

As competitive and non-competitive events increased in number, so did the diversity of prizes. In 1915, cash purses totaling $5,102 went to sixty competitors. Besides cash, decorative saddles were awarded to winners of the cowboys' bucking-bronco and steer roping contests and the cowgirls' relay race. Prizes for the top three finishers in

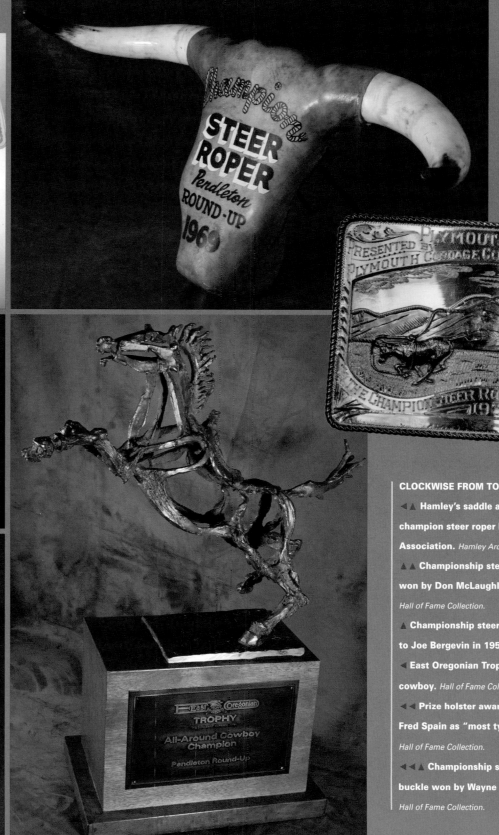

CLOCKWISE FROM TOP LEFT

◄▲ Hamley's saddle awarded to the 1957 champion steer roper by the Rodeo Cowboys' Association. *Hamley Archive.*

▲▲ Championship steer roper horns won by Don McLaughlin in 1969. *Hall of Fame Collection.*

▲ Championship steer roper buckle awarded to Joe Bergevin in 1959. *Hall of Fame Collection.*

◄ East Oregonian Trophy for best all-around cowboy. *Hall of Fame Collection.*

◄◄ Prize holster awarded in 1911 to Fred Spain as "most typical cowboy." *Hall of Fame Collection.*

◄◄▲ Championship saddle bronc buckle won by Wayne Davis in 1938. *Hall of Fame Collection.*

REWARDS

RANCH AND RODEO

BY GEORGE MURDOCK

The traditional skills cowboys use on working ranches are still reflected in almost every rodeo program. Tie-down roping, bronc riding, and team roping showcase cowhand expertise.

▼ *"Let 'er Buck." Howdyshell Collection.*

It is often said that rodeo is the only American sporting event to grow out of an occupational activity—ranching.

Yet the relationship between modern rodeo events and the actual use of those skills in everyday ranching isn't unlike the relationship between what we have come to know as "Chinese food" and what people eat in China. The roots are perhaps similar, but some level of aberration has been necessary for popular consumption.

Ranch chores have historically included such things as roping, breaking horses, riding, herding, and branding, so there was a natural evolution into

On the "Tony" Vey R
near Pendleton Ore

▲ **Tony Vey Ranch.** *Low Collection.*

some arena events as working ranch competitions began to transform into formal rodeos.

Some of the earliest cowboy competitions found their roots in challenges that highlighted gatherings at railheads after long cattle drives. With the expanding railway system and the advent of cattle cars, those drives faded into history. The introduction of barbed wire, together with the railroads, led to a decreasing occupational demand for cowboys. Some of the most skilled began to appear in Wild West shows and at a new form of rodeo that included paying customers.

The traditional skills cowboys use on working ranches are still reflected in almost every rodeo program. Tie-down roping, bronc riding, and team roping showcase cowhand expertise. The bronc riding events include both saddle and bareback.

Barrel racing, a keen competition for women, has also become a standard at most rodeos. Bull riding and steer wrestling are not directly related to the duties of working cowboys but provide plenty of spectator appeal.

Other events that sometimes appear on a program range from steer roping and wild cow milking (both events at the Round-Up) to pole bending and goat tying (not seen in Pendleton, though popular across America). Some of these can be traced to working ranches, while others are offered for competitive or entertainment value. A modified version of tie-down roping, goat tying is a timed event where a goat is tethered on the end of a rope and the contestant rides across the arena, steps down from the horse, catches the goat, and ties it down. In pole bending, also a timed event, six poles are spaced twenty-one feet apart, and with a running start, the mounted contestant weaves down and back among them, slalom fashion. The idea is to record the fastest time while leaving the poles still standing. Both events require expert horsemanship, but neither reflects life on the ranch.

Modern ranchers still pretty much break horses the old-fashioned way, but the object is to reduce the level of bucking rather than to spur it to greater heights. Cowboys must eventually mount a horse during the breaking process, and some of the subsequent action is similar to bareback and saddle bronc riding. Both rodeo events, however, have been modified to demonstrate superior skill and provide more excitement for the crowd.

▲ Martha Boyer, Round-Up princess, takes part in the L. E. "Verne" Pearson cattle drive in 1959, the year Pearson's daughter Vicki was queen. *Courtesy of Martha Boyer.*

Bull riding, now arguably the most popular sport in rodeo, finds its roots in front of the grandstand, not as a day-to-day trade for cowboys out on the range. Certainly, on some distant ranches, little buckaroos or even well-oiled cowpokes have taken rides on cows and bulls alike—but most likely for less than eight seconds.

Tie-down roping, team roping, and steer roping are probably the purest of the modern circuit's rodeo sports with relation to the occupation of ranching. These events represent skills that today's cowboys utilize in much the same form. Bronc riding, however, was the event that set the sport in motion, as hired hands from various ranches gathered on weekends to see who could tame the rankest horse, thereby earning recognition as the top hand in the area.

Not all rodeos present the audience with a wild cow milking contest, as the Round-Up does. The idea of getting milk out of uncooperative mothers is still very much a part of calving season—particularly when the weather is cold and a rancher is anxious to get a newborn calf up and going. Sometimes, out of desperation, cowboys rely on makeshift arrangements for confining the anxious mother. But mostly, they have some sort of stall or stanchion where they can collect more than a measurable drop of milk. Rarely is a crew around to help chase and rope the cow.

Despite the twists and turns along the path to creating rodeo as we know it today, the events share one thing in common: the sport remains the soul of the Wild West—alive, still, in Pendleton, Oregon.

———

George Murdock, editor of the East Oregonian, *is a Pendleton rancher.*

▼ **Pearson cattle drive, 1959. Until fences and freeways barred the way in the 1960s, the Pearsons drove five hundred cows and calves a hundred miles from their winter range in Juniper Canyon up to their summer range in the Blue Mountains.** *Courtesy of Martha Boyer.*

Three generations of Hamleys with

Round-Up champions.

▲ J. J. Hamley with King Merritt, 1935.

▲▶ Lester Hamley with Everett Shaw,

1948.

▶ Dave Hamley with Jeff Knowles, 1999.

Hamley Archive.

Hamley & Company was closely associated with the Round-Up from its 1910 inception. J. J. Hamley awarded a trophy saddle to Bert Kelly, winner of the bucking contest that first year. The first championship saddle, valued at $250, was judged "Best in the World" while on display at Cheyenne. In later years, practically every Round-Up champion owned at least one Hamley saddle. The company's influence extended beyond the champions to all cowboys, Hollywood stars, and politicians—to whoever wanted to own the best. The quality of Hamley saddles was unequaled and internationally recognized.

In 1919 the Round-Up committee called a meeting of rodeo representatives from Walla Walla, Washington; Boise, Idaho; and Cheyenne, Wyoming. They asked the Hamley & Company saddlery to design a standardized bronc saddle to replace the various types of saddles being used in competition. The design was so successful that the Hamley bronc saddle, with little modification, is still in use today. In 1960 the company began making the saddles without a horn. Originally it was called the "committee" saddle, then later,

PRESIDENT T.D. TAYLOR OF THE ROUNDUP. AND FIRST PRIZE #350. SADDLE.

No 257

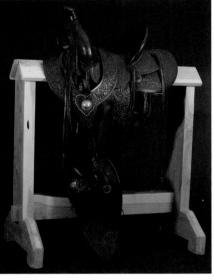

◄ Hoot Gibson poses before a row of Hamley saddles, n.d. *Helm Collection.*
▲ Til Taylor's saddle, made by E. L. Power in 1910. *Hall of Fame Collection.*
◄ Til Taylor with the prize saddle of 1912, donated by Hamley's for the bucking contest. L. W. Minor of Wallowa, Oregon, won the saddle. *By W. S. Bowman in Low Collection.*

▲ Inside Hamley & Co. saddlery, 1907.

OHS Collection, OrHi 61768.

▶ Everett Bowman, all-around champion of 1932, with prize Hamley saddle.

Hamley Archive.

the "association" or just plain "bronc" saddle. Association saddles remain the standard for the cowboy bucking-horse rider.

Hamley's made saddles on site in Pendleton until 1968 and continued to sell custom orders made off site until 1982, shortly after the final Hamley, David, retired. David had sold the company in 1980. The new owner lacked experience in the western world, and the venture was unsuccessful until Loren and Margaret Woods took over management in 1984. They ran the business until 1995, when another change in ownership occurred.

Pendleton saddle maker Randy Severe made finely worked saddles on site at Hamley & Company from 1995 to 1998. As late as 2000, Hamley's built the saddles for the movie *All the Pretty Horses*, starring Matt Damon and Penelope Cruz. But business management was tumultuous, and Hamley's survival was in question until 2004, when business partners Parley Pearce and Blair Woodfield of Walla Walla, Washington, purchased the faded legend and began restoring Hamley & Company to its former grandeur.

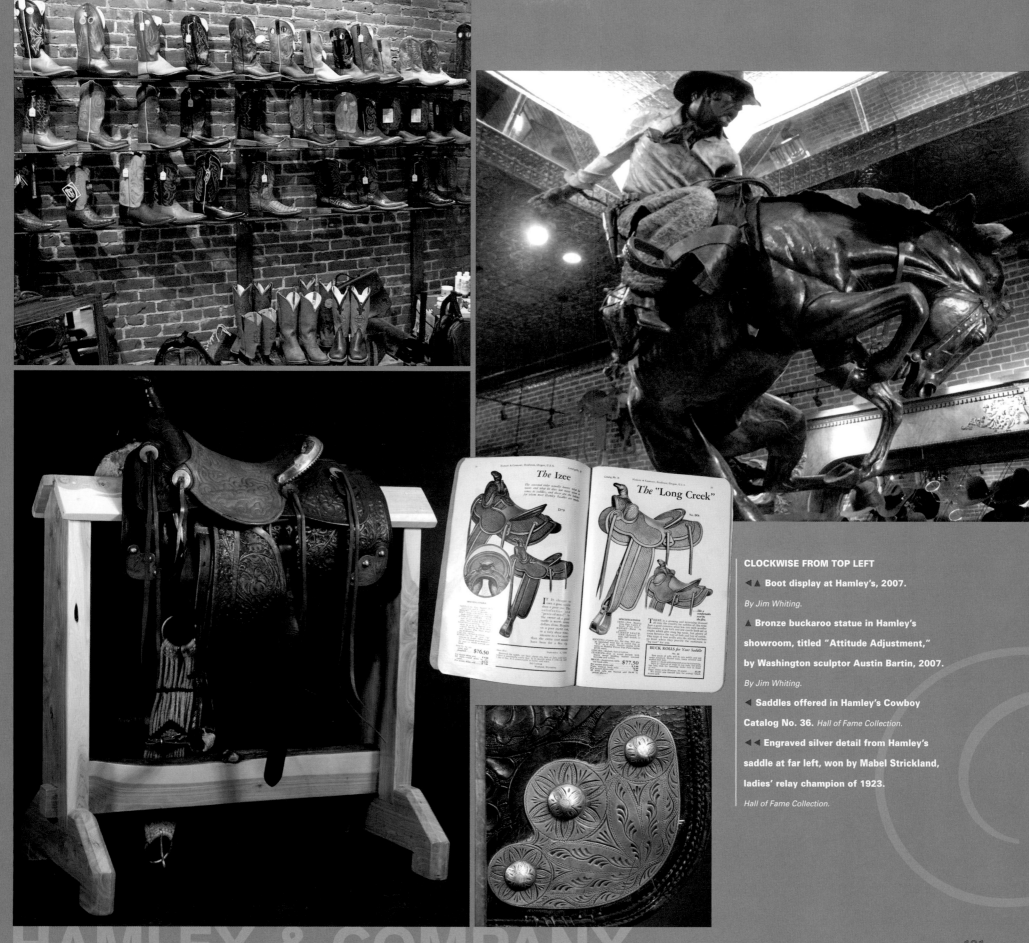

HAMLEY & COMPANY

Today saddles, western wear, and tack are just part of the mix. The store now includes a museum-quality western art gallery, the third-floor Slickfork Saloon, and an elegant old-time Steakhouse in an adjacent building. High-brows and low-brows intermingle.

Locals remember the 1950s, when famous roper and Hollywood actor Montie Montana rode his paint horse "Rex" through the swinging front doors and joined the throngs to shop in the store one Round-Up day. Although no one has ridden a horse into the store lately, it is once again a lively landmark in the Pendleton scene.

Pendletonian Elnor Purchase Alkio remembers traveling back East with her Oregon pioneer dad and mom, Mr. and Mrs. William Purchase, in their Buick in the 1930s. Somewhere in the middle of Wyoming, a cowboy came galloping up beside their car, thrust an envelope at Mr. Purchase, and asked, "Will you mail this letter for me?" It was addressed to "Hamley's, Pendleton, Oregon."

Today there is no need to flag down a passing Buick. The internet and the online Hamley catalog bring the store directly to its customers. (Old editions of the print catalogs have become collectors' treasures.) Like the Round-Up, Hamley & Company plans to be around at least another hundred years.

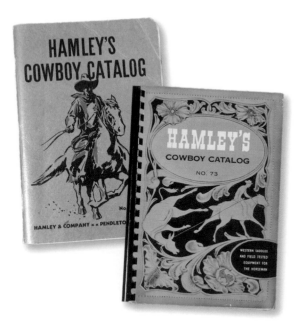

▲ Hamley's catalogs numbers 36 and 73.

Hall of Fame Collection.

▼ One day's shipment of mail to Hamley & Company, n.d. *Low Collection.*

SEVERE BROTHERS SADDLERY

Since 1955, the Severe brothers have been hand stamping and tooling beautiful, one-of-a-kind saddles. The family have achieved national recognition as artists in the saddle making world—by their peers, by cowboys, and by such august institutions as the Smithsonian.

It started on a ranch in southern Idaho when Bill and Duff Severe's sheep-herder father taught his sons the art of braiding rawhide and turning it into handsome pieces of cowboy gear. The brothers settled in Pendleton and worked for Hamley & Company for ten years before they founded their own shop in 1955. Over the years, the business grew, garnering national and international recognition along the way. Eight times, the Smithsonian Institute in Washington, D.C., has singled out Severe saddles for exhibit as prime examples of traditional western saddle-making. Celebrities and politicians (the late President Gerald Ford among them), as well as many working cowboys and pleasure riders, have been on their client list.

The brothers are gone now. Bill died in 1993, and Duff passed away in 2004. Bill's son Randy, schooled by Duff in the art of tooling, carries on the creative tradition. Robin and Monty, Randy's brothers, carve the saddle trees. Randy's sons, Jarad and Ryan, help to keep the family heritage strong. Some of Duff's miniature saddles, finely detailed models of his life-size saddles, are on display in the Duff Severe Museum at the entrance to the Pendleton Underground Tour.

Round-Up is a special time for the Severes. Over the years, the saddle shop has built many trophy saddles awarded to rodeo champions. Steer roping, calf roping, bronc riding, and barrel racing saddles all bear the Severe Brothers stamp. Many of the competing PRCA cowboys (members of the Professional Rodeo Cowboys Association) who pass through Pendleton take advantage of Severe hospitality and stay at the "Hotel de Cowpunch," dormitory-style accommodations upstairs in the World War II army barracks that houses the saddle shop.

For years Bill and Duff worked in the arena as volunteers during the rodeo. Randy has served on the Round-Up's board of directors since 2000 and currently oversees the livestock for the show. Each of his three daughters—Jodi, Darla, and Darci—has been Round-Up royalty.

Duff Severe grew up working with horses and watching his father and other cowboys craft rawhide gear. "They'd take an old, bloody, hairy hide and clean it up, and pretty soon they'd have something beautiful braided out of it," he says. "That really impressed me."

—*National Geographic*, January 1992

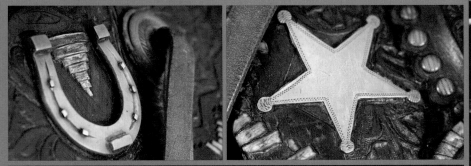

▲ **Duff Severe, revered Pendleton saddlemaker.** *Hall of Fame Collection.*
◄ **Severe Brothers saddle with silver and gold details, won in 1969 by champion steer roper Don McLaughlin.** *Hall of Fame Collection.*

SEVERE BROTHERS

COWBOY FIVE STAR
By Ann Terry Hill

Since 1955, the cowboy dormitory above the Severe Brothers saddle shop in a former barracks near the Pendleton airport has been the place of choice to stay for most of the cowboys who pass through this rodeo town. Campfire coffee is always brewing, and the cowpokes know that around the year, they have a bunk-style bed where they can roll out their sleeping bags free of charge to any PRCA member. The cowboys have often passed the hat, and several years they had enough spare change to send Bill and Duff Severe, founders of the saddlery, to the National Finals Rodeo (NFR) in Las Vegas. Randy Severe, Bill's son, keeps the tradition alive.

Rodeo icon Casey Tibbs, just back from a trip to Paris, France, christened the place "Hotel de Cowpunch" in the 1950s. With his soft South Dakota accent, he added a French flair to the billet.

The place is steeped in atmosphere. Earthy smells of leather drift up from the saddle shop on the ground floor. Abandoned milk cans serve as stools around the corner table where cowpokes play cards, read, or listen to music. Autographed pictures from 1955 to the present cover the walls, and hats that survived the arena foray decorate a cor-

▲ Bob Edson of the PRCA (at right) presents an award to Bill and Duff Severe (left and center). *Howdyshell Collection.*
► Casey Tibbs awaits his turn to ride, ca. 1956. Bob Chambers, longtime Round-Up announcer, is at right. *Howdyshell Collection.*

The Severes are a family of entertainers to boot. Well known for their musical talents, they are often invited to sing the national anthem to open each day's rodeo. During Round-Up week, you might find them harmonizing on Main Street as "The Singing Severes."

Randy sums up the family's pride in the construction of a Severe saddle. "I want to make the best and most beautiful saddle you can find, and then make the next one more beautiful than that."

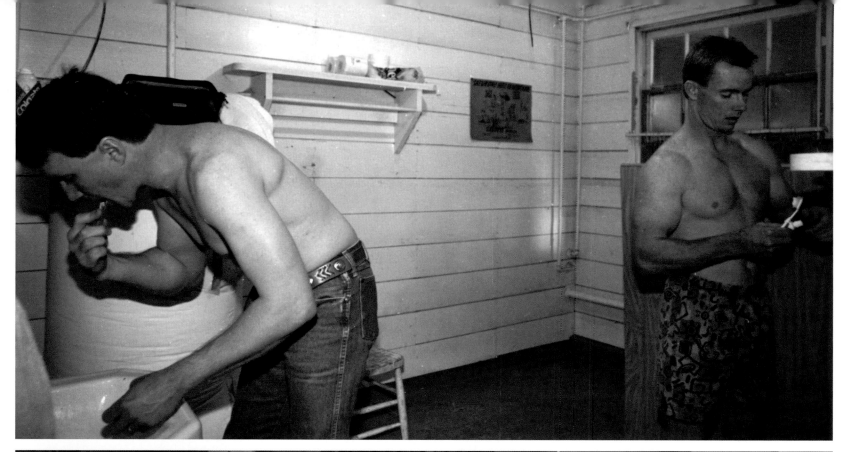

◄ Inside the Hotel
de Cowpunch, 2006.
By Don Cresswell,
EO Archive.

BOB CROSBY
WINNER OF
ROOSEVELT T:
PENDLETO
1928
(DOUBLE

▲ **Bob Crosby in his favorite black hat, 1928.** *By R. Doubleday. Courtesy of Betty Branstetter.*

COWBOY VOICES

BY ANN TERRY HILL

To Bob [Crosby], no hat was worthy of the name unless made by Stetson. What cow country men wore between boots and sombrero was of little importance, but the garments for feet and head must be of the very best quality.

—Thelma Crosby, *Bob Crosby, World Champion Cowboy,* 1966

▼ Crosby prepares for competition.

Howdyshell Collection.

BOB CROSBY

Jar the floor, Honey!" was Bob Crosby's daily 3 A.M. wake-up call to his wife Thelma. For years, the couple slaved extraordinarily long hours to keep the family ranch in New Mexico, the Cross B, going. Even after Crosby had established himself as king in the rodeo world, the 3 A.M. call was standard, a reflection of his work ethic.

With the help of Eve Ball, Thelma Crosby wrote the biographical *Bob Crosby, World Champion Cowboy,* first published in 1966. Roberta Crosby Burkstaller, the couple's daughter, republished the book in 2006 through Wild Horse Press in Walnut Springs, Texas.

Although Crosby owned many new hats, according to Thelma, his battered, weathered old black Stetson became his symbol of achievement. He always wore the black hat when he had a significant competition coming up, and he was seldom photographed without it. Crosby was wearing that hat when he won all three of his world championships, including when he retired the Roosevelt Trophy in Pendleton in 1928.

In the 1920s, rules for the world championship contest were standardized. Judges determined the winners by the number of points a cowboy won at both Cheyenne and Pendleton in a single season. At both rodeos, contestants were required to enter both a horseback event and a cow event—bulldoggers and ropers had to also participate in bronc-busting or wild horse racing, and bronc riders had to enter a bulldogging or roping contest. The points were averaged over three years. Crosby won the miniature Roosevelt Trophy in 1925 and 1927 (he stayed home and practiced in 1926, his daughter said in a 2008 telephone interview). In 1928 he won the big gold and silver trophy itself.

"Wild Horse" Bob Crosby, as the popular cowboy was called, was a giant in the arena and out. In his daughter's words, "He was the most exciting cowboy. The crowd would go wild in Pendleton whenever he rode into the arena."

SHOAT WEBSTER

Shoat Webster retired the Sam Jackson Trophy at Pendleton in 1951 after winning the all-around championship three years in a row (the first two wins won him "legs" on the trophy; the third made it his to take home). He considered this his greatest success. The trophy had been sought after for twenty-one years. Webster returned in 1952 to win a leg on the Oregon Journal Trophy, making him the all-around champion four years in a row.

Pendleton loved "Shoat" (whose given name was Howard Chouteau Webster) and his famous horse "Popcorn." Shoat returned the admiration.

"I loved the people and the rodeo," he said. "I loved Pendleton. I don't know if the people were more fun or if the winning was more fun, but Pendleton is one of the best places I ever rodeoed. I loved that old dirt arena and coming off that slope onto it. Steer roping was probably my favorite event. I won the most money doing that, and that was what I was noted for." (Telephone interview with Ann Terry Hill, 2006)

Webster is part Shawnee, enrolled under the Cherokee. His uncle Fred Lowry was his roping inspiration and mentor. From the age of twelve or thirteen, he always had a rope in hand. He was known to practice on his sisters and the chickens.

Among his many honors, Webster is included in the National Cowboy and Heritage Museum Rodeo Hall of Fame. He was inducted into the Pendleton Round-Up and Happy Canyon Hall of Fame in 1975. His 1951 Hamley trophy saddle, with an oak-leaf stamp, and the coveted Sam Jackson Trophy are exhibited at the Professional Rodeo Cowboys Association Museum in Colorado Springs. In all, Shoat Webster won three Hamley saddles.

JIM SHOULDERS

Always the champion, Jim Shoulders won the bull riding in 1958, the bareback riding in 1958 and 1959, and the all-around plus one leg on the Oregon Journal Trophy in 1958. In 1999 he was named to the Round-Up and Happy Canyon Hall of Fame. In a 2007 interview, he said, "I like Pendleton because they give a lot of money and it's always a celebration. My wife Sharon made her first visit there in 1999. She's seen a lot of rodeos, and she couldn't

▼ Shoat Webster, 1950. *Howdyshell Collection.*

▶ Jim Shoulders, 1958. *Howdyshell Collection.*

believe how wild it is. She was impressed. Pendleton really got her attention."

Reminiscing about his rodeo days, Shoulders said, "I didn't go to Pendleton for years, until they became a *real* rodeo and had bull riding. When they put bulls back [in 1944], I went."

Jim Shoulders died in June 2007. He was buried in a pine box with horseshoe handles and his personal brand burned into the wood.

DEAN OLIVER

Rodeo legend Dean Oliver was Round-Up champion roper in 1957, 1971, and 1976. He was inducted into the Round-Up and Happy Canyon Hall of Fame in 1996. At age twenty, when most ropers are well on their way, Oliver hadn't even started his rodeo career. But he made up for lost time in the '50s, '60s, and '70s. By the end of his career, he had won an unprecedented seven national world titles. Still active in 2008 at the age of seventy-seven, he has been named member-at-large on the prestigious PRCA Executive Council.

In a 2008 telephone interview, Oliver remembered the Round-Up. "I always looked forward to coming to Pendleton. It is a true part of the West, from the Indians to the races to the rodeo.

"I never minded coming off that grassy slope. I had my horse shod with cork shoes so he wouldn't slip. It is so unique to chase those calves down that slope.

"I won in Pendleton three times and placed many times. It's a good rodeo, and I liked competing there. The directors and the people all go out of their way for the cowboys. The town is rodeo minded. It is one of a kind—there isn't any other rodeo like it. The town is a nice place to come to, too."

HARLEY MAY

Harley May won the steer roping contest in 1961. He remembers it as one of the biggest thrills of his life. Going into the final round, he was third against roping champions Ike Rude and Joe Snively.

After the event, May recounted, Snively and Rude, who were traveling together with John Pouge, didn't even take time to unsaddle their horses. Without a word, they loaded them in the trailer and headed down the road. Pouge later recalled that they traveled seventy miles in silence. Then Rude, whose usual reply to anything was "Things are downhill and in the shade," spoke up. "We let that god-damned bronc rider beat us." They continued on without another word.

May returned to Pendleton several times and won the bulldogging in 1962. He remarked, "Pendleton is a 'cowboy up' rodeo. You have to be a cowboy to win anything there." At age fifty-two, he returned to Pendleton acting as pilot for several young cowboys. Since he was there, he thought, "Hell, I might as well enter the steer wrestling." He placed third. (Telephone interview with Ann Terry Hill, 2006)

JACKIE WRIGHT

Round-Up bareback champion in 1965, Jackie Wright rode "War Paint" fifteen out of seventeen times (though never in Pendleton), a record. He vividly remembers this horse and the trips he had on him. In his words,

"Paint" was always cranky. He'd kick you if he got the chance. When Christensen Brothers got him he was six or seven years old, and flashy with his paint markings. His name was "War Paint," and that's what they featured at the rodeos.

The first time I had him was at Grants Pass [Oregon]. He threw me off on the track. I've never been thrown so hard in my life. I had him again in about two weeks, and he threw me off again. He really bucked me hard.

I got to trying to figure this out. I was pretty young, but I'd rode some pretty rank horses by then, and I was wondering why he bucked me off. One reason I found was you couldn't pull on his head . . . you give him so much rein and had to slip him a little as he went out through [the gate]. But the main reason was when we were in the chute and he heard the click of the gate, he knew he was up and that was his cue. He'd rear in there with you, and lots of times, in those little chutes, they used to have boards across the top, and he'd either take some of them out as you went through or you'd have to duck.

After two hundred and thirty years, Thom Jeff and the other Framers of the Constitution would recognize the dignity, nobility, and working savvy at play in the classic combo of a Stetson or Resistol hat, jeans, chaps, high boots, low spurs, and a bright bandana that constitute the elements of what I have to argue is our hands-down *national* costume.

—Marianne Wiggins
(quoted in Kendrick, 2008)

▲ A cowboy takes a break. *Howdyshell Collection.*

▶ **Ron Currin rides in the wild horse race, 1959.**

Howdyshell Collection.

RON CURRIN

that among the prizes presented to him was a steer-head roping dummy made by Bill Severe that had a picture of his father, Clark, between the horns. In 2007 Pake commented to Stan Timmermann that he was going to buy some extra steers for his ranch so he could practice and win Pendleton one more time.

Pake not only rodeos, but he is a singer and fiddle player as well. The front and back covers of his first independent album, "Rodeo Man" (1980), featured pictures of a man roping a steer in the "short go" championship round at Pendleton.

CURRIN BROTHERS

The four Currin brothers, Ron Jr., Tony, Steve, and Mike, would be famous at the Pendleton Round-Up even if they weren't local. The Currin boys always add a bit of theater to Round-Up events. Each brother has won an event, and Tony has won twice. They are the sons of Ron Currin Sr. and Judy Lazinka Currin of Heppner. Members of a rodeo family supreme, the brothers have become legends in their own time.

Tragically, Mike Currin died in a plane crash in 1990. The three remaining brothers shared thoughts about Pendleton in April 2008.

Tony Currin won the bulldogging contest in 1987 and 1989. "Round-Up is a family tradition," he said enthusiastically. "I think I've only missed one in my life. It is our favorite rodeo. It is one of a kind—a bit dangerous, and you are a little leery coming off that slope. But it was a real thrill for me, one you never forget. When I was a kid I used to dream about winning a saddle in Pendleton. I've ended up winning two of them."

Ron Currin Jr. attended his first Round-Up in 1960 when he was three weeks old and his mother carried him to the show in her arms. He hasn't missed a Round-Up since. Ron won the bulldogging in 1995 and said, "It's a great thrill for a boy from eastern Oregon to win at the Pendleton Round-Up."

Steve Currin won the bulldogging in 1991. He is probably even better remembered for the shows he put on in other years. In 1989, when he was a rookie, his steer somersaulted over his head. He managed to grab its tail and get enough momentum to pull himself up, get a hold on the steer's head, and throw it at the far end of the arena—all in twenty-four seconds. Another year, his steer "dog fell" (to the wrong side) twice. Steve climbed on his back and rode him out of the arena. Cowboys and spectators alike refer to him as the Round-Up specialty act.

Mike Currin was 1988 all-around winner. At Saturday's show, he was dressed in his western best, including a fine hat. When he won, he was so excited that while taking his victory lap, he spontaneously threw his hat into the south grandstand. Miraculously, his mom, Judy Lazinka Currin, caught it.

The Currin family preserved Mike's memory by presenting the Mike Currin Memorial Award, a saddle that went to the high-point cowboy on the Columbia River Circuit, from 1990 to 2006. At one time or another, all three of Mike's brothers won this award.

ETBAUER BROTHERS

Another set of brothers, the Etbauer trio, have also had an impact in Pendleton. Over the years, all three have won the saddle bronc championship. Interviewed by telephone in April 2008, Robert said, "Pendleton was one of my favorite rodeos. Got my first major win there [in 1987]. I enjoyed it then and I do now. It is unique. The only time the grass arena ever bothered me was when I landed on it!"

Billy Etbauer, in his forties and still competing at Pendleton in 2008, won the saddle bronc title in 1994. "Pendleton is just a great old rodeo," he said in an interview. "It takes you back in time. They keep trying to get better and better stock, and you just hope you draw a good one and don't make the grass."

Dan Etbauer, saddle bronc winner in 1990 and 1996, said, "Pendleton is one of the most prestigious rodeos, and I dreamed of winning it when I was a kid. I got lucky enough to win it twice. I got the highest mark of my career there, an eighty-nine, on "Sundown" in '96. I also broke a wrist and tore up a knee there a couple of other years when I wasn't so lucky."

TOM SOREY

Four Round-Up championship saddles decorate the wall of Tom Sorey's den. This Pendleton cowboy triumphed in steer roping in 1996 and 1999 and won the Mike Currin Memorial Award the same years.

▲ **Mike Currin, 1988.** *Howdyshell Collection.*

▼ **Wallace Smith drawing, 1924—a sketch by the designer of the Round-Up bucking horse logo.** *From Smith's 1925* Oregon Sketches.

A Parthian Kick

"It is special to win here because it's my hometown rodeo," Sorey said in an April 2008 interview. "The hometown rodeos are the hardest to win because you are trying so hard to shine in front of your family and friends. Years ago I told my wife that someday she would see my name on the Winners' Board. To win twice was a special thrill."

What does he think about Pendleton's turf? "Roping on the grass never bothered me. I was too busy thinking about getting the rope on and the steer down. Just make a good run, that's what I wanted."

BUTCH KNOWLES

If you aren't born a Lazinka or born to one, you can marry into the family as Butch Knowles did when he wed Mary Healy, one of Kathryn Lazinka Healy Thorne's daughters. Butch made a name for himself and added to the family luster by winning the saddle bronc riding at the Round-Up in 1986 and again in 1991. "It is such a big deal in our family," he said when interviewed in 2008. "I played football in that arena when I was in high school, and I dreamed of riding broncs there."

For the last nineteen years, Butch has been an analyst on national television for the Professional Rodeo Cowboys Association. "Now, whenever I'm on a plane, I always hear

people speak of Pendleton, Calgary, and Cheyenne. Those are the traditional rodeos."

Remembering his bronc riding days, he says, "The chutes in Pendleton are a little bigger than at other rodeos, and it's a little tricky to get down on the horse. When you compete in Pendleton—there is nothing like it."

MIKE BEERS

In 1997, roper Mike Beers of Powell Butte, Oregon, took permanent possession of the East Oregonian Trophy by winning his third all-around title. The others came in 1985 and 1995. Beers, whose career earnings approach $2 million, broke his pelvis and shoulder in 2007 but managed to compete again by the end of the year. He attended the 2007 Round-Up in a wheelchair.

In 2008 he commented about Pendleton: "There is nothing like winning in Pendleton. Getting to do the lap around the arena is the ultimate. It's the only rodeo we go to that's on grass. The thrill you get when you nod for your steer—you don't even see him coming off that slope on the west end. The rush is like nothing else."

FRED WHITFIELD

A black cowboy from Texas, Fred Whitfield was Pendleton's calf roping champion in 1995, 1996, and 2005. With each successive win, his time improved (from 12.03 seconds, to 10.1 seconds, to 9.8 seconds). This is a roper who gets better and better. He speaks of the Round-Up with the typical cowboy mixture of pride and humility. In a 2008 interview, Whitfield said, "Pendleton is unique. Some guys go a lifetime and never win it. I've won it three times and hold the calf roping record there. I've always thrived on roping on a football field. But there will be a time when some guy comes along and wins for the fourth time, and my record will be history."

BRAD GOODRICH

Calf roping champion at the 2004 Round-Up, Brad Goodrich echoes the sentiments of the old-timers. "The Pendleton Round-Up is the best," he said in a 2008

▼ Happy Canyon princess Raeann Crane with all-around winner Mike Beers and sons in 1995. *Courtesy of Raeann Crane.*

interview. "It's the most traditional and true-to-life rodeo there is. I make no secret that it's my favorite of all the rodeos. Winning the calf roping at Pendleton was the greatest win in my career—one of the greatest thrills of my life."

Goodrich said he was competing less in 2008, but he would be in Pendleton. "I'll be competing there until my boots are 'toes up!'"

ROD HAY

In a 2008 interview, Rod Hay, Canadian saddle bronc rider who won in Pendleton in 2003, 2004, 2005, and 2006, had this to say about the Round-Up: "Pendleton isn't like the other rodeos. You get to mount up and ride around the track when you win, which is exciting. It is definitely the one to be a champ at." About the grass arena, he added, "The grass doesn't make much difference when you're on top, but it sure does when you hit it!"

CASH MYERS

Two-time winner of the all-around title and with two legs up on the East Oregonian Trophy in 2008, roper Cash Myers hoped to retire the trophy. He and Trevor Brazile (who had one leg up) had a friendly competition to see who could win it for keeps. Interviewed by telephone in 2008, Myers spoke with enthusiasm about Pendleton. "It's a throw-back rodeo—the whole atmosphere that goes with it," he said. "I don't know any cowboy that doesn't like it. It means a lot to me to have won the East Oregonian Trophy twice [in 2005 and 2007], with all the great cowboys listed on it." Myers won again in 2008 and took the trophy home.

TREVOR BRAZILE

In 2007 Trevor Brazile became the Professional Rodeo Cowboys Association's first triple-crown winner since 1983, when his father-in-law, Roy Cooper, earned the distinction. Brazile won three world titles at the National Finals Rodeo in Las Vegas: tie-down roping (calf roping), steer roping, and the all around. In Pendleton eight years earlier, he won both the calf roping and the all around, gaining a leg on the East Oregonian Trophy. In a 2008 interview, Brazile said,

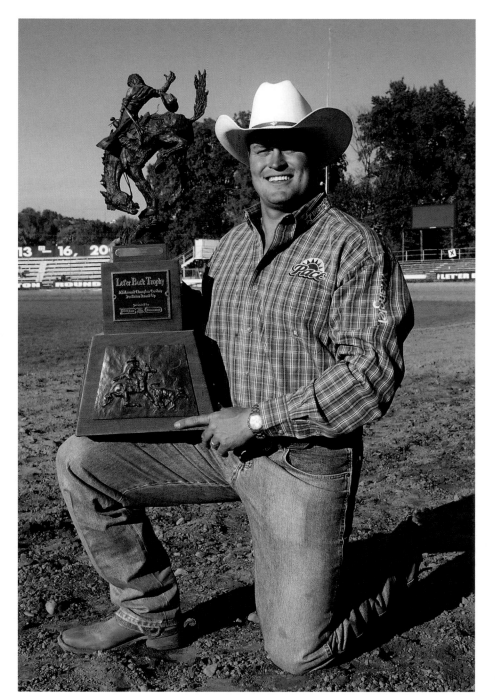

◄ Cash Myers with the East Oregonian Trophy in 2005. Retiring the trophy in 2008, Myers said, "More than anything pride don't go away. You can spend that money but you can't spend that pride."

EO Archive.

"It's a cool deal to win the East Oregonian Trophy once. Anyone who wins it three times and retires it definitely deserves it."

Brazile agrees with his fellow cowboys that the Round-Up is one of a kind. "Everybody I know that has cowboy pictures in their home has a picture up of the Pendleton Round-Up. It is the rodeo that is unique. It has a cowboy element that no other rodeo has."

WESTWARD HO! PARADE

BY ANN TERRY HILL

The parade is like history in motion, paying tribute to tribal ancestors and early pioneers alike. No vehicle can be motorized or feature pneumatic tires.

—*East Oregonian,* September 2007

▼ Six-horse team pulls a wagon train in the 2007 Westward Ho! Parade. *EO Archive.*

Nostalgia and tradition combine to make Westward Ho! one of the most memorable parades in the West. Since Round-Up's beginning in 1910, parade-goers have come from across the country to enjoy the spectacle, a resurrection of historic, non-motored conveyances. No motorized vehicles are allowed. Everything that moves is powered by four-legged critters and humans. Horses, oxen, mule teams, buffalo, and donkeys make the trek through town on an annual basis, outfitted as they were in the 1800s. People in the parade represent miners, mountain men, pioneers on the Oregon Trail. They include cowboys and cowgirls and Indians, royal

▲ **Chief Gary Burke of the Confederated Tribes of the Umatilla Indian Reservation parades in the 2007 Westward Ho!** *EO Archive.*

courts and bands from around the state, politicians, local businesses, and Northwest universities. The players change over the years, but overall, the parade accurately depicts the Old West.

Each year, the Westward Ho! starts promptly at 10 a.m. on Friday of Round-Up week. It is announced with a gunshot and led by the parade's Grand Marshal, the current queen and court, and the Round-Up board of directors. Dozens of volunteers help to bring it about. Every five years, the Round-Up courts and Happy Canyon princesses of the past ride, giving crowds a chance to see how rodeo garb has changed over the years. In 2005, Ruth Porter Piquet, a Round-Up princess in both 1933 and 1934, led this group. She plans to be around in 2010 for the centennial.

Many of the historic wagons stored under the grandstand perished in the 1940 fire. The few original covered wagons that remain are maintained by volunteer Bill Dawson, who spends each summer getting the wagons in working order. Dawson succeeds the late Gerald Swaggart, who held this responsibility for several decades.

Each year, the parade director selects the Grand Marshal, someone with enough Round-Up history to be worthy of leading the parade. Abe Schiller, part-owner of the famed Flamingo Hotel in Las Vegas, was the first to hold the title, in 1957. In earlier years, many dignitaries and movie stars rode in the parade, but none had the distinction conferred by the Grand Marshal title. Honorees who have held the position include cowboys and cowgirls, Indians, volunteers, private citizens, and past board members. Grand Marshals may choose to ride a horse or to ride in a buggy at the head of the parade. Most choose to appear on horseback. Riderless horses accompanied by family members have sometimes led the parade, since the honorees had recently died.

The Dress-Up Parade, another Round-Up festivity, is held as a kick-off on Saturday morning before Round-Up week. The parade is made up of merchant floats, Indians in regalia, bands, royal courts, and many horse clubs. This parade was originally held on the Saturday night prior to Round-Up, but it got so rowdy that organizers changed it to Saturday morning.

▲▲ A six-horse team pulls an old-fashioned log-hauler in Westward Ho! Parade. *Howdyshell Collection.*

▲ Governor Holmes of Oregon (center) and Governor Rosellini of Washington (right) ride in the 1958 Westward Ho! Parade. *OHS Collection, CN 010718.*

▶ A mule-drawn prairie schooner in Westward Ho! 2007. *By Jim Whiting.*

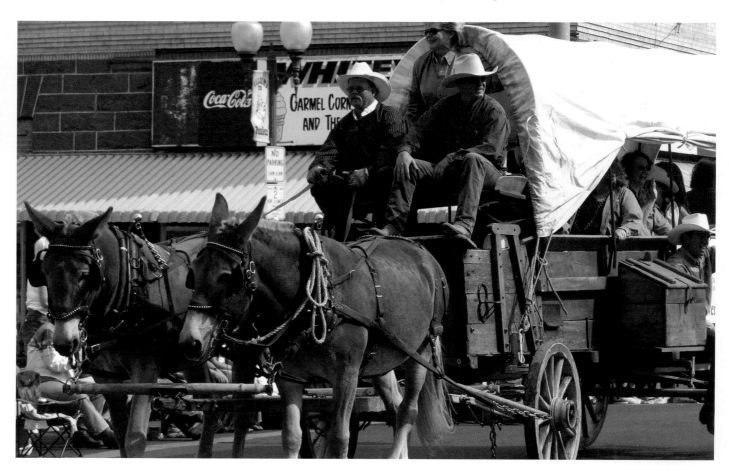

CLOCKWISE FROM TOP LEFT

▲ images from the 2007 Westward Ho!
Parade. Rex Buck Jr. is at lower right.
By Jim Whiting.

▼ Pendleton Woolen Mills float in the
2007 Dress-Up Parade, which allows
motorized vehicles. *PWM Archive.*

WESTWARD HO!

▲ Announcer's box in 1916. A six- by six-foot crow's nest twenty feet off the ground stood just off the track in the arena.

The megaphone was bolted to a protective railing. *By Lisa G. Paterson in OHS Collection, bb003690.*

BEHIND THE MIKE

BY ANN TERRY HILL

Foghorn's ability to project his voice through a megaphone (in the years before microphones were invented) made him famous, and his glib commentary on the shows pleased the crowds and helped build the popularity of the sport.

▼ Red Cross workers rush to help a cowboy in the early years. The announcer keeps the crowd informed. *By W. S. Bowman in Low Collection.*

Rodeo announcers are the glue that holds the show together. They control the tempo of arena events, and they can make or break a rodeo. If they have the crowd's attention, they project the general excitement or disappointment. The crowd feels it and is with them.

Announcers have been an integral part of the show for decades. Foghorn Clancy was the first. His name was a carry-over from the days he hawked newspapers and was known as the "town crier" in Mineral Wells, Texas. After watching Clancy get unceremoniously thrown from a mount in the San

▲ Swan dance winners, 2007. From left, Wilma Buck, Aurlyn Stwyer, Charlene Tilloquots, and Katrina Walsey. *By Jim Whiting.*

INDIAN VILLAGE

BY ANN TERRY HILL

Today's village is composed of two hundred to three hundred teepees. It is unique in the world of rodeo as the largest annual Indian encampment in North America.

▼ Indian Village in 2007. *By Jim Whiting.*

Since 1910, Indians have been as much a part of the Pendleton Round-Up scene as the cowboys and the roughstock. The Indian Village to the north of the stadium is perhaps the most beautiful spot on the Round-Up grounds. For almost a century, it has been the center of activity for the Native American community during Round-Up week. The teepees are set up mainly by members of the Confederated Tribes of the Umatilla Indians, though members of other Northwest tribes also come and camp. Teepee sites are handed down through generations, and many families occupy the same space in the village their ancestors did.

| ▲ **Happy Canyon, 2007.** *By Gary Ogilvie.*

HAPPY CANYON—
GOING STRONG SINCE 1913

BY ANN TERRY HILL

The last scene of Happy Canyon's first act shows the exodus of Indians as they pack their teepees and belongings and move to the reservation. It is a poignant finale.

The epic story of the West is nothing new to Pendleton. This story has been told and retold since 1913 at Happy Canyon, the nighttime pageant of the Pendleton Round-Up. Faces and animals have shifted over the decades; even the venue has changed. But the roles are coveted and handed down from generation to generation. Kevin Hale, Happy Canyon president in 2007 and 2008, commented in a 2008 interview: "Happy Canyon is in a sense a family reunion. As much as anything, it is a community celebration. We try to promote and preserve it as part of the real West."

◄ Only men performed in the frontier town scenes in Happy Canyon's early years. Ron Hudson, champion cowboy and Round-Up president in 1989–1990, donned a calico dress to greet Dean Foquette.

Howdyshell Collection.

HAPPY CANYON

▲▲ Caroline Motanic Davis (at left) and her daughter Toni Minthorn ride in the 1974 Westward Ho! Parade. *Howdyshell Collection.*

▲ Beaded pins, followed by engraved silver pins, gave the wives of Happy Canyon directors a free pass for life. *Courtesy of Wes Grilley.*

► Happy Canyon Court, 1961. Left to right: Lois McFarland, Beverly Strong, and Bertha Carter. *Howdyshell Collection.*

Grandmothers, grandfathers, fathers, mothers, sons and daughters, both Indian and white, keep this show going. The parts are treasured hand-me-downs, and some have been in the same family for decades.

Since 1955, when Caroline Motanic was chosen as the first Happy Canyon princess to represent the show and travel around the Northwest as a Round-Up ambassador, Happy Canyon has chosen one or two princesses annually. Several princesses have traveled abroad to Japan and Hong Kong, and even to the Oval Office at the White House. The show itself is a huge undertaking involving about 425 people, most of whom are volunteers.

The original idea for the pageant came in 1913 after the Umatilla-Morrow County Fair, which was held on what is now the corner of Main and Frazier in Pendleton. Town leaders decided they needed something to entertain the nighttime crowds during Round-Up.

Roy Raley, the first president of the Round-Up, wrote the first show, which was basically the Wild West part of the pageant. Two years later, Raley enlisted Anna Minthorn Wannassay, a Cayuse tribal member, to write the Indian portion of the pageant, a sellout in the first year and for

many years to follow. There is no script for the Indians, who know their parts by the music played. The animals often know their parts as well as the human cast members.

In 1956, the Happy Canyon show was moved from its original site on Southwest Emigrant Avenue to the arena behind the Pendleton Convention Center on the Round-Up grounds at Southwest Court. The show was revised in 2001, with speaking parts added. This proved unsuccessful. Several years later, Indian and pioneer narrators were added, and the crowd seemed to approve. Happy Canyon evolves slowly, but its essence endures.

Gambling was a popular part of post–Happy Canyon festivities until 1970, when District Attorney Joe Smith of Pendleton declared it illegal and shut it down for the year. In 1971, the Oregon State Legislature enacted the Happy Canyon Gambling Act, pushed through by Ruff Raymond. The act is still in effect and benefits Happy Canyon as well as many other non-profit organizations.

Aside from the pageant, which is presented each of the four nights of Round-Up, Happy Canyon and the Round-Up now co-produce a kick-off concert held in the Happy Canyon arena at the start of Round-Up week. Another highly successful pre-rodeo event is the Pro Bull Riding, or the US Bank/Pendleton PBR Classic held in the Happy Canyon arena Monday and Tuesday nights before the actual Round-Up begins. Happy Canyon and the Round-Up co-sponsor this thrilling event. Top professional bull riders from all over the country compete for large purses while gearing up for the Round-Up rodeo.

Happy Canyon presents several other activities during Round-Up. The annual Hall of Fame banquet co-sponsored by Happy Canyon and the Round-Up features the year's new inductees and launches the week of festivities.

To commemorate Happy Canyon's ninetieth anniversary in 2006, Pendleton Woolen Mills issued a commemorative blanket. Designed by the Happy Canyon board of directors, the blanket features a colorful design incorporating the Happy Canyon logo and a commemorative leather patch.

Happy Canyon's future includes upgrading the facilities yet preserving the pageant's authenticity. President Hale said, "The show will continue to showcase the cultures of both the Native Americans and the whites, and how traditions are handed down from family to family."

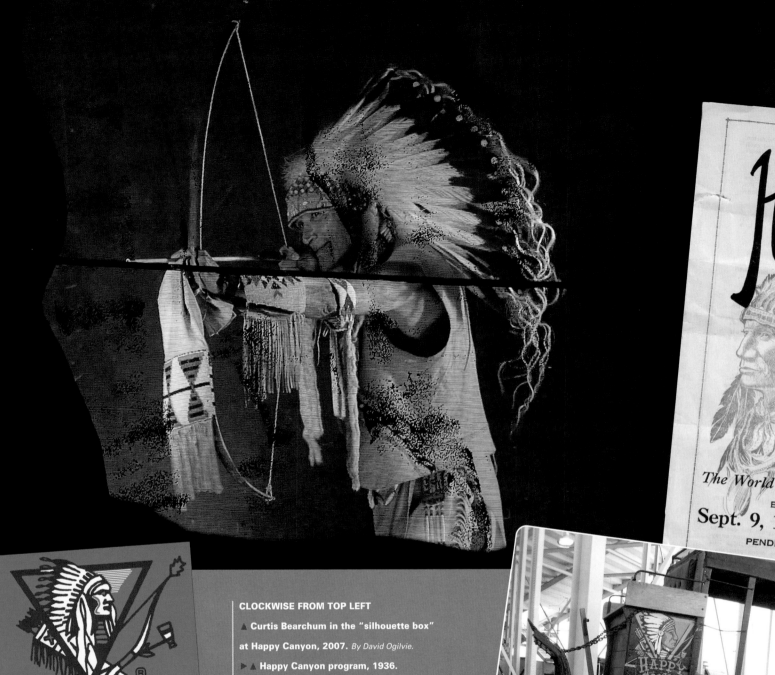

CLOCKWISE FROM TOP LEFT

▲ Curtis Bearchum in the "silhouette box" at Happy Canyon, 2007. *By David Ogilvie.*

▶ ▲ Happy Canyon program, 1936.

Hall of Fame Collection.

▶ Stagecoach used in the show, 2007.

By Jim Whiting.

◀ Happy Canyon logo.

Happy Canyon

The World's Most Unique Show!

EVENINGS OF

Sept. 9, 10, 11, 12, 1936

PENDLETON, OREGON

CLOWNS AND BULLFIGHTERS

BY ANN TERRY HILL

"Get out there and entertain the crowd."

Monk remembers, "We got a pretty good paycheck.

It sure beat working in the harvest, so we had

letterhead printed and went to work."

▶ Monk Carden, ca. 2003, clowning around in his nineties. *Courtesy of Umatilla Historical Society.*

A. O. "MONK" CARDEN

Monk Carden spent his youth clowning around at rodeos—Pendleton, Ellensburg, Heppner, and Union, Oregon. Born in February of 1909 and still going strong in April 2008, he is nationally recognized as the oldest living rodeo clown. He jokingly enters clown reunion parties being carried on a stretcher. He is, in fact, a year older than the Pendleton Round-Up, and he hasn't missed many of the shows. A. O. "Monk" Carden is a true Pendleton native. Northwest Carden Street in town is named for his pioneering ancestors.

MOENS & CARDEN

| ▲ George Moens (left) and Monk Carden perform in the Round-Up arena, n.d. *Low Collection.*

233

▲ ▲ Carden and Moens clowning, ca. 1928.

Howdyshell Collection.

▲ Fleeing an angry brahma bull, ca. 1958.

Howdyshell Collection.

Carden has done things to make people laugh all his life, and he's still clowning for the folks in his retirement community and at the annual Rodeo Clown Reunion, where he is revered. "It was much different back in the days when I was doing it for a paycheck," he says. "We were athletic, but we didn't have to fight bulls."

Monk got his start at the 1928 Pendleton Round-Up when the hired rodeo clown broke his leg and couldn't go on. The rodeo president, Henry Collins, had seen his acrobatic acts and said, "Get out there and entertain the crowd." He and his long-time partner George Moens, now deceased, did just that, and a business was born. Monk remembers, "We got a pretty good paycheck. It sure beat working in the harvest, so we had letterhead printed and went to work." To the delight of the crowds, the team performed at the Round-Up from 1928 to 1934. They were inducted into the Hall of Fame in 1978.

Unlike today's clowns, who face off with angry bulls, Monk risked his life in the arena riding backwards on a mule, riding a trick horse, and doing gymnastic stunts, acquiring many bruises along the way. His one similarity with modern clowns is that he didn't wear baggy, falling-down pants, which would have hindered his acrobatics.

Although in retirement, Monk keeps close contact with his clown compatriots, annually attending the Rodeo Clown Reunions held throughout the West, which are coordinated by Gail Hughbanks Woerner, author of *Fearless Funnymen* and a noted historian on rodeo clowns. Monk's ambition was to bring the Rodeo Clown Reunion to Pendleton, which he did successfully in 2006 with Woerner's help. When he's not working on that project, he stays busy doing pen-and-ink line drawings. To this day, he'll suit up and put on his clown makeup at the drop of a hat, if you ask him.

RODEO HEROES

When a cowboy is down and a bullfighter or barrelman has a 2,000-pound bull like "Zorro" or "Dirty Harry" coming at him, there's no time to panic. His objective is to save the cowboy's life and give him time to get to the fence before the animal tramples him. He doesn't think of his own safety. At the same time, he is supposed to make it look easy and to entertain the crowd, getting a few laughs along the

◄ Clowns Wilber Plaugher (right front) and George Doak rush to push photographer Joe Howdyshell out of harm's way, 1970s. *Howdyshell Collection.*

▼ George Doak, clown and bullfighter, 1976. *Howdyshell Collection.*

way. Don't be fooled. Even though they're dressed in crazy clown attire, usually with painted smiles on their faces, for the men in the arena this business is dead serious and dangerous.

Barrelmen and bullfighters make their living the old-fashioned way—traveling from rodeo to rodeo in their campers. They are rodeo's unsung heroes. Insurance companies won't even look at them. They do it for the love of the sport and the chance to help out fellow cowboys.

The first clown acts were in the 1920s, when it became clear that someone was needed in the arena to distract the bulls and help cowboys get to safety. The clowns quickly became top crowd pleasers, returning to enthusiastic fans year after year. George Doak, a popular performer and Pendleton Round-Up and Happy Canyon Hall of Fame

inductee in 1983, entertained rodeo audiences in Pendleton for nineteen years.

Returning to Pendleton in 2006 for the Rodeo Clowns Reunion, Doak reminisced about the Round-Up. "I've had many fond memories, but Pendleton I considered my second home, and that's why I'm so glad to be here this year. There are so many people here that are like blood relatives to me. I didn't ride in many parades, but I always did in Pendleton because it was so much fun. I had my little mule."

Doak laughed as he remembered the Let 'er Buck Room. "I didn't drink while I was rodeoing, but I went in there. It scared me because I got in there and I couldn't get out!"

The 1960s and 1970s brought an era of specialized bull-fighters and barrelmen, so called because they jump into a barrel when an angry bull comes after them. Two of the best

in the business, barrelman Flint Rasmussen and bullfighter Joe Baumgartner, have performed their duties and entertained crowds for more than a decade. By 2008, Baumgartner had appeared fourteen consecutive times as bullfighter at the National Finals Rodeo (NFR), while Rasmussen had appeared eight times. Rasmussen has won the Pro Rodeo Clown of the Year award eight times and the Coors "Man in the Can" five times.

Baumgartner has fought bulls in Pendleton since 1992. "It takes nerves of steel, and being quick on your feet," he says. "If you're scared, you won't be able to do the job." He does his homework long before he enters the arena. "I know which are the bad bulls, and I'm ready for them," Baumgartner explains. "I don't just walk in cold. It seems like every stock contractor has at least one animal in his string that I have a conflict with. But if the animal isn't bucking, it isn't doing its job."

Baumgartner's worst moments have been when a cowboy got hung up on the bull after the ride, and the bullfighter had to deflect the bull's attention from the cowboy to himself to save the rider from injury or even death. In 2007 he broke a leg at the bull riding in Pendleton while blocking a bull from running over a fallen rider. "Injuries are just part of the job," he says, "and the job is what keeps me young and the adrenalin flowing."

Slim Pickens, born as Louis Burton Lindley Jr. in 1919, was an expert rider by the age of four and a rodeo performer by the age of twelve. He was the highest-paid rodeo clown in the business in the 1950s, when he moved on to a Hollywood career. Pickens was inducted into the Pendleton Hall of Fame in 2006.

◄ Slim Pickens tries to revive a downed bronc rider with his milk-squirting skunk, 1949. *Howdyshell Collection.*

FACING PAGE ◄ Bullfighter Donnie Griggs grabs "Popcorn" the bull while trying to help bull rider Chad Eubank of Texas; bullfighter Lloyd Ketchum assists, 2007. *EO Archive.*
▲ Joe Baumgartner (left) and clown Flint Rasmussen, Pendleton favorites, in 2006. *By Ann Terry Hill.*

Flint Rasmussen is living his childhood dream. As a kid, he would stand in front of the mirror strumming a tennis racket, pretending he was in the spotlight. He worked his way through college as a rodeo clown in Montana. After teaching math and history in high school for a couple of years, he decided to make performing his career. He had seen many rodeo acts, which struck him as all the same: exploding cars, talking mules, and imploding outhouses. He vowed to be different, and his fast-paced acts have become one of the big draws in rodeo today.

Rasmussen was the barrelman and clown at Pendleton for years, retiring in 2005 after signing a contract with the PBR (Professional Bull Riders) as their exclusive barrelman. Now Pendleton rodeo fans get to watch him at the PBR Monday and Tuesday nights of Round-Up week or on television. Remembering his years in Pendleton, he said in 2008, "It's like no other rodeo. It is unique. When I arrived there it was like pulling into my own hometown. The committee members are such good friends. They made me feel like I was one of them."

Rasmussen's acts are spontaneous. He works closely with the announcer, who knows what is going to happen about 20 percent of the time. The rest is all freelance, like his advice at the 2004 Pendleton Round-Up to a Canadian bull rider who scored a seventy-two: "Don't worry, Buddy. With the exchange rate what it is, your ride was a ninety-four!"

Rasmussen applies his athletic skills to his dance routines in the arena. But when a bull and a cowboy are at center stage, he is the fast-moving man in the middle who can jump on or into the barrel in a second, a major distraction for fighting-mad bulls. He can also make a quick exit, stage left, if things get too harried.

PENDLETON.

ROUND-UP ROYALTY

BY ANN TERRY HILL

Through the decades, reigning queens and courts have attracted international attention to the Round-Up as well as helping to keep Pendleton in the spotlight nationally and regionally.

From 1910 on, Pendleton had a Round-Up queen and court. In fact, it is said that the very first rodeo queen reigned at Pendleton. Bertha Anger and her court were such successful Round-Up ambassadors that other rodeos quickly followed suit, and today, even the smallest rodeo has a queen and court. Queen Bertha, dressed more like a bride than a cowgirl, rode on a float at the 1910 celebration. She would have been amazed at the athletic horsewomen who succeeded her as rodeo royalty.

Initially the role of Round-Up queen was a recognition of daughters of local ranchers and prominent business families. It has evolved into

◄ Queen Muriel Saling, 1912. *Low Collection.*

FACING PAGE ◄ Queen Jean Frazier with the 1933 Round-Up court. *By Rice in OHS Collection, CN 005990*

[Most rodeo queens] stuck to the flashy promotional duties. Over time, both Indian and white women became symbols of the rodeo rather than actors in the arena.

—Joan Burbick, *Boston College Magazine,* Winter 2003

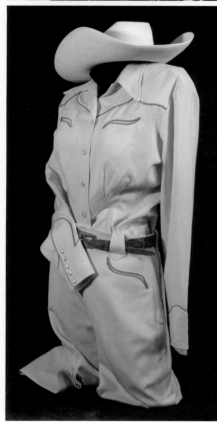

a highly sought-after assignment that comes after winning a tryout. Any young woman between the ages of eighteen and twenty-three, with a high school diploma or the equivalent, can compete. She is judged on her social skills, her looks, and her communication skills, as well as her horsemanship and ability to make the Round-Up court's famed run-in. The behind-the-scenes commitment of parents and chaperones is essential to the success of every queen and court.

Through the decades, reigning queens and courts have attracted international attention to the Round-Up as well as helping to keep Pendleton in the spotlight nationally and regionally. In the early years, several Hollywood stars served as queens, including Josie Sedgwick (an action heroine in early westerns) in 1924 and Mabel Strickland (the Walla Walla cowgirl who went on to Hollywood) in 1927. But for the most part, the women honored as royalty came from Pendleton or nearby. Several went on to win state and national titles.

▲▲ Josie Sedgwick, Hollywood actress, was Round-Up queen in 1924. *Howdyshell Collection.*

▲ Gabardine shirt and pants worn by the Round-Up courts in the 1950s. *Hall of Fame Collection.*

▶ Vicki Pearson, 1959 Round-Up queen, is crowned Miss Rodeo America at the Flamingo Hotel in Las Vegas, Nevada. At right is Abe Schiller of the Flamingo, and at left is the Flamingo's "Annie Oakley." *Courtesy of Vicki Pearson Batus.*

Round-Up queen Vicki Pearson won the title of Miss Rodeo America in 1960. Queens Julie Rugg, Marilyn Foster, Judy Lazinka, and Janice Healy, along with princesses Jan Beamer and her daughter Robin Bothum, held the title of Miss Rodeo Oregon after serving as Round-Up royalty.

Queen Gladys McDonald (1913) was the first member of the royal courts to ride a horse, starting a tradition that has persisted ever since. Outfits, entries, and faces have changed, but for every young woman who has participated, serving as rodeo royalty is a cherished experience that leaves indelible memories.

Kathryn Furnish Ramey, Round-Up princess in 1929 and in 2008 the oldest living member of a Round-Up court, had this to say:

In those days we had to furnish our own outfits. They gave us the gloves, but we had to give them back afterwards. We all wore white silk blouses, and our skirts were white corduroy with black leather trim. I had my own boots. They loaned us horses. We rode into the center of the arena, and then one by one we were introduced and galloped forward, waving. Afterwards we just went into the grandstand and sat in some empty seats.

One year I happened to sit right in front of one of the relay stations, and I will never forget Lorena Trickey doing the flying leap change [from horse to horse in a relay] and catching her pants on the saddle horn. It pulled her pants off!

The cowboy who was handling her racing string was a quick thinker. He pulled off his blue sweater, covered her up, and together, they nonchalantly walked out of the stadium. It brought the crowd to its feet. (Telephone interview with Ann Terry Hill, 2006)

For Ruth Porter Piquet, 1933 and 1934 princess, "Being on the court two years in a row was quite an honor. The Round-Up asked me to be queen; however, my dad wouldn't let me. He said it would spoil me." The courts had to furnish their own outfits, and Fox Hastings lent Ruth a red leather fringed skirt to wear. Ruth reported that it was too large, and Fox said, "Just take it down to Hamley's and have them move the snaps."

◀ The 2007 Round-Up court strike a pose in their matching Pendleton Woolen Mills dusters. *By Jim Whiting.*

▲ Queen Julie Rugg with all-around champion Chris Lybbert in 1976. *Howdyshell Collection.*

▼ Queen Tiah DeGrofft and her 2001 court in front of their horses' Round-Up stalls. *Courtesy of Liz Johnson Bronson.*

"I once got to ride Bob Crosby's famous little quarter horse," Ruth remembered. "And I knew Yakima Canutt and all those famous cowboys. Knew Montie Montana and got to have dinner on the Portland Rose—the train that came up for the Round-Up that people lived on. The court got to join the dignitaries. We didn't travel in those days—I think we did go over to Heppner."

Ruth was on queen Shirley Thompson's court in 1934, the first court to make the daring fence-jumping entry. She remembers that "in 1933, the last day of the show, we rode into the arena, and my horse got so excited, he ran as fast as he could around the track. The crowd loved it, and the directors decided to make the entry more exciting. So in 1934, we were the first court to actually jump the wooden rail fence and come to a sliding stop in front of the south grandstand." (Telephone interview with Ann Terry Hill, 2006)

As of 2006, Ruth was still riding in the Westward Ho! Parade and looking forward to participating in the 2010 centennial celebration.

Others remember that the jump was conceived by Dan Bell and Yakima Canutt in an effort to make the entry of the queen and court more spectacular. When skeptics cited safety concerns, Bell replied, "Well, they better know how to ride!"

Whatever its origin, the run-in remains one of the most thrilling moments of the Round-Up. At 1:15 each afternoon of the show, the boom of a cannon starts the entry. The national anthem is sung, then the flagbearers ride into the arena followed by the members of the court, who enter from the east and west sides at full gallop and jump the fence between the track and the infield, stopping in front of the south grandstand. Then the queen, in white buckskins, makes her entry across the arena from the north gate in

241

▲▲ **Princess Liz Johnson dashes across the arena on her horse "Trader," 2001.**

Courtesy of Liz Johnson Bronson.

▲ **Queen Andrea Beck makes her grand entrance in 1985. She was the first Round-Up queen to jump the fence with both hands in the air.** *Howdyshell Collection.*

a heart-stopping ride. At the Round-Up's seventy-fifth anniversary in 1985, queen Andrea Beck made the entrance still more memorable: she dropped the reins and jumped the fence with both hands high in the air. It was a Round-Up first, since emulated by several other queens.

The Round-Up courts travel widely, sometimes with their horses. They have represented Pendleton at festivities throughout the United States and abroad.

Esther Motanic, Round-Up queen in 1926, was the first Indian queen. Melissa Parr followed in 1932, then Virginia Wilkinson (1948), Leah Conner (1952), and Diana McKay (1953). Splendid in their traditional regalia and also skilled horsewomen, these queens emphasized the strong links among the Indians, the Pendleton community, and Round-Up tradition.

In 1955, the Happy Canyon board named Caroline Motanic the first Happy Canyon princess, and Happy Canyon has had princesses ever since, largely replacing Indian representation on the Round-Up courts. Two Happy Canyon princesses have also served on the Round-Up court: Toni Minthorn (Happy Canyon princess, 1978; Round-Up princess, 1982) and Debra Weathers Croswell (Happy Canyon princess, 1985; Round-Up princess, 1988).

During their year of reign, the Happy Canyon princesses also travel widely. They have hobnobbed with United States Presidents, civic leaders, movie stars, and popular entertainers. Raeann Crane and her cousin Jaimie Crane, 1995 Happy Canyon princesses, built lasting friendships on a trip to Japan and have entertained Japanese guests at later Round-Ups. With her mom Tessie Williams as chaperone, Nancy Parker spread the Happy Canyon word to Hong Kong and Hawaii. Nancy recalls meeting entertainer Don Ho (of "Tiny Bubbles" fame) in Honolulu as a highlight. Wherever they travel, the elegant princesses represent not only their own family and culture, but also their close ties to the Round-Up and Happy Canyon.

In many cases, the camaraderie and friendships forged on Round-Up courts last a lifetime. Former queens and princesses hold Round-Up traditions dear, as Joyce Trowbridge Hales (1947 princess) wrote in a poem she composed to honor Kelly McCormmach (1963 queen). Today the poem is read aloud each year at a luncheon to salute the current queen and court.

CLOCKWISE FROM TOP LEFT ◄◄ Queen Julie King and the 1951 court with visiting Hawaiians. *Courtesy of Julie King Kilkenny.* ▲▲ Tessie Williams (front left) with 1998 Happy Canyon princesses, Stacy McKay (left) and Lucy John, at the Saturday morning dance contest. In background at left is Nettie Queahpama Shawaway at age ninety-nine. *PWM Archive.* ▲ Happy Canyon princess Sophia Bearchum (left) and Round-Up queen Janet Horne greet Governor Mark Hatfield, 1964. *By Jim Vincent, courtesy of Sophia Bearchum Enos.* ▲ (center) Esther Motanic, 1926 Round-Up. *Howdyshell Collection.* ◄ Royal court of Haramachi, Japan, with Happy Canyon princesses Raeann Crane and Jaimie Crane, 1995. *Courtesy of Raeann Crane.* ◄◄ Nancy Parker (right), Happy Canyon princess in 1975—1976, with her mother, Tessie Williams, court chaperone, in Waikiki, Hawaii. *Courtesy of Nancy Parker Minthorn.*

QUEENS & PRINCESSES

PAST ROUND-UP ROYALTY

The crotch of our pants came to our knees,
Our shirts didn't come with snaps,
The hats we wore didn't always fit,
So we held them on with chin straps.

Nevertheless we had lots of fun,
And really thought we looked great.
We married the guys who held our horses
While awaiting our ride out the gate.

Now we're busy raising Queens and Cowboys,
Just Round-Up wives we've all become,
Our Queen and Princess days may be over,
But our Round-Ups have only just begun.

Not all of us were born in the saddle,
Some of us weren't ranch gals, true—
But when the bomb goes off each day of Round-Up,
We still jump the fence with each of you.

Joyce Trowbridge Hales lived what she wrote. Kelly McCormmach had been the flower girl at her wedding to John Hales (Round-Up president, 1949–1951). Their daughter Heather was a princess in 1973 and a queen in 1974. Heather married Doug Corey (Round-Up president in 1991 and Happy Canyon president in 2005), and their daughter Cydney was princess in 2003 and queen in 2004. Many families around the area—including the Rosenbergs, Lazinkas, Lieuallens, Boylens, Cimmiyottis, Pearsons, Coreys, Levys, Harveys, Severes, Kings, Williamses, and Kilkennys—can claim similar interconnections. Bloodlines are strong. Round-Up royalty is a sorority that runs deep with family ties and Round-Up and Happy Canyon relationships.

Darlene Tucker Turner (daughter of famed Joseph, Oregon, stock contractor Harley Tucker and princess in 1960 on Martha Boyer's court) can't decide if it was more fun to be on the court or to watch each of her three daughters become princesses. The Round-Up celebrated its fiftieth anniversary the year Darlene was princess, and the court wore gold-colored western suits instead of the customary gabardine pants and shirts.

▲▲ Luncheon gathering of former Round-Up queens, 1954. Joan Pearson is at front center; Leah Conner is to her right; and Melissa Parr at left. *Courtesy of Joan Pearson Corley.*

▲ Queen Darla Severe (left) and princess Jennifer Levy race clown Flint Rasmussen in 2003. *Courtesy of Mac Levy.*

Nancy Collins Rivenburgh, daughter of Henry Collins (Round-Up president, 1920–1932), a princess in 1950 on Kathryn Lazinka's court, remembers her summer as wonderful fun. She confesses that "Kite (Kathryn) was indeed the expert rider of the group, and I think sadly that I was the worst. But nevertheless we made it without too many disasters. I fell off (actually I think I was bucked off) my horse during the parade in Milton-Freewater, and my hat consistently blew off every day that I left the chute to race across to the grandstand."

Much to the delight of the Round-Up public, some queens entered Round-Up competitions. In 1955 the crowd stood up and gasped as queen Katherine Wyss, competing in the relay race in a regal white shirt, took a dirty spill around the west-end turn when her horse stumbled and fell on the muddy track. In true cowgirl spirit, she got up and walked away—muddy and shaken—but returned to compete the next day.

Janet Horne (princess in 1963 and queen in 1964) recalls her many "celebrity" memories. "We met Walter Brennan, Michael Landon, and lots of politicians. Sophia Bearchum, Happy Canyon princess, and I greeted Nelson Rockefeller at the airport when he was campaigning for the U.S. presidency. I remember how intrigued he was with a real Indian princess. Both Sophia and I thought that was hilarious."

In 2000 and again two years later, Round-Up courts, accompanied by the Happy Canyon princesses in 2002, traveled to Washington, D.C., where they were greeted at the White House by Presidents Bill Clinton and George W. Bush.

In 2003 queen Darla Severe and princess Jennifer Levy put on an extra show for the crowd. Both girls were high-school track stars, and they challenged athletic rodeo clown Flint Rasmussen to a footrace across the arena. Stripping down to their running shorts and track shoes, the girls pulled out all stops, and the race was neck and neck. As spectators cheered wildly, Rasmussen won by the length of his clown's nose.

Pendleton's link with western Oregon has grown ever stronger through the years. Queen Leah Conner was invited to visit Portland and attend the Ice Follies in 1952. And ever since Joan Pearson's 1954 reign, Round-Up and Happy Canyon representatives, with the courts acting as ambassadors, have made an annual trek, complete with

▲▲ 2000 Round-Up court in the Oval Office with President Bill Clinton and Senator and Mrs. Gordon Smith. *Courtesy of Brittany Smith Ware.*

▲ 2002 Round-Up and Happy Canyon courts at the White House with President George W. Bush, Senator and Mrs. Gordon Smith, Randy and Rosemary Severe, Matt Duchek, and Pat Chapman.

◄ Katherine Wyss, 1955 queen, greets Miss Oregon, Dorothy Mae Johnson, who went on to be first runner-up to Miss America. *Howdyshell Collection.*

horses, to the Portland Rose Festival and participated in the Rose Parade.

In 1956, queen Sandra Curl's court and Happy Canyon princess Caroline Motanic made a spectacular arrival in Portland for the Rose Festival, traveling by yacht from Bonneville Dam down the Columbia, then up the Willamette to disembark at the sea wall in downtown Portland. (Their horses came by land.) The girls were greeted by Rose Festival dignitaries and the mayor of Portland. The stunt, initiated by Round-Up director Dan Bell, generated national publicity for the Round-Up and Happy Canyon as well as for the Rose Festival.

For Rose Festival queens and princesses, an annual exchange visit to Pendleton is a highlight of the year. The Round-Up and Happy Canyon royalty entertain the Rose Festival court with barbecues, hoedowns, and visits with the tribes, introducing them to a way of life not generally known to city teens, and they love it.

The selection of Whitney White as 2007 queen brought one family's participation in the Round-Up full circle. Whitney is the great-granddaughter of Clarence M. Bishop, who with his brother Roy Bishop founded the Pendleton Woolen Mills and was involved with the Round-Up since its inception. Like many other Pendleton families, the Bishops have carried the tradition of participating and contributing down through decades. Whitney's mother, Rebecca Bishop, was a princess in 1974, and her aunt Melinda Bishop MacColl served on the 1970 court.

I would have to say, nothing beats being queen. I think for me, it's been a lot about the tradition—making my mark in history, continuing my family's heritage, and building on the traditions of the Pendleton Round-Up. Representing the Pendleton Round-Up was a tremendous honor, a huge personal accomplishment, and definitely the chance of a lifetime.

—Whitney White, 2005 Round-Up princess and 2007 Round-Up queen

◄ Queen Whitney White jumps the fence in 2007.
By Nicole Barker in EO Archive.

▲ Tessie Williams (center, with braids) and her family host the Round-Up court at an Indian-style feast in the village, an annual tradition, ca. 1975. *Courtesy of Nancy Parker Minthorn.*

9/11

The terrible events of 9/11, seared on the soul of every American, took place on a Tuesday before the Wednesday start of the 2001 Round-Up. Tiah DeGrofft, 2001 queen, shared her memories in a 2006 letter:

As past Royalty, I think it is imperative that we share our stories and keep the tradition of the Round-Up alive. Each year the experience of being on the court should be spectacular for all the young women serving in this position.

I present a gift to the court annually and remind them that they have much to be proud of, but they carry a lot on their shoulders . . . from memories of past court members who have made our famed run, to the little girls who dream of having the chance, and the desire of the moms who never had the opportunity.

Come September, Pendleton's heroes have always been the cowgirls. They are loved and supported with pride and admiration and placed high on a pedestal that no other community can match. The famous, heart-pounding, life-threatening run across the slippery grass infield makes the best of champions pause, turn their heads, and smile at the salute these young women give the world.

September 11, 2001, was one of the largest tragedies this country has ever seen on its own soil. The terror of 9/11 is something that no one will soon forget, but it is ingrained on my memory because it was Tuesday of Round-Up the year I was queen. I can remember sitting in my motel room trying to get ready for the day's events and watching the heartbreaking scenes from New York City on my television screen with my princesses, Liz Johnson, Rachel Faber-Luciana, Laina Mathews, and JaDee VanHouten. There was much deliberation as to whether or not the rodeo would even take place. Luckily, president Mark Rosenberg and his board of directors decided that they needed

to give people a place to come, to feel safe, and to escape the sadness all around us.

Wednesday as I sat behind the north gate waiting to do my run-in, I remember looking around me and seeing the emotion on the faces of the crowd as *The Star-Spangled Banner* was sung and the flag was presented in the breathtaking way the Round-Up salutes it. After I crossed the infield and paused at the south grandstand, I looked around at the crowd once again. I will never forget the tears falling from so many eyes as complete strangers stood, embraced each other, and cheered. I get goose bumps every time I see the grand entry, but nothing will ever give me the chills the way it did on that memorable day.

A quote from a Eugene newspaper in the front-page introduction to the 2006 souvenir program sums up our world-famous Round-Up, and both of my courts lived up to it in every word: "In good times and bad, Pendleton has gone on with the Round-Up. People over on the Umatilla have always been willing to take a chance. Maybe that's the real cowboy spirit. Maybe it's a little bit tougher brand of civic spirit. Anyhow, in Pendleton, the show goes on."

▲ Queen Tiah DeGrofft and the 2001 Round-Up court with Mabel and Mort Bishop Jr.
Courtesy of Liz Johnson Bronson.

9/11

▲▲ Ella Lazinka Ganger as Grand Marshal of the 1963 Westward Ho!
Parade. Four nieces, all former Round-Up royalty, escort her: left to
right, Kathryn Healy Thorne, Judy Currin, Jean Barbouletos, and Mary
Lou O'Rourke. *Courtesy of the Lazinka family.*

▲ Roy Bishop (at left) in Indian encampment with American Indian
beauty winner Melissa Parr, ca. 1925. *PWM Archive.*

Whether working behind the scenes at the annual event or performing on the Happy Canyon stage, they play roles that have become cherished family tradition.

Bert Kelly, Ella and Rhoda Lazinka, and Herman Rosenberg were all contestants in the first Round-Up. Kelly became the first bucking champion. Ella Lazinka took the honors in the 1910 women's relay, and Herman Rosenberg, a local rancher, competed in the wild horse race along with teammates George Fletcher and Lee Caldwell. R. W. (Robin Wesley) Fletcher was one of the originators of the Mounted Cowboy Band and the Hick Band still performing today at Happy Canyon. Lucy Lieuallen Woodward (daughter of James T. and Lucy Lieuallen) rode in the first Westward Ho! Parade. Iva Hill, sister of wheat farmer Jim Hill Sr., was a princess on the Round-Up court in 1910 and 1911. The Bishop family, particularly Roy, was instrumental in the Indians' decision to participate from the beginning. This family, owners of Pendleton Woolen Mills, has made key contributions to the Round-Up's success ever since.

Little is known about the early pioneers, but some of the facts can be reconstructed by talking to descendants, reading historical accounts and old programs, and checking records at the Hall of Fame. Bert Kelly left many descendants who have participated over the decades. His great-great nephew Leland Kelly won the bulldogging contest in 1970, and Leland's brother Dick worked as a Round-Up announcer for KUMA radio station. Bert Kelly's saddle is on display at the Hall of Fame.

The Lieuallen family has many links to the Round-Up over the years, including board members C. L. Lieuallen, Lawrence Lieuallen, Revella Lieuallen, and Sheldon Lieuallen, and Round-Up princesses Christine (1944), Marlene (1949), Bette Bell (1950), and Mary Kay (1988 princess; queen in 1990).

The Lazinka clan is one of the most enduring. Ella Lazinka and her sister Rhoda competed in the women's relay in 1910, and Ella won. This was just a start. Their father, Henry Leopold Lazinka, an immigrant from Prussia, headed a family that has contributed multiple queens, princesses, cowboy champions, Happy Canyon cast members, Hall of Fame inductees, and a Grand Marshal over the years. His progeny show no sign of fading from the picture. A descendant of the original Lazinka family almost certainly shows up somewhere on each year's roster.

In 2007, Kathryn Lazinka Thorne, the eldest child of Henry (son of Henry Leopold Lazinka) and Jennie Lazinka, shared her thoughts on a lifetime of Pendleton Round-Up. "The first Round-Up I vividly remember was in 1940, when Marion Hughes was queen. She was riding with a broken jaw, but still managed to smile and wave at the crowd. I also remember Montie Montana and his impressive trick riding that year. From that first Round-Up, it became an infectious disease. With my family's love of riding, it became something we couldn't pass up." (Interview with Ann Terry Hill, 2007)

Kathryn and all her sisters—Jean, Judy, and Mary Lou—have been queens or princesses. In 1963, their aunt Ella was Grand Marshal, and the four nieces rode in the parade as her honor guard. Ella Lazinka was inducted into the Round-Up and Happy Canyon Hall of Fame in 1987. Their dad, Henry (Ella's brother), drove the ox team in the Westward Ho! Parade for many years.

The offspring of Ella's nieces continue to play a major role in the celebration. Judy married Ron Currin. Together they had four sons and a daughter who carried on the tradition of winning Round-Up honors. Their daughter Jennifer was queen in 1991. All four of their boys won Round-Up championships. The entire Currin family was inducted into the Hall of Fame in 1996.

Two of Kathryn's daughters, Patti Jean and Janice, were also queens. Two of her granddaughters, princesses Annie Hisler (2000) and Hailey Davis (2008), have been third-generation royalty, and two of her grandsons, Brian and Blake Knowles, steer wrestle and rope.

"So how do you not be involved in Round-Up?" Kathryn asks. "It has been exciting to see the younger generations perform in the events and know that it has been going on for a hundred years. My heart is still in my throat when the bomb goes off, the American flag is shot into the air, and they play the national anthem for the introduction of queen and court at every show."

The Bishops have been part of Round-Up since its inception. Much of the Indian participation in Round-Up can be attributed to the good will and good word of this family, which has earned the trust of the Native Americans. Roy Bishop extended the first invitation to the Indians to participate, promising them a place by the river to camp,

▲▲ Rhoda (left) and Ella Lazinka, 1912. *Courtesy of the Lazinka family.*

▲ Judy Lazinka Currin and Ron (second and third from left) with their children. The entire Currin family was inducted into the Hall of Fame in 1996. *Courtesy of the Lazinka family.*

Grand March—5th Annual at Pendleton (Moorehouse)

▲ Pendleton Woolen Mills ad, ca. 1965, showing the Indian Village. Mort Bishop Jr. made it a policy to promote the Round-Up with every Pendleton ad. *PWM Archive.*

▲▶ Mounted Cowboy Band in the grand march, 1915. *By L. Moorhouse in OHS Collection, bb003678.*

▶ Jim Hill Sr. drives twelve-mule team. *Courtesy of the Hill family.*

bestowed on only one other person in recent history (Leonard King). Mark Rosenberg, Jim's son, was Round-Up president in 2001 and 2002 and made the decision to carry on with the Round-Up after the terrorist attacks on 9/11, a day before the show was to open. His brave decision was later applauded. When asked about this decision in 2008, Mark Rosenberg said: "Actually, it was a pretty easy choice to go on. About four hundred cowboys were already in Pendleton, slack [qualifying rounds] had already started, and to pull the plug then would have bankrupted the Round-Up. Emotions ran high, and many people asked, 'How could you do this with such an emergency?' But we'd already amassed about $1 million in expenses, and if we'd had to refund all those tickets, it would have been financial ruin. A lot of businesses and people outside the Round-Up were also depending upon that income. I saw no other option but to go on."

Iva Hill, a princess in 1910 and 1911, was part of another family that counted Round-Up and Happy Canyon as important traditional events. Jim Hill Sr. drove the twelve-mule team with a one-line jerk line, hauling three wagons in the Westward Ho! Parade until his death in 1955. His sons, Fred and Jim Jr., grandson Fritz, granddaughter Terry, and great-grandson Jason have all contributed over the years. Fred, a 2008 Hall of Fame inductee, was a Round-Up president and a Grand Marshal, and his daughter Terry was both a princess and a queen (1956 and 1957). With World War II double amputee Shorty Kaufman, Jim Jr.

initiated the enduring Happy Canyon role of Doc Kill-um (which involves a hasty on-stage double amputation) shortly after the war. That role was handed down to his nephew Fritz and is currently performed by Fritz's son, Jason.

Asked to reflect on the history of the Happy Canyon Old Town part shared by three generations of Hills, Fritz said in 2008: "Having this role stay in the family from the 1940s to the present isn't an obligation. It's a gift. The miracle—after sixty plus years—is that the Hills have never lost a patient, have healed many people with laughter, and have never had to have malpractice insurance."

The Fletcher family has been integral to the Round-Up and Happy Canyon since 1910. After the first Round-Up, R. W. (Robin Wesley) Fletcher came up with the idea of a horseback band. The Pendleton Mounted Cowboy Band led the Westward Ho! Parade in 1911, its first public appearance. It met its demise in 1938 but came back to life in 1985 and remains alive and well today. Fletcher later originated the Happy Canyon Hick Band, which still performs on the Happy Canyon stage.

R. W. Fletcher and his wife had seven children, all musically talented. In 1916 R. W. formed the Fletcher

It takes a special talent to make music while aboard a horse. The original Pendleton Mounted Cowboy Band, with eighteen mounted musicians, traveled throughout the Northwest promoting the Round-Up. It played in the Calgary rodeo's first show in 1912.

▲ Airplane flying over mule-drawn freighter, ca. 1948, labeled "Progress." *By Dennis, in Low Collection.*

◄ Original cowboy band, 1910. R. W. Fletcher is fourth from right in the front row; young Wesley Fletcher stands beside him. *By L. Moorhouse, courtesy of Betty Branstetter.*

▲ **Wesley Fletcher in 1911.**
By W. S. Bowman in Helm Collection.

▶ **The musical Fletcher family lined up in a row and the jazz band ready to perform.** *Courtesy of Betty Branstetter.*

◀ **R. W. Fletcher as the first Happy Canyon sheriff, a role that continues in the Fletcher family.** *Howdyshell Collection.*

FLETCHER FAMILY

Family Jazz Band, which included six of his children. The family traveled from Canada to Mexico and as far east as Denver promoting the Round-Up and Happy Canyon.

R. W. Fletcher played the sheriff in Happy Canyon for many years. On his death, R. A. (Robin Allen) "Bob" Fletcher, the son of R. W., took over the role until 1956, when his son Bill assumed the role. R. A. was a past president of the Happy Canyon board; his son Robin Allen Jr. has played many roles at the night show and also served on the Happy Canyon board. R. A.'s wife, Ruth Fletcher, did the makeup for Happy Canyon cast members for almost four decades. Robin Jr.'s children and grandchildren now make up the fourth and fifth generations of the family participating in the pageant. Robin and his daughter Becky Fletcher Waggoner agree that "being part of these two events [Round-Up and Happy Canyon] has been an important part of our family's year. It is more than a holiday. It has become a part of our family identity and our lives. The 'family reunion' aspect of getting together year after year with the same families, where the children grow up together, establishes life-long friendships." (Interview with Ann Terry Hill, 2008)

Beryl Grilley, matriarch of another influential Round-Up family, rode horseback daily when she was in her nineties. In an interview in 2006, ninety-seven-year-old Grilley reflected on how much fun it was as a kid to ride her horse to town along with another kid, Don Hawkins, and to take part in the grand entry at the Round-Up. In her teens she was a greeter for the Journal Special, the train that came from Portland each Round-Up. Later she was a Round-Up court chaperone, a 1997 Hall of Fame inductee, and Grand Marshal of the Westward Ho! Parade in 1999. Her husband Don was a Round-Up director in the '40s, and their children, Wes and Gayle, took up the passion. Wes was Happy Canyon director of show from 1970 to 1980 and Happy Canyon president in 1980 and 1981. Gayle was a Round-Up princess in 1954 and rode for years in the famed Happy Canyon quadrille (a square dance with eight mounted cowboys and cowgirls).

Brothers Mike and Bruce Boylen are both "Round-Up babies," born on September 14 two years apart. Their grandfather was a timer at the first Round-Up. One of their prized possessions is a white 1910 Round-Up button given to their dad, E. N. "Pink" Boylen. At the age of ten he sold programs, and the button allowed him to get into the show free.

Pink Boylen went on to a Round-Up career that spanned more than forty years, during which he served as director of competitive events, arena director, ticket booth

▲ ◄ **Beryl Grilley and granddaughters Mary Frances and Ginnie ride sidesaddle in the 1980 Westward Ho!** *Howdyshell Collection.*

▲ ▲ **Parley Pearce of Hamley's visits Fritz Hill in the Hill family box, south grandstand, 2007.** *By Jim Whiting.*

▲ **Left to right: E. N. "Pink" Boylen, queen Julie King, and Oregon governor Douglas McKay, 1951.** *Courtesy of Julie King Kilkenny.*

► Verne Terjeson inducts E. N. "Pink" Boylen into the Pendleton Hall of Fame, 1973. *Howdyshell Collection.*

▼ Lou Levy created the Junior Indian Beauty Pageant and has helped with the event for more than sixty years. *Courtesy of the Levy family.*

In his 1975 book *Episode of the West*, E. N. "Pink" Boylen noted that the Round-Up and Happy Canyon Hall of Fame was the "first ever started on the North American continent by an individual western show." He envisioned it as "a shrine to a great American heritage; namely, the cowboy and the Pendleton Round-Up."

director, and pennant bearer. In 1976 he was named Grand Marshal of the Westward Ho! Parade. Pink Boylen was a member of the Round-Up board of directors who founded the Hall of Fame, to which he was inducted in 1973. One of his many lasting contributions to Pendleton and the Round-Up is his book *Episode of the West: The Pendleton Round-Up, 1910–1951*, a historical review of the period published in 1975.

Pink Boylen's family followed his lead. Both his sons, Mike and Bruce, were on the Happy Canyon board and active members of the cast, including riding in the quadrille. Bruce won day money in bulldogging in 1960. They started volunteering at the rodeo when Mike was twelve, sharing duties with the Terjeson twins, Rich and Ron. About the same time they began helping with the Northwest Bucking event and ushering at Happy Canyon. Mike rode in his first parade when he was three. Pink Boylen's daughter Donne was a princess in 1944 and queen in 1945.

Mike and Bruce speak fondly of their Round-Up memories. Says Mike: "My everlasting memory is of all the help there that is volunteer. It's a real key to the success and the reason the town has supported it so much." (Interview with Ann Terry Hill, 2007)

Another family that has influenced Round-Up over the years is that of L. L. Rogers. His daughter Mildred Rogers was queen in 1925. She married Berkeley Davis, who was Round-Up president. Their son Pat was on the board of directors, and his daughter Susan was queen in 1971. Rogers' niece Joan Barnett was queen in 1949, her daughter Julie Rugg was queen in 1976, and Julie's daughter Cheyenne Williams was a princess in 2008, becoming third-generation royalty.

Since the mid-1900s and into the present millennium, one of the dominant clans in and around Pendleton has been the Corey/Levy family. Sisters Joan and Helen Hoke married George Corey and Lou Levy, respectively, and these two branches of the family have produced scores of Round-Up and Happy Canyon contributors. Fathers, daughters, sons, cousins, uncles, aunts, you name it—all have played roles as presidents, directors, queens, princesses, Happy Canyon cast members. Several important firsts are attributed to members of the family:

- Lou Levy started the Junior American Beauty Indian Pageant in 1962.
- The first Buckle Club party (named for the directors' silver buckles) was held in the grassed-in area between the George Corey and Lou Levy homes in the mid '50s.
- Doug and Heather Corey, Round-Up court chaperones in 1985 (the Round-Up's seventy-fifth anniversary year), brought back the leathers the courts had worn in early years. The same year, Round-Up directors wore red satin shirts reminiscent of the early rodeo stars.
- Steve Corey was instrumental in introducing women's barrel racing as a Round-Up event in 2000.
- Steve and Doug Corey, both past presidents of the Round-Up, played a large part in bringing sponsors to the Round-Up and making the Sponsor Building (The Roy Raley Room) on the Round-Up grounds, opened in 2006, a reality.
- Doug Corey, honored for twenty-six years of volunteer work related to animal welfare, was inducted into the PRCA Hall of Fame in 2007.

▲ ◄ Five-year-old Don Hawkins bulldogs a goat in the 1927 Happy Canyon show. *Courtesy of Helen Hawkins.*

▲ The same photo on a leather purse presented to the women of the family by Jennifer Hawkins, 2007. *By Jim Whiting.*

◄ Corey family Christmas card in 2007, the year George Corey was Grand Marshal of Westward Ho! Joan and George Corey are at center front; their sons Doug and Steve are at left front and right back, respectively. *Courtesy of Steve Corey.*

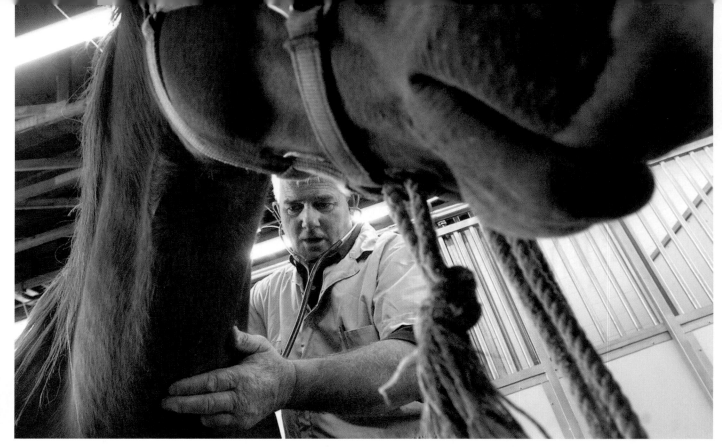

As grandchildren in the Corey/Levy clan begin to marry and have children, we can be sure that new generations will continue the family's one hundred percent commitment to Round-Up tradition.

The Hawkins family has been on the Round-Up scene from its very early years. Patriarch Don Hawkins remembers riding his horse to town to participate in the grand entry into the arena. All three Hawkins brothers, Don, Wray, and Bob, served as Happy Canyon directors, and Don went on to serve on the Round-Up board of directors.

One of Don's major contributions came after the Let 'er Buck Room—the rowdy bar under the south grandstand during Round-Up week—opened to the public in 1969. Don oversaw the operation from 1970 to 1977. Each Round-Up he still makes a pilgrimage to the bar, picking up the commemorative chip for the year (the chips were his idea in the first place) and sipping a Pendleton Whisky with friends and family. The Hawkins brothers were inducted into the Hall of Fame in 1995. Their sister, the late Mary Jane Hawkins, was a Round-Up princess in 1938.

Tim Hawkins, Don's son, is carrying the tradition of participation to a new level. He is chairman of the Pendleton Round-Up Centennial 2010 Committee, a full-time job in itself, while he continues to farm and contributes to Round-Up as a board member with regular duties. Asked to comment on the centennial year, Tim Hawkins said: "Our goals for the celebration have been both to honor our tradition and to kick off our next hundred years. This milestone has given many of us a chance to reflect on the past and look forward to the future of this world-class event. It is hard to comprehend the number of people this rodeo represents—from the boards who have directed it for the past one hundred years, to our Native American friends who help distinguish our rodeo from all others, to the countless volunteers who have made the Pendleton Round-Up greatly admired and respected in the world of rodeo."

Yet another family, owners of the *East Oregonian*, have played a major role in the success of the Pendleton Round-Up. The Aldrich, Bedford, Forrester, and Brown families, all interrelated, have been contributing since 1910. J. W "Bud" Forrester served as Round-Up director of publicity from 1952 to 1954. The Pendleton newspaper has been around longer than the Round-Up, and each year it has given vital coverage and support to the event. The *EO* (as locals fondly call it) accurately records Round-Up events, publishing statistics that become part of the historical record. It also reports on Round-Up-related activities and serves as a major source and voice for the celebration. Every year since

1973, the newspaper has presented the Let 'er Buck Trophy to the all-around winner. To permanently win the prize, the cowboy must win it three times. Mike Beers retired the first East Oregonian Trophy in 1997. Cash Myers retired the second in 2008. The 2009 winner will have a leg on a new trophy designed by Pendleton artist Michael Booth.

Many other families have left indelible footprints on the Round-Up and Happy Canyon in its first century. Among these are the James Sturgis family, the John and Mike Kilkenny clan, the Lester and Howard J. "Tom" King families, Sam Cook and son Don Cook, Dr. Richard Koch and family, the Ruff Raymond and son Royal Raymond families, Finis Kirkpatrick, the Irvin Mann Sr. and Irvin Mann Jr. families, the Robert Hopper and son Michael Hopper families, and the Hodgen clan. These are just a few of the families that make up the backbone of the Round-Up and Happy Canyon. The commitment of each of these families is a part of their heritage. The rodeo and pageant they have sustained through love and tradition can never be replicated by newer, more commercial ventures.

▲▲ *East Oregonian* offices, Pendleton, 1887. *OHS Collection, OrHi 23379.*

▲ Edwin B. Aldrich, editor then owner of the *East Oregonian* between 1908 and 1950. *Courtesy of Steve Forrester.*

◄ Judging the Junior Indian Beauty Contest in 1968: left to right, Jim Hill, Mrs. Glenn Jackson, Si Zentner, and J. W. "Bud" Forrester. *Howdyshell Collection.*

FROM GENERATION TO GENERATION: TRIBAL PARTICIPATION

BY ROBERTA CONNER

The Happy Canyon Pageant could not exist without the full involvement of Umatilla tribal members, who pass roles down through generations.

From the earliest Happy Canyon cast to the present year's show, tribal participants are proud to present their ancient lifeways, songs, dances, and history—this is not an act. Most of today's Happy Canyon Indian performers are third- and fourth-generation participants who have inherited their roles from the earliest Indian cast. A 1925 participant roster listed eighty names of Indian participants, and many surnames listed match today's names.

Johnson Chapman's role was Indian leader. Indian women on the roof were Mrs. Jim Crawford, Sophie Sampson, Agnes McKay, Matilda Chapman,

◄ Allen Patawa, tribal headman, ca. 1938.
Howdyshell Collection.

FACING PAGE ◄
Lucien Williams and Delia Lowry, n.d.
Howdyshell Collection.

Elizabeth Chapman, and Susie Koplots. Walt Davis, Abe Shawaway, George Spino, Thomas Standing, and Tom Mox Mox were "braves" on the roof. Mrs. Felix Paul and Susie Williams were in the main arena. Melissa Abraham, Mrs. Shawaway, Teewax, and Mollie Minthorn led the "vanishing race," and Mary Red Elk was the maiden in the canoe. Hiato was the medicine man, and drummers included John Abraham and Fred Dickson. Arthur Motanic, Philip Bill, Aaron Minthorn, and Joseph Thompson were hunters and rode around the emigrant wagon joined by Dan White, Willie Williams, Lucien Williams, Isadore Whitebull, and Louis Van Pelt. The "main body" included Mr. and Mrs. Poker Jim, Captain Sumkin, and forty more cast members with last names Minthorn, Sampson, Lloyd, Patawa, Conner, Van Pelt, Red Elk, Mox Mox, Red Hawk, Whirlwind, Black Hawk, Wild Bill, Halfmoon, Parr, Martin, Red Crow, Wak Wak, Shillal, Allen, Lincoln, Washington, Crawford, Bay, Wannassay, and Shay.

Here are just a few profiles from the dozens of tribal families who have played pivotal roles in the Happy Canyon show for four generations.

ANNA MINTHORN WANNASSAY

After the Happy Canyon Pageant was a few years old, Roy Raley asked Cayuse tribal member Anna E. Minthorn Wannassay to help him add to the frontier show the story of the first people of this landscape—the Columbia River Plateau people now known as the Cayuse, Umatilla, and Walla Walla Tribes. At that time, the tribal story was not portrayed anywhere else. For many in the audience, this pageant and the Indian roles in the Round-Up were undoubtedly their only education about these tribes.

The script changes incorporated tribal village life before contact with white men leading up to encounters with pioneers. At the time, hundreds of Indians, primarily from the Confederated Tribes of Umatilla, camped for the Round-Up each year. From this legion of tribal people, roles were matched up with persons willing to portray them.

Three of Anna's grandnieces have served as Happy Canyon princesses: Anna Minthorn, Michelle Spencer, and Talia Minthorn. Currently, granddaughter Mitzi Rodriguez leads the welcome dance in the village scene.

ROYALTY FROM CHOWISIIPUM: THE BEARCHUM FAMILY

Fourteen Happy Canyon princesses trace their ancestry back to one Wallulapam woman—Chowisiipum. Her three daughters, Rosaline Tashwick, Sophie Charley, and Angeline Mox Mox, camped with their families at Round-Up. Rosaline was a Round-Up princess in 1932. She was in the Happy Canyon show when all the Indians came in dressed in their finest regalia on horses also decorated in fine trappings. The riders would all dismount and dance in the main arena.

Granddaughter Cecelia Charley Bearchum remembers first seeing Happy Canyon when her father, Thomas Charley, was in the cast at the old show site in downtown Pendleton. Cecelia began as a tribal visitor coming in from the east, then she moved to the village scene as the woman scraping the hide. Her son Curtis has been a dancer in the show and now is a fisherman. All four of her daughters have served as Happy Canyon princesses. Cecelia remembers when the selection of the girls was handled by the tribes at the Longhouse. She also recalls that when her eldest daughter, Brenda, was a princess, she insisted that the princesses be chaperoned when they traveled to ensure they were respected and well cared for. Later, her daughter Sophia would serve as chaperone.

The fourteen princesses descended from Chowisiipum are Brenda, Frances, Sophia, and Eleanor Bearchum; Joyce and Sharon Hoptowit; Marilyn and Ashleigh Wolf; Claudette and Vanessa Enos; Naomi Bearchum; Lucy John; Stacy McKay; and Bridget Kalama.

▲ Sophia Bearchum, Happy Canyon princess in 1964. *Howdyshell Collection.*

▲▶ Left to right: Elaine, James, and John Hoptowit, 1964. *Howdyshell Collection.*

▶ Ashleigh Wolf, center front, 1999 Indian Beauty Contest winner. *Howdyshell Collection.*

DESCENDANTS OF POKER JIM

The descendants of Poker Jim can be found throughout the Happy Canyon Pageant. His sons Clarence, Richard, and Robert all played parts in Happy Canyon and Round-Up history. Clarence succeeded his father as a Round-Up chief, and his brothers Richard and Robert rode, competed, danced, and trick-roped in their earlier years. Poker Jim's grandchildren Ellen Cowapoo, William Burke, Raymond "Popcorn" Burke, Ernestine Crawford, Videll Bronson, and Richard Jr. "Summer" Burke all camped, paraded, and participated in Happy Canyon roles as well as Round-Up.

Poker Jim's great-grandchildren have all taken part in Happy Canyon, on foot and on horseback, as dancers, scouts, warriors, raiders, pulling travois, in the wedding party, and in the village scene. Today, the Burkes, Crawfords, Bronsons, and Cowapoos all have fifth- and sixth-generation family members taking on roles handed down through the years.

Seven of Poker Jim's great-granddaughters have been Happy Canyon princesses: Alvina Burke Huesties, Judy Burke Farrow, Althea Huesties Wolf, Esther Huesties, Lawanda Bronson, Ronna Cowapoo, and Monika McGuire. Another descendant, Kylie Bronson, was a Round-Up court princess.

CLOCKWISE FROM TOP LEFT

▲ Clarence Burke, at left, with father, Poker Jim, in 1930. *Howdyshell Collection.*

▲▶ Melinda Bishop presents prize blanket to Indian Beauty Contest winner Laverne Burke, 1975. *PWM Archive.*

▶ Round-Up chief Clarence Burke with winners of the 1973 Junior Indian Beauty Contest. From left, Allison White, Lawanda Bronson, and Babette Cowapoo. The two at right are members of the Burke family. *Howdyshell Collection.*

POKER JIM &

LEFT HALF CLOCKWISE FROM TOP ▲ Left to right: Round-Up chiefs Clarence Burke, William Oregon Jones, Gus Conoyer, and Tom Joe. ▲ Richard Burke. ◄ Raymond "Popcorn" Burke with winner of the Junior Indian Beauty Contest. ◄◄ Richard Burke with young dancers. *Howdyshell Collection.*

RIGHT HALF ▲▲▲ Robert Burke. ▲▲ Left to right: Happy Canyon princesses Alvina Burke (1963) and Judy Burke (1966). ▲ Left to right: Ronna Cowapoo (1973) and Monika McGuire (1994). *Howdyshell Collection.*

THE BURKE FAMILY

▲ Pendleton Whisky bottle, 2008.

Courtesy of Hood River Distillers.

▼ Sign posted in the Let 'er Buck Room

in 2007. *By Jim Whiting.*

string seen in Pendleton include "Wild Card," "Surprise Party," and "Broadway"—the bareback horse on which the most money ever has been won.

The roping calves Sankey supplies are all fresh, meaning they've never been roped. In the fall of the year, it's not easy to come up with 130 to 150 never-roped calves, but Darrell Sewell provides the stock from his ranch in Idaho. Sewell also provides the steer roping stock, which he brings in from Mexico.

Brent Palmer of Milton Freewater, Oregon, furnishes the team roping stock and bulldogging steers. Cows for the wild cow milking contest come from Larry Hoeft of Bar 41 Ranch, Pilot Rock, Oregon.

Famous broncs of the past have included Christensen Brothers' "War Paint" and "Miss Klamath." Harry Knight provided "Joker," "Midnight," and "Five Minutes to Midnight," while Joe Kelsey thrilled the crowds with his broncs "Snake," "Devil's Dream," and "Badger Mountain." Over the years, contractors such as Harley Tucker of Joseph, Oregon; Harry Vold of Colorado; and John Growner of Red Bluff, California, have added to the excitement with their champion strings, making the cry of "Let 'er Buck" as meaningful today as it was when "Long Tom" was the horse to master in the early 1900s.

LET 'ER BUCK ROOM

Almost as famous as the Round-Up itself, the Let 'er Buck Room has enjoyed a reputation for rowdiness since the day it opened its bar beneath the south grandstand in 1958. Originally a private club primarily for directors and their guests, it opened to the public in 1969, and the legends and lines to get in have grown each year. It is said that some people come to Pendleton to attend the rodeo, and some come just to take part in the Let 'er Buck Room action. The busy bar is open only during Round-Up week. The stories it has spawned are colorful and not exaggerated. Cowboys, Buckle Bunnies (women who chase cowboys), and ordinary people looking for a taste of the Old West rub shoulders here, and the meeting is electric. Everyone is out to have a good time, although a few old-fashioned brawls have broken out. The atmosphere is like spontaneous combustion, and the crowd is so loud that you couldn't hear a gunshot.

Not too much has changed since the beginning. Western trappings decorate the walls, and the long, unpretentious bar has lines ten deep of people waiting to get a drink. Visitors must buy chips to pay for their drinks. (In the '70s, six chips cost $5.00 and bought six drinks; in 2007, one $4.00 chip bought one bar drink, and a shot of Pendleton Whisky—spelled the Canadian way—cost $6.00.) Patrons have their choice of whisky, scotch, gin, vodka, or rum with or without a mixer, but no exotic drinks are poured. The room was expanded in 2007, taking over space formerly occupied by the Hall of Fame. The crowds expanded with it, though at least for the first year, the long lines of partiers waiting to get in were eliminated.

The story is told that one year, a Let 'er Buck patron drank so much that he was dead drunk on his feet, but he didn't fall over until the bar closed and the crowd that had held him up emptied out. Women were known to shed their bras and toss them over the long-horn steer horns hanging over the entrance to the ladies room. "The crazy stuff doesn't happen so much anymore," says Billy Morrison, Round-Up director in charge of the room in 2008. "OLCC [Oregon Liquor Control Commission] regulations have tightened since the early '80s, and Let 'er Buck Room employees now monitor the crowds. Those who have had too much to drink are quickly escorted out. Also, the Fire Marshal has put limits on the crowd, making control much easier."

"All the same," Morrison says, "there are stories there you just can't tell. People come in and think they are in the Wild West. Some people buy a ticket for the show, get in the Let 'er Buck Room, and never come out."

For years, young ladies in the Let 'er Buck Room known as "Buckle Bunnies" would bare all from the waist up then don a T-shirt proclaiming the deed. Steer horns above the entrance to the ladies' room were hung with discarded bras. Authorities banned the practice in 2002.

HALL OF FAME

Everybody needs to celebrate "old memories and heritage. That's what the Hall of Fame is for," said former Hall of Fame president Stan Timmermann, interviewed in 2008.

The Hall of Fame is a dream sparked by far-sighted community leaders Lester King and Verne Terjeson, among many others. The original Hall of Fame opened in 1969 in the Round-Up Pavilion on the Round-Up grounds. Later it moved to a room under the south grandstand, where it became a gathering spot for old-timers in town for the show. In 2006 it moved into its permanent building across the street from the Round-Up stadium.

Fund-raising for the new building was a giant community effort. Grants, yard sales, and Bucking Horse Christmas wreath sales helped in reaching the goal. Volunteer hours amassed were uncountable.

In September 2007, Dr. Nels Nelson, publicity director for the Hall of Fame, told the *East Oregonian* that "moving into the new quarters has allowed the organization to display larger memorabilia and allows visitors to wander freely with plenty of room among the displays." Spacious wall displays and floor exhibits give the public insight into what the Round-Up and Happy Canyon have been about since 1910.

Matt Duchek, president of the Hall of Fame in 2008, commented that "there is no way to experience [Round-Up and Happy Canyon] unless you are here that week, and the Hall of Fame provides a glimpse of the excitement, the pageantry, the fun that goes on."

Duchek said that "the mission of the Hall of Fame is to promote and preserve the history of Round-Up and Happy Canyon. We are international, and we want the people visiting from as far away as Japan, Italy, and Venezuela to understand. We have wagons, saddles, guns, props from Happy Canyon, pictures, and a wealth of other things we can change around. We also have queens' outfits, hats, and a buggy and a sheepherder's wagon. One of the star attractions is the 'stuffed' icon bucking horse 'War Paint.' " Visitors are astounded by the sheer size of the animal.

Each year two or three outstanding Round-Up and Happy Canyon supporters are inducted into the Hall of Fame. The inductee can be a cowboy, cowgirl, or Indian, a community member, an exceptional volunteer, a family—

anyone who has made a major contribution to the Pendleton event. Even outstanding animals are given an honored place in the Hall of Fame (see page 294).

The Hall of Fame depends on volunteers to look after its displays and collections and to keep its doors open to the public. Jack Sweek has been a pillar since the beginning. A former roper and the son of Calvin Sweek, who served as vice-president of Round-Up in 1933, Jack knows and savors all phases of the rodeo experience. His input has been invaluable. Betty Branstetter, until her retirement in 2007, was key to everyone's research project because she could find whatever was needed. "Just ask Betty" was the most common answer to any question. Pat Terjeson, Betty Holeman, and Helen Hawkins hung most of the Hall of Fame plaques, which commemorate inductees through the years. Bob Chambers and his wife Vicky spent two months working to get the new Hall of Fame ready to open. Chambers enlisted the help of his dad, Bob Sr., to go through thousands of photos to provide the background for displays.

It seems that everyone in the community owns a piece of the Hall of Fame. You will find their names inscribed on bricks that were sold to help finance the project. About three thousand visitors come through the doors annually, and they are always welcomed with pride and Let 'er Buck spirit. A gift shop adjacent to the museum offers clothing, accessories, books, and other mementos that keep Round-Up memories alive.

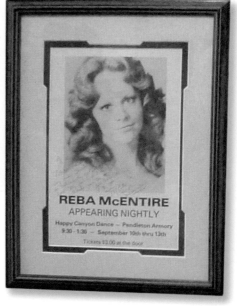

▲ Inscribed Reba McEntire posters from 1980 and (at left) from 2000 in the Hall of Fame Collection, 2007. *By Jim Whiting.*

In 1980 Reba wrote: "Never have I been treated any nicer. Thanks for making an old country girl feel right at home." In 2000 she inscribed her photo: "To Happy Canyon: Thanks for everything! Especially for believing in me many years ago."

HISTORY ON EXHIBIT

By Michael Bales

Interviewed in 2008, Betty Branstetter, a former Hall of Fame board member, described some of the Hall of Fame's artifacts from decades ago as if the events happened yesterday.

A saddle display includes those won by cowboy Bert Kelly in the first Round-Up bucking-bronc championship in 1910, Casey Tibbs in the same event in 1959, and cowgirl Mabel Strickland in the 1923 cowgirl relay race. The saddle and other gear of Umatilla County sheriff Tillman D. Taylor are also on display. Taylor was Round-Up president from 1911 until 1920, when he was killed trying to stop a jailbreak.

Photographs line the walls, including those of Hall of Fame members, Round-Up queens, and Indian princesses. Among the exhibits is a rope Montie Montana used in his dazzling trick displays, along with his hat and boots. Montana, a frequent performer in the 1930s and 1940s, took part in Round-Ups and Happy Canyon Pageants at various times from 1927 to 1997.

A mannequin is dressed in the leather outfit that 1929 queen Kathleen McClintock wore: white top with black piping and white fringe, and white divided skirt with black fringe.

An Indian teepee looms large. More striking still is "War Paint," the only animal member of the Round-Up Hall of Fame preserved and displayed at the museum. A taxidermist posed him in a bucking position, fitting considering that the ornery paint horse threw ninety percent of his riders in a career that spanned more than twenty years. Considered among the toughest buckers in rodeo history, "War Paint" was put to sleep in 1975 at the age of forty.

Branstetter said that before the museum moved into its new building, "War Paint" was spiffed up. Among other things, his eyes were restored and insect holes, which children thought were marks from cowboys' spurs, were patched.

◄ Memorabilia left and above: Drum of the Pendleton Drum and Bugle Corps, silk souvenir scarves, seventy-fifth anniversary commemorative coins, commemorative buttons, and Round-Up souvenir programs. *Hall of Fame Collection.*

▲ Above: "War Paint" throws Shirley Bothum in 1963. *Howdyshell Collection.*

◄ Woolly chaps. *Hall of Fame Collection.*

HISTORY ON EXHIBIT

VOLUNTEERS

Since the inception of the Round-Up, volunteerism has made it happen. Scores of people in the community give hundreds of hours without any thought of pay. Call it civic pride, call it Round-Up fever. It's the glue that cements this event into an annual happening and brings a widespread community together. Volunteers work for the individual directors of Round-Up, Happy Canyon, and Hall of Fame, who are also volunteers. (Round-Up has seventeen directors, Happy Canyon has twelve, and the Hall of Fame has fourteen.) Each year it takes close to a thousand volunteers to get the job done. That's about double the number of contestants in the arena.

Jack Shaw explained the importance of volunteers to the *East Oregonian* in 2007: "Once you've been on the board and seen the three, four, or hundred and fifty that work for you, it's pretty simple. You need them. All the volunteers. Hell, that's what makes it work." Shaw, sixty-four in 2007, has been volunteering since his years in junior high school.

"Volunteers are the unsung heroes of Round-Up," said George Corey, age ninety-two in 2008 and a Round-Up

▲ Happy Canyon director's buckle, a lifetime pass to Round-Up and Happy Canyon.
Courtesy of Wesley Grilley.

◄ Photographers Ralph Vincent (left) of the *Oregon Journal* and Bus Howdyshell of Pendleton, 1944. *Howdyshell Collection.* Howdyshell's metal lifetime pass to Round-Up and Happy Canyon and his baffle camera, a Speed Graphic manufactured by Graflex Inc. *Hall of Fame Collection.*

▼ R. W. Fletcher puts up posters for the 1939 Round-Up. *Courtesy of Betty Branstetter.*

▲ When the directors call a workday, dozens of volunteers show up. *Howdyshell Collection.*

▶ Lou Levy (at right) gives prizes to Junior Indian Beauty Pageant winner Lawanda Bronson in 1973. Chief Clarence Burke is at left. *Howdyshell Collection.*

▲ Director's buckle—a lifetime pass to the Round-Up and Happy Canyon—that belonged to Donald Grilley in the 1940s. *Courtesy of Wesley Grilley.*

it." Over the years, both Corey's sons, Doug and Steve, have taken countless hours off from their jobs to attend to Round-Up duties as volunteers.

In 2008, Lou Levy, patriarch of the Levy family, had been volunteering for sixty-two years. To his credit goes the creation of the Junior Indian Pageant sixty-two years ago. The pageant, held in Roy Raley Park, features Indian girls twelve and under. "I felt the public should have a chance to see the young Indian girls with their beautiful outfits," Levy told the *East Oregonian* in 2006. He still actively participates in the Round-Up, along with his family of six children and his grandchildren, all of whom have been queens, princesses, workers, volunteers, and gracious ambassadors.

With pride, volunteers like the Swearingen brothers, Mervin and Wayne, count a collective ninety-seven years of service in 2008 and have no thought of retiring. Many volunteers start out when they are kids, age twelve or thirteen, working the livestock or as pennant bearers for the Round-Up queen and court and the board of directors. Happy Canyon starts them even younger in the street scenes, the immigrant scenes, and the "coming out of the trunk" scene. Reese Furstenberg, daughter of former queen Megan Corey Furstenberg and her husband Tyson, holds the honor of being the youngest volunteer yet, coming out of the trunk in 2007 when she was only six weeks old.

The volunteers come from across the country. Colby Marshall (from Alexandria, Virginia) and Dick Beach (from Boeme, Texas) have made the pilgrimage to Pendleton for many years. Former queen Tiah DeGrofft flies in annually from Rhode Island to offer her services. In some cases, the volunteers are involved for months. Community leaders and business executives are generous in allowing their employees time off during Round-Up.

Don Hawkins, a volunteer since he was a kid at both Round-Up and Happy Canyon (eighty-six years old in 2008) summed it up: "They couldn't put on a show without the volunteer help."

COWBOY BREAKFAST

The coffee goes on at 4:30 a.m., and the cooks are busy adding ingredients to the dry mix for the buttermilk pancake batter. By 6 a.m., the grill is hot and the volunteers of the

director twice in the 1960s. "A lot of people aren't on boards but put in hours of labor without getting much, if any, credit. They do it for the love of the event and to be part of

VFW are ready to start feeding the hordes of hungry Round-Up visitors lining up in Stillman Park for a generous serving of ham, eggs, pancakes, and coffee at a minimal price ($6.00 for adults and $4.00 for children in 2008). The Veterans of Foreign Wars, Post 922, and the Women's Auxiliary have put on this breakfast annually since 1949. It is their chief fundraiser, with proceeds going to causes such as youth programs, scholarships, and the Veterans Affairs Hospital in Walla Walla, Washington. Fred Bradbury, one of the chief volunteers, estimates they feed four thousand people during the four days of Round-Up. "We go through 12,000 eggs and 1,200 pounds of ham each year," he said in 2008.

MAIN STREET COWBOYS

Since 1951, when city leader Morris Temple founded the Main Street Cowboys, the group has had a strong presence in Pendleton at Round-Up and other events throughout the year. Temple gathered together city businessmen who wanted Main Street to be represented during Round-Up. The purple and chartreuse shirts they wear along with their cowboy hats, a uniform easily spotted by visitors, are their trademark.

In 2008, the Main Street Cowboys had a membership of about sixty merchants. During Round-Up week, they put in

an average of eighty to a hundred volunteer hours per man and keep the downtown humming with "The Greatest Free Show on Earth."

Main Street is closed off and devoted to block after block of entertainment, food booths, concessions, and a carnival at the south end. The Cowboys rent chartreuse and purple benches to merchants and to the public to use for advertisements or announcements. Each year about 360 benches are placed strategically around town. Revenue from the rent of the benches supplies a major part of the group's funding for the year.

One of the major events sponsored by the Main Street Cowboys is the annual Dress-Up Parade, a family-oriented activity held the Saturday prior to the rodeo. By the early 2000s, this parade had about 155 entries, including merchants, bands, rodeo courts, and riding clubs. Originally the Dress-Up Parade was held on Saturday night; but it sometimes got rowdy, so the Cowboys moved it to Saturday morning with good results. The parade is pure fun and leaves everyone in a Round-Up mood.

◄ A volunteer makes pancakes at the 2007 VFW Cowboy Breakfast. By Jim Whiting.

▼ Listening to a band on Main Street. Howdyshell Collection.

▼▼ The Main Street Cowboys' float in the 2007 Dress-Up Parade. By Jim Whiting.

APPENDICES

ROUND-UP PRESIDENTS
BY ANN TERRY HILL

Dozens of community leaders have held the volunteer position of Round-Up president. Butch Thurman, president in 2007 and 2008, considers being "the face of the Round-Up" a great thrill and a bigger responsibility. "It definitely takes three or four hours a day during the year, and a lot more than that during the actual week," Thurman said in 2008. "My job is to keep all the balls in the air, to show guidance if needed. The main job is to run the meetings and represent the Round-Up during my term. There are about twenty-five sub-committees, and the president appoints those committees and must make sure they are all moving forward."

The Round-Up organization is steeped in tradition and heritage. Thurman noted that seven current board members had fathers who were on the board before them: Butch himself is the son of Roy Thurman; Troy LeGore is the son of Jerry LeGore; Kevin Hudson the son of Ron Hudson; Tim Hawkins the son of Don Hawkins; Mike Thorne the son of Glenn Thorne; Larry Williams the son of John Williams; and Billy Morrison the son of Bill Morrison. "Seven of us are at the table where our fathers sat before us," Thurman said with a smile.

Like many former Round-Up presidents, Thurman owns horses, but he is not a cowboy. Riding well in the entry became a personal goal. Says Butch: "When the cannon goes off, your chest tightens up and you know you have to gallop around the arena behind the court—those girls can ride with their hair on fire. I didn't want to get left in the dust."

1910–1911
J. Roy Raley

1912–1919
Til B. Taylor

1920–1932
Henry W. Collins

May–June 1933
L. G. Frazier (interim)

1933–1938
Dr. W. D. McNary

1939–1940
William Switzler

1941–1944
Sam R. Thompson

1945–1948
Fay S. LeGrow

1949–1951
John Hales

1952–1953
Berkeley A. Davis

1954–1956
Finis Kirkpatrick

1957–1958
Jack Stangier

1959–1960
John Bauer

1961–1962
Fred Hill

1963–1964
Verne Terjeson

1965–1966
Ford Robertson

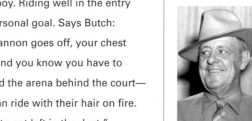

1967–1968
Leonard King

1969–1970
John Mulligan

1971–1972

Bob Hales

1984

Jerry Schubert

1993–1994

Paul Rice Jr.

2004–2005

Tom Weeks

1973–1974

Frank Tubbs

1985–1986

Don Cook

1995–1996

Mark Perkins

2006

Marv Anderson

1975–1976

Glenn Thorne

1987–1988

Larry Rew

1997–1998

Mike Hopper

2007–2008

Butch Thurman

1977–1978

John S. Fisk

1989–1990

Ron Hudson

1999–2000

Garry Zollman

1979–1980

Royal Raymond

1991

Doug Corey

2001–2002

Mark Rosenberg

1981–1983

Jim Rosenberg

1992

Bob Burns

2003

Steve Corey

ROUND-UP CHIEFS AND PROMINENT TRIBAL HEADMEN

1910–1943

Gilbert Minthorn, Cayuse, Indian organizer at 1910 Round-Up; participated until his death

1911–1936

Poker Jim, Walla Walla, Round-Up chief until his death

1911–1926

Cayuse chief **Cap Sumkin,** led Westward Ho! Parade every year

1911–1950s

Tribal headmen participating in Round-Up:

Jim Badroads, Cayuse; Amos Pond, Umatilla; Jim Kanine, Walla Walla; Allen Patawa, Cayuse; **Paul Showaway,** Umatilla; George Red Hawk, Cayuse; Sam Morris, Nez Perce; Johnson Chapman, Cayuse; Uma Sumkin, Cayuse; John Abraham, Walla

Clarence Burke, George Spino, Willie Wocatsie

Walla; Fred Dixon, Cayuse; Leo Sampson, Walla Walla; Tom and Phillip Shillal, Umatilla; Charlie Whirlwind, Cayuse; **George Spino,** Umatilla; Tom Johnson, Cayuse; Harry Dick, Cayuse; Mitchell Lloyd, Umatilla; Henry White, Umatilla; Anthony Red Hawk, Cayuse; Andrew Barnhart, Umatilla; John Moses, Nez Perce; Tom Joe, Umatilla

1936–1987

Clarence Burke, Walla Walla, became Round-Up co-chief, succeeding his father Poker Jim

1936–1950

Willie Wocatsie, Walla Walla, became Round-Up co-chief with Clarence Burke

1952–1954

Luke Cowapoo succeeded Willie Wocatsie as co-chief

1954–1958

William Oregon Jones succeeded Luke Cowapoo as Round-Up co-chief

1958–1965

Jesse Jones Sr. succeeded William O. Jones as Round-Up co-chief

1978–1984

William Minthorn a.k.a. Cayuse chief Blackhawk joined Clarence Burke as co-chief

1983–2006

Raymond Burke named a Round-Up co-chief

Left to right: Raymond Burke, William Burke, Jesse Jones Jr., and Marvin Burke, 1988

1988–

William Burke and Jesse Jones Jr. named Round-Up co-chiefs

1990–

Carl Sampson named chief of the Walla Walla

2007–

Gary Burke, son of Raymond, assumed his father's role as Round-Up co-chief

1910

Bertha Anger

Genevieve Clark

Iva Hill

Edna Thompson

Edna Wissler

1911

Laura McKee

Norma Alway

Irma Baer

Iva Hill

Muriel Saling

1912 & 1916

Muriel Saling

1913

Gladys McDonald

1914 & 1917

Lula Matlock

1915

Doris Reber

1918, 1919, & 1920

No queens

1921

Helen Thompson

Daphne Gibbs

Elsie Fitzmaurice

Kathryn Thompson

Thelma Thompson

1922

Thelma Thompson

Jessie Drumheller

Adeline Scroggins

Jean Skeen

Helen Thompson

1923

Jessie Drumheller

Elizabeth Hailey

Thelma Thompson

1924

Josie Sedgwick

1925

Mildred Rogers

Doris Churchill

Mary Clark

Agnes McMurray

Katherine McNary

1926

Esther Motanic

Louise Martin

Minnie Patawa

1927

Mabel Strickland

Mary Bond

Elizabeth Crommelin

Jean Frazier

Janet LaFountaine

1928

Mary Duncan

Dorothy Barthell

Kathleen McClintock

Lois McIntyre

Roberta Morrison

1929

Kathleen McClintock

Kathryn Furnish

Dena Lieuallen

Allegra McCormmach

Adelyn McIntyre

1930

Lois McIntyre

Evelyn Cresswell

Mildred Hansell

Virginia Sturgis

Annabel Tullock

1931

Betty Bond

Barbara Castleman

Jean Cronin

Jessie Thompson

Shirley Thompson

1932

Melissa Parr

Rose Badroads

Rosaline Kanine

Carrie Sampson

Margaret Sheoships

1933

Jean Frazier

Cathryn Collins

Dorothy Doherty

Anne Kistner

Ruth Porter

Sally Seigrist

1934

Shirley Thompson

Hazel Barton

Margaret Brosnan

Ruth Porter

Mary Robison

Betty Tubbs

1935

Helen Hansell

Helma Karstens

Maxine Conley

June Lemons

Velma Powell

June Thompson

1936

Mary Robison

Jeanette Potter

Edna Rice

Beverly Simpson

Patricia Ward

Eva Wilcox

1937

Cathryn Collins

Irene Bannister

Betty Jane Holt

Marion Hughes

Barbara Kirkpatrick

Helen Shafer

Alta Bell Troxel

1938

Jean McCarty

Lila Ellen Boone

Josephine Brock

Mary Jane Hawkins

Ann Little

Betty Jean Tippett

Betty West

1939

Barbara Kirkpatrick

Jane Boyer

Patty Cowan

Lavern Herndon

Maxine McCurdy

Jean Richards

Peg Thompson

1940

Marion Hughes

Shirley Brady

Adarene Fisk

Wanda Piper

Betty Troxel

1941

Maxine McCurdy

Mary Hassell

June Kirkpatrick

Helen Proebstel

Anne Thompson

1942 & 1943

(no Round-Ups)

1944

Janet Thompson

Donne Boylen

Marilyn Glenn

Christine Lieuallen

Pat Mann

Jerry McIntyre

Susan Sturgis

1945

Donne Boylen

Beverly Barrett

Mary Esther Brock

Gloria Gibbs

Barbara Tippett

1946

Jackie Hales

Patti Folsom

Pauline Lieuallen

Suzanne Lieuallen

Marge McKenzie

1947

Patti Folsom

Marion Andrews

Charlotte Montag

Joyce Trowbridge

Janet Young

1948

Virginia Wilkinson

Veva Bill

Laura McKay

Thelma Parr

Edna Quaempts

Gladys Sheoships

Myrna Williams

1949

Joan Barnett

Kathryn Lazinka

Marlene Lieuallen

Barbara Owens

Barbara Raymond

1950

Kathryn Lazinka

Nancy Collins

Francine Hisler

Bette Belle Lieuallen

Shirley Warner

1951

Julie King

Creagh Brennan

Kathleen Folsom

Thelma Harvey

Jean Lazinka

1952

Leah Conner

Audrey Blackhawk

Diana McKay

Martina Quaempts

Bernice Ryan

1953

Diana McKay

Linnea Sampson

Loretta Quaempts

Doris Scott

Yvonne Scott

1954

Joan Pearson

Judy Greve

Gayle Grilley

Ann Kirkpatrick

Katherine Wyss

1955

Katherine Wyss

Sharon Bryant

Sandra Curl

Lili Mae Mascal

Deanna Whitely

1956

Sandra Curl

Tammy Dix

Claudette Edwards

Terry Hill

Judy Thompson

1957

Terry Hill

Gayle Austin

Judy Fisher

Susan King

Linda Pearson

1958

Judy Lazinka

Loretta Anderson

Jan Beamer

Marcia Bull

Kay Smutz

1959

Vicki Pearson

Martha Boyer

Linda Ferris

Silva Harvey

Ruth Tibbets

1960

Martha Boyer

Diane Bartsch

Mary Lou Lazinka

Darlene Tucker

Nancy Smith

1961

Mary Lou Lazinka

Marilyn Foster

Carla Meyers

Jan Thompson

Lynn Whitacre

1962

Marilyn Foster

Jeanne Brogoitti

Patty Buchanan

Nancy Howard

Pat Wehrli

1963

Kelly McCormmach

Kay Brunner

Janet Horne

Barbara Moore

Mary Ann Storie

1964

Janet Horne

Sandra Beach

Judy Curcio

Kay Oliver

Linda Oylear

1965

Judy Curcio

Shannon Mahoney

Maureen

    McCormmach

Jan McCurdy

Kristin Weber

1966

Paulette Rice

Marsha McCormmach

Susan Olsen

Austene Trowbridge

Margaret Winget

1967

Susan Olsen

Jackie Broun

Sheila Mabry

Sandi Philippi

Jo Anne Price

1968

Mary Thompson

Melissa Davis

Linda Levy

Susan Lindstrom

Gayle Rosenberg

1969

Gayle Rosenberg

Linda Denton

Shirley Hindman

Susan Trowbridge

Julie Tubbs

1970

Sally Kamm

Melinda Bishop

Rachel Brunner

Donna Doherty

Patti Healy

1971

Patti Healy

Jeri Krebs

Judy Purchase

Brenda Ricco

Teri Thompson

1972

Susan Davis

Mary Hibberd

Becky Raymond

Betsy Shaw

Shelly Simpson

1973

Becky Raymond

Carol Cassens

Shannon Cimmiyotti

Heather Hales

Jan Kaser

1974

Heather Hales

Becky Bishop

Suzanne Dick

Patsy Hopper

Nancy Kilkenny

1975

Lori Anderson

Michelle Evans

Susan Fitterer

Ann Lorenzen

Jan Terjeson

1976

Julie Rugg

Mary Ann Koch

Diane Levy

Jennifer Raymond

Betty Jane Thompson

1977

Jennifer Raymond

Julie Courson

Kathie Schubert

Joyce Tubbs

Cindy Wyss

1978

Kathie Schubert

Kristy Howell

Nancy Pinkerton

Cindy Ridley

Kim Sherrell

1979

Rilla Livingston

Bridget Boylen

Janice Healy

Susan Shields

Leslee Temple

1980

Janice Healy

Cindy Dougherty

Liz Lybarger

Nita Nichols

Lisa Snow

1981

Susan Koch

Sarah Branstetter

Cyd Cimmiyotti

Patti Kilkenny

Katy Thorne

1982

Katy Thorne

Susan Insko

Toni Minthorn

Kari Sherrell

Cindy Turner

1983

Cyd Cimmiyotti

Andrea Beck

Lisa Martin

Anita Palmer

Tara Temple

1984

Lisa Martin

Cindy Insko

Nancy Miller

Katy Sorey

Candi Turner

1985

Andrea Beck

Jody Gugin

Ellen Kilkenny

Tina Simpson

Shannon VanDorn

1986

Ellen Kilkenny

Gregory Cimmiyotti

Lisa Ferguson

Linda Sue Maiden

Wendy Wagner

1987

Lisa Ferguson

Serena Baker

Robin Bothum

Bille Jensen

Sara Mautz

1988

Linda Sue Maiden

Mary Kay Lieuallen

Tami Simpson

Sandi Turner

Debra Weathers

1989

Tami Simpson

Theresa Alden

Mary French

Toni Hagen

Janelle Pace

1990

Mary Kay Lieuallen

Mollie Bothum

Katie Rosenberg

Annette Tolley

Whitney Wagner

1991

Jennifer Currin

Diana Erickson

Sarajane Hendrix

Tonya Johnson

Lois Ward

1992

Sarajane Hendrix

Kristen Applegate

Rebecca Hatley

JoAnna McEwen

Josie Perkins

1993

Jodi Rice

Michele Allen

Carrie Ann Levy

Raeann Shook

Jill Yost

1994

Carrie Ann Levy

Megan Gass

Kimberly Hoeft

Sunny Swanson

Mary Wachter

1995

Kimberly Hoeft

Corey Loiland

Molly McEwen

Marty Perkins

Jodi Severe

1996

Jodi Severe

Jamie Bealer

Kimberly Kelty

Jolene Sallee

Alison Shook

1997

Jamie Bealer

Megan Corey

Kristen Elliott

Josilyn Evans

Natalie Johnson

1998

Megan Corey

Shana Anderson

Kristen Hagen

Cicely Loftus

Casey Seeger

1999

Josilyn Evans

Juliann Bealer

Maci Childers

Tiah DeGrofft

Sarah Levy

2000

Shana Anderson

Annie Hisler

Darci Severe

Brittany Smith

Amy VanderPlaat

2001

Tiah DeGrofft

Rachel Faber-Luciana

Liz Johnson

Laina Mathews

JaDee VanHouten

2002

Brittany Smith

Jaime Clarke

Abby Ely

Haley Davis

Darla Severe

2003

Darla Severe

Cydney Corey

Lindsey Joseph

Jennifer Levy

Jill Sorey

2004

Cydney Corey

Emily Johnson

Tiah Pahl

Jill Quesenberry

Jessi Wells

2005

Jennifer Levy

Sarajane Rosenberg

Shanna Smith

Abby VanderPlaat

Whitney White

2006

Sarajane Rosenberg

Kylie Bronson

Celeste Hillock

Darlene Thompson

Lindsee Williams

2007

Whitney White

Tiffany Jo Aliverti

Dana Grieb

Lacey Mayberry

Beth Ann Sullivan

2008

Lacey Mayberry

Hailey Davis

Kathryn Hixson

Katie Partlow

Cheyenne Williams

HAPPY CANYON PRESIDENTS

1916–1921	Joe Tallman
1921–1922	James Sturgis
1922–1924	James Johns
1925	L. C. Scharpf
1926	Les Hamley
1927–1929	Philo Rounds
1930	Elmer Storie
1931–1939	John Murray
1940	John Kilkenny
1941–1944	Fay Hodges
1945–1948	Raley Peterson
1949	Homer Beale
1950–1951	Syd Laing
1952–1955	Jack Duff
1956–1957	Whitey Breaid
1958–1960	Bill Duff
1961–1962	Don Buchanan
1963–1965	R. A. "Bob" Fletcher
1966–1967	Don Hawkins
1968–1969	Russ McKennon
1970–1971	Emile Holeman
1972–1973	Bill Morrison
1974–1975	Mike Kilkenny
1976–1977	Bob Hawes
1978–1979	Rich Koch
1980–1981	Wes Grilley
1982–1983	Stan Timmerman
1984–1985	Steve Corey
1986–1987	Mark Rosenberg
1988–1989	Tim Hawkins
1990–1991	Jim Duff
1992–1993	Dennis Hunt
1994–1996	Kelly Hawkins
1997–1998	Bob Blanc
1999–2000	Wayne Low
2001	Terry McCartor
2002	Matt Duchek
2003	David Stuvland
2004	Jack Matlock
2005–2006	Doug Corey
2007–2008	Kevin Hale

HAPPY CANYON PRINCESSES

1955–1956

Caroline Motanic

1957

Marie Alexander

1958–1959

Anna Jane Wilkinson

1958

Joyce Hoptowit

1959

Anna Marie Pond

1960

Brenda Bearchum
(Miss Indian America in 1961)

1960–1961

Bertha Carter

1961

Lois McFarland

1961

Beverly Strong

1962

Margaret Henry

1962

Judy Hines

1963

Alvina Burke

1963

Sharon Hoptowit

1964

Sophia Bearchum

1964

Donna Minthorn

1965

Patty Crane

1965

Marilyn Wolf

1966

Frances Bearchum

1966

Judy Burke

1967

Louise Spino

1967

Mildred Naneges

1968

Lillian Moses

1968

Carla Walker

1969

Eloise Baptiste

1969

Bernadine Robertson

1970

Jeri Murr

1970

Cathy Sampson

1971

Judith Moses

1972

Rosalie Alexander

1972

Darlene Terry

1973

Ronna Cowapoo

1973

Alva Jo Sheoships

285

1974–1975	1976	1979	1981	1984	1987	1989	1992
Katherine Minthorn	Marcella Lloyd	Lawanda Bronson	Mary Craig	Gretchen Hines	Bridget Kalama	Alisa Portley	Anna Minthorn

1974	1977	1979	1982–1983	1985	1988	1990–1991	1993
Michelle Liberty	Eleanor Bearchum	Janene Barnes	Lona Pond	Debra Weathers	Rita Allman	Fawn Williams	Esther Huesties

1974	1977	1980	1983	1985–1986	1988	1991	1993–1994
Lorena Thompson	Teri Parr	Julie Minthorn	Sandra Craig	Janine Winn	Ethel Jackson	Irene Jackson	Shannon Galloway

1975–1976	1978	1981	1984	1986–1987	1989–1990	1992	1994
Nancy Parker	Toni Minthorn	Ada May Patrick	Louisa Allman	Michelle Spencer	Rachel Jones	Teara Farrow	Monika McGuire

1995	1997	1999	2001	2003	2005	2007
Jaimie Crane	Naomi Bearchum	Victoria Allen	Tara Burnside	Talia Minthorn	Lela Buck	Chelsey Dick

1995	1997	1999	2001	2003	2005	2007
Raeann Crane	Adrienne Farrow	Donna Nez	Sydelle Harrison	Shaina Watlamet	Rosaline Hines	Monece Moses

1996	1998	2000	2002	2004	2006	2008
Claudette Enos	Lucy John	Vanessa Enos	Ashleigh Wolf	Keri Kordatzky	Neville Benson	Brittany Cline

1996	1998	2000	2002	2004	2006	2008
Althea Huesties	Stacy McKay	Drew Johnson	Jacy Alexander-Sohappy	Ashley Picard	Crystal Pond	Tyera Pete

SADDLE BRONC CHAMPIONS

1910	Bert Kelly		
1911	John Spain		
1912	L. W. Minor		
1913	A. E. McCormach		
1914	**Red Parker**		

Red Parker, John Judd, Lee Caldwell,
Champions, 1914

Red Parker: Champion Cowboy
of the World, 1914

1915	**Lee Caldwell**
1916	Jackson Sundown
1917	Yakima Canutt
1918	**Hugo Strickland**
1919	**Yakima Canutt**

1920	**Tex Smith**
1921	Hugo Strickland
1922	Howard Tegland
1923	Yakima Canutt
1924	Paddy Ryan
1925	Bob Askins
1926	Shark Irwin
1927	Bob Askins
1928	Turk Greenough
1929	Pete Knight
1930	Pete Knight
1931	F. E. Studnick
1932	Pete Knight
1933	Floyd Stillings
1934	Chuck Wilson
1935	Pete Knight
1936	Pete Knight
1937	Bill McMacken
1938	Wayne Davis
1939	Jack Wade
1940	Nick Knight
1941	Doff Aber
1944	Bob Burrows
1945	Bill McMacken
1946	Jim Luke
1947	Gene Pruett
1948	Jerry Ambler

Ray Bell, Yakima Canutt, H. Strickland, Tex Smith: Champion Buckers of the World, ca. 1919

1949	**Bud Linderman**
1950	Bill Linderman

Bud Linderman on "Reservation," 1950

1951	Buster Ivory
1952	Arlo Curtiss
1953	Arlo Curtiss
1954	Gene Pruett
1955	Deb Copenhaver
1956	Alvin Nelson
1957	Alvin Nelson
1958	Les Johnson
1959	Casey Tibbs
1960	Joe Chase
1961	Marty Wood
1962	Kenny McLean
1963	Kenny McLean
1964	Jim Tescher
1965	Shawn Davis
1966	Jim Bothum
1967	Jerry Hixon
1968	Larry Mahan
1969	J. C. Bonine
1970	Hugh Chambliss
1971	Doug Brown /
	Marty Wood *(tie)*
1972	Darrel Kong

1973	Dennis Reiners /
	Don Farmer *(tie)*
1974	Brian Claypool
1975	Bill Pauley
1976	Doug Vold
1977	Bob Gottfriedson
1978	Melvin Coleman
1979	Joe Marvel
1980	Ivan Daines
1981	Bob Brown
1982	Charles Stovner /
	Mel Hyland *(tie)*
1983	Kent Cooper
1984	Brad Gjermundson
1985	David Bothum
1986	Butch Knowles
1987	Robert Etbauer
1988	Kyle Wemple
1989	Lewis Feild
1990	Dan Etbauer
1991	Butch Knowles /
	Jack Nystrom *(tie)*
1992	Kyle Wemple
1993	Dan Mortensen
1994	Billy Etbauer
1995	Jess Martin
1996	Dan Etbauer
1997	Ryan Mapston
1998	Todd Hipsag
1999	Dan Mortensen
2000	Ira Slagowski
2001	Glen O'Neill
2002	Glen O'Neill
2003	Jesse Bail / Rod Hay *(tie)*
2004	Rod Hay / Glen O'Neill *(tie)*
2005	Rod Hay
2006	Rod Hay /
	Cody DeMoss *(tie)*
2007	Chet Johnson
2008	Morgan Forbes

BULLDOGGING CHAMPIONS

1911	**Buffalo Vernon**

McCoy, Briscoe, Blanchett, Vernon—
Champion Steer Bulldoggers of the
World, 1911

1912	Art Acord
1913	Wallie Padgett
1914	Sam Garrett
1915	Frank Cable
1916	Frank McCarroll
1917	Paul Hastings
1918	Ray McCarroll
1919	Jim Massey
1920	Yakima Canutt
1921	**Yakima Canutt**

Yakima Canutt, World Champion
Bulldogger, 1921

1922	Mike Hastings
1923	Lloyd Saunders
1924	Buck Lucas
1925	Mike Hastings
1926	Norman Cowan
1927	Dick Shelton

1928	Dick Shelton
1929	Dick Shelton
1930	Paddy Ryan
1931	Frank McCarroll
1932	Hugh Bennett
1933	Dick Truitt
1934	James Irwin
1935	Everett Bowman
1936	Dick Truitt
1937	Shaniko Red
1938	Cliff Gardner
1939	Bill McMacken
1940	Everett Bowman
1941	Fritz Truan
1944	Homer Pettigrew
1945	Buckshot Sorrels
1946	Dave Campbell
1947	Claude Hensen
1948	Al Garrett
1949	Shoat Webster
1950	Dub Phillips
1951	Barney Wills
1952	Gordon Davis
1953	Bob Nordtone
1954	Dud Taylor
1955	Leonard Saye
1956	Sherman Sullins
1957	Carl Mendes
1958	Gene Miles
1959	Wilbur Plaugher
1960	Bob A. Robinson
1961	Harry Charters
1962	Harley May
1963	Max Griffith
1964	John W. Jones
1965	Bill Linderman
1966	Walter Wyatt
1967	Roy Duvall
1968	Donnie Yandell
1969	Walter Linderman
1970	Leland Kelly

1971	Fred Larson
1972	Frank Shepperson
1973	Dave Meyers
1974	Lee Phillips
1975	Danny Torricellas
1976	Pat Nogle
1977	Fred Larson
1978	Jim Zolman
1979	Danny Torricellas
1980	Carl Hansen
1981	Lane Johnson
1982	Tom Ferguson
1983	Danny Torricellas
1984	Arlen Driggers / Byron Walker *(tie)*
1985	Byron Walker
1986	John Jones
1987	Tony Currin
1988	Mark Waltz
1989	Tony Currin
1990	John W. Jones Jr.
1991	Steve Currin
1992	Trav Cadwell
1993	Sam Kayser
1994	Danny Torricellas
1995	Ron Currin Jr.
1996	Todd Suhn
1997	Rope Meyer
1998	Herbert Theriot
1999	Jason Lahr / Tommy R. Cook *(tie)*
2000	Birch Negaard / Teddy Johnson (tie)
2001	Brock Andrus
2002	K. C. Jones
2003	Josh Lessman
2004	Tommy R. Cook
2005	Tommy R. Cook
2006	Brad Gleason
2007	Todd Suhn
2008	Casey Martin

STEER ROPING CHAMPIONS

1911	Roy Ross
1912	Dell Blancett
1913	Ed McCarty
1914	Tom Grimes
1915	George Wier
1916	George Wier
1917	Charlie Wier
1918	Ed McCarty
1919	Fred Beesan
1920	Ray Bell
1921	Tom Grimes
1922	Hugo Strickland
1923	Tom Grimes
1924	Hugo Strickland
1925	King Merritt
1926	Hugo Strickland
1927	**Bob Crosby**

Bob Crosby roping, 1927

1928	Bob Crosby
1929	Dick Truitt
1930	Jake McClure
1931	Ike Rude
1932	**Everett Bowman**

Everett Bowman, Champion, 1932

1933	Bob Crosby
1934	Bob Crosby
1935	King Merritt
1936	Carl Arnold / Ike Rude *(tie)*

1937	Bill McMacken
1938	Ross Henry Meeks
1939	Asbury Schell
1940	Clay Carr
1941	Bob Harverty / Everett Bowman *(tie)*
1944	John Rhodes
1945	John Bowman
1946	John Bowman
1947	Clark McEntire
1948	Everett Shaw
1949	Shoat Webster
1950	Cotton Lee
1951	Shoat Webster
1952	Oran Fore
1953	**Ike Rude**

Ike Rude, 1953

1954	Don McLaughlin
1955	Carl Sawyer
1956	John Dalton
1957	Clark McEntire
1958	Clark McEntire
1959	Joey Bergevin
1960	Duane Reece
1961	Harley May
1962	Don McLaughlin
1963	Dewey Lee David
1964	Joe Snively
1965	Everett Shaw
1966	Richard Walker
1967	Jim Prather
1968	Allen Keller
1969	Don McLaughlin

1970	Dewey Lee David
1971	Irv Alderson
1972	Joe Snively
1973	Ben Patterson
1974	John Dalton
1975	James Allen
1976	Walt Arnold
1977	Kenny Call
1978	Arnold Felts
1979	Terry McGinley
1980	Walt Arnold
1981	Jim Davis
1982	Guy Allen
1983	Guy Allen
1984	Pake McEntire
1985	Pax Irvine
1986	H. Baumgardner
1987	Tommy Hirsig
1988	Charles Good
1989	Guy Allen
1990	Neil Worrell
1991	J. D. Yates
1992	Buster Record
1993	Roy Angermiller
1994	J. D. Yates
1995	Mike Thompson
1996	Tom Sorey
1997	Jim Davis
1998	Guy Allen
1999	Tom Sorey
2000	Clay Cameron
2001	J. D. Yates
2002	Jarrett Blessing
2003	Jason Stewart
2004	Mike Beers
2005	Doug Clark
2006	Cash Myers
2007	Rich Skelton
2008	Scott Snedecor

CALF ROPING CHAMPIONS

Year	Champion	Year	Champion
1927	Ed Bowman	1970	Donnie Yandell
1928	Bob Crosby	1971	Dean Oliver
1929	Jake McClure	1972	Donnie Yandell
1930	Jake McClure	1973	Jim Gladstone
1931	E. Pardee	1974	Keene Wright
1932	Bob Crosby	1975	Bob Ragsdale
1933	Everett Shaw	1976	Dean Oliver
1934	Dick Truitt	1977	Larry Ferguson
1935	Everett Bowman	1978	Roy Cooper
1936	King Merritt	1979	Phil Lyne
1937	Lloyd Depew	1980	Steve Bland
1938	John Thomas	1981	Steve Bland
1939	Roy Lewis	1982	Pax Irvine
1940	Richard Merchant	1983	Phil Lyne
1941	Buck Standifer	1984	Dan Webb
1944	Floyd Peeters	1985	Joe Lucas
1945	John Bowman	1986	Mike McLaughlin
1946	Vern Castro	1987	Steve Hilmeyer
1947	Dean Merritt	1988	Clay Tom Cooper
1948	Toots Mansfield	1989	Joe Lucas
1949	Chuck Sheppard	1990	Johnny Emmons
1950	Shoat Webster	1991	K. C. Jones
1951	Toots Mansfield	1992	Tiny Bertsch
1952	B. J. Pierce	1993	Herbert Theriot
1953	E. V. Dorsey	1994	Brent Lewis / Troy Pruitt *(tie)*
1954	Dell Haverty	1995	Fred Whitfield / Mike Beers *(tie)*
1955	B. J. Pierce	1996	Fred Whitfield
1956	Joe Bergevin	1997	Mark Nugent
1957	Dean Oliver	1998	Trent Walls
1958	Roy Savage	1999	Trevor Brazile
1959	Johnny Leonard	2000	Herbert Theriot
1960	Harry Charters	2001	Blair Burk
1961	Harry Charters	2002	Ricky Hyde
1962	Sonny Davis	2003	Jerome Schneeberger
1963	Dale Smith	2004	Brad Goodrich
1964	Sonny Davis	2005	Fred Whitfield
1965	Bud Corwin	2006	Joe Beaver
1966	Don McLaughlin	2007	Alwin Bouchard / Tim Pharr *(tie)*
1967	Lee Farris	2008	Brad Goodrich
1968	Bob Ragsdale		
1969	Olin Young		

TEAM ROPING CHAMPIONS

1991	Kory Koontz / Rube Woolsey
1992	Bobby Harris / Jake Milton
1993	Doyle Gellerman / Walt Woodard
1994	Jake Barnes / Clay O'Brien Cooper
1995	Shane Schwenke / Monty Joe Petska
1996	Liddon Cowden / Brent Lockett
1997	Rich Skelton / Speed Williams
1998	Brent Lockett / Chance Kelton
1999	Matt Tyler / Bobby Harris
2000	Billie Holland / Mike George
2001	Richard Eiguren / B. J. Campbell
2002	Liddon Cowden / Brent Lockett
2003	Jake Barnes / Boogie Ray
2004	Travis Tryan / Matt Zancanella
2005	Tee Woolman / Cory Petska
2006	Joe Beaver / Nick Simmons / Jake Stanley / Russell Cardoza *(tie)*
2007	Charly Crawford / Cody Hintz
2008	Luke Brown / Monty Joe Petska

BULL RIDING CHAMPIONS

Year	Champion	Year	Champion
1944	Johnny Tubbs	1980	Eddie Rawden
1945	Frank Voros	1981	Bobbie Delvecchio
1946	Alex Dick	1982	Jody Tatone
1947	Tom McBride	1983	Charlie Sampson
1952	Steve Johnson	1984	Rob McDonald / Sam Poutous *(tie)*
1956	Buck Rutherford	1985	Lane Frost
1957	Joel Sublette	1986	Charlie Sampson / Philip Fournier *(tie)*
1958	Jim Shoulders	1987	Lane Frost
1959	Duane Howard	1988	Clint Branger
1960	Bob Wegner	1989	Johnny Chavez
1961	Bob Wegner	1990	Joe Wimberly
1962	Ronnie Rossen	1991	Michael Gaffney
1963	Larry Davis	1992	Cody Custer
1964	Bob Wegner	1993	Shannon Wortman
1965	Paul Mayo / Gils Garstead *(tie)*	1994	Adam Carrillo
1966	Kenny Stanton	1995	David Fournier
1967	Larry Mahan	1996	Scott Breding
1968	Paul Mayo	1997	Hank Reece
1969	Larry Mahan	1998	Kelly Armstrong
1970	Kenny Stanton	1999	Royd Doyal
1971	John Dodds	2000	Danell Tipton
1972	Brian Claypool	2001	Tyler Fowler
1973	John Dodds	2002	Casey Baize
1974	Harold Haptonstall / Monte Condon *(tie)*	2003	Fred B. Boettcher
1975	Kenny Stanton	2004	Corey McFadden
1976	Doug Brown	2005	Bryan Richardson
1977	Barney Brehmer	2006	Mike Moore
1978	Don Johnson / Butch Kirby *(tie)*	2007	Clint Craig
1979	Gary Leffew	2008	J. W. Harris

BAREBACK CHAMPIONS

1948	Bob Maynard		Marvin Garrett *(tie)*	**1999**	Pete Hawkins
1949	Bud Linderman	**1989**	Mark Garrett /	**2000**	Scott Johnston
1950	Casey Tibbs /		Lewis Feild *(tie)*	**2001**	Larry Sandvick
	Jim Hailey *(tie)*	**1990**	Lewis Feild	**2002**	Ken Lesengrav
1951	Casey Tibbs	**1991**	Mark Garrett	**2003**	Davey Shields Jr.
1953	Eddy Akridge	**1992**	Deb Greenough	**2004**	Clayton Foltyn
1954	Dell Haverty	**1993**	Lance Crump	**2005**	Cody DeMers /
1955	Ralph Buell	**1994**	Denny McLanahan		Cimmaron Gerke
1956	John Hawkins	**1995**	Marvin Garrett		*(tie)*
1957	Bob Cullison	**1996**	Pete Hawkins	**2006**	**Will Lowe**
1958	Jim Shoulders	**1997**	Kelly Wardell	**2007**	Cleve Schmidt
1959	Jim Shoulders	**1998**	Brian Hawk	**2008**	Will Lowe
1960	Johnny Mitchell				
1961	Don Mayo				
1962	Buddy Peak				
1963	Dave Reidhead				
1964	Kenny Stanton				
1965	Jackie Wright				
1966	Larry Mahan				
1967	Tony Haberer				
1968	Bob Mayo				
1969	Larry Mahan				
1970	Ace Berry				
1971	Joe Alexander				
1972	Ace Berry				
1973	Royce Smith				
1974	Scottie Platts				
1975	Scottie Platts				
1976	Russell McCall				
1977	Joe Alexander				
1978	Steve Dunham				
1979	Joe Alexander				
1980	John McDonald				
1981	Mickey Young				
1982	J. C. Trujillo				
1983	J. C. Trujillo				
1984	Lewis Feild				
1985	Randy Taylor				
1986	Robin Burwash				
1987	Duane France				
1988	Wayne Herman /				

Will Lowe, Bareback Champion, 2006

BARREL RACING CHAMPIONS

2000	Gloria Freeman
2001	Kelli Currin
2002	Charmayne James
2003	Charmayne James
2004	Jolee Lautaret
2005	Maegan Reichert
2006	Linzie Walker
2007	Linzie Walker
2008	Linzie Walker

ALL-AROUND COWBOY WINNERS

1912

Hoot Gibson

1913

A. E. McCormach

1914

Sammy Garrett

1915

Lee Caldwell

1916

Jackson Sundown

1917

Yakima Canutt

1918

Hugo Strickland

1919

Yakima Canutt

1920

Yakima Canutt

1921

Darrel Cannon

1922

Mike Hastings *(tie)*

1922

Hugo Strickland *(tie)*

1923

Yakima Canutt

1924

Hugo Strickland

1925

C. W. Cash

1926

Hugo Strickland

1927

Bob Crosby

ROOSEVELT TROPHY

1923

Yakima Canutt

1924

Paddy Ryan

1925

Bob Crosby

1926

Norman Cowan

1927

Bob Crosby

1928

Bob Crosby *(trophy retired after three wins)*

SAM JACKSON TROPHY

1929

Dick Truitt *(no trophy)*

1930

Jake McClure

1931

ke Rude

1932

Everett Bowman

1933

Everett Shaw

1934

Dick Truitt

1935

Everett Bowman

1936

Carl Arnold *(tie)*

1936

Ike Rude *(tie)*

1937

Bill McMacken

1938

Ross Henry Meeks

1939

Bill McMacken

1940

Clay Carr

1941

Fritz Truan

1942 & 1943

(no Round-Ups)

1944

Gene Rambo

1945

John Bowman

1946

Hugh Bennett

1947

Clark McEntire

1948

Everett Shaw

1949

Shoat Webster

1950

Shoat Webster

1951

Shoat Webster
(trophy retired after three wins)

OREGON JOURNAL
TROPHY

1952

Shoat Webster

1953

Eddy Akridge

1954

Dell Haverty

1955

Leonard Saye

1956

John Dalton

1957

Clark McEntire

1958

Jim Shoulders

1959

Don McLaughlin

1960

Harry Charters

1961

Harry Charters

1962

Sonny Davis

1963

Mac Griffith

1964

Sonny Davis

1965

Paul Mayo

1966

Don McLaughlin

1967

Larry Mahan

1968

Allen Keller

1969

Olin Young

1970

Kenny Stanton

1971

James Allen

1972

Eldon Dudley

EAST OREGONIAN TROPHY

1973

Walter Arnold

1974
John Dalton
1975
Walter Arnold

1976

Chris Lybbert

1977

Jeff Knowles

1978

Byron Walker

1979

Danny Torricellas

1980

Steve Bland

1981

Phil Lyne

1982

Roy Cooper

1983
Phil Lyne
1984
Roy Cooper

1985

Mike Beers

1986

Harold Baumgardner

1987

Tom Ferguson

1988

Mike Currin

1989

Lewis Feild

1990
Lewis Feild

1991

K. C. Jones

1992

Bret Boatright

1993

Ron Currin Jr.

1994

J. D. Yates

1995

Mike Beers

1996

Todd Suhn

1997
Mike Beers

1998

Herbert Theriot

1999

Trevor Brazile

2000

Birch Negaard

2001

Cody Ohl

2002

B. J. Campbell

2003

Kyle Lockett

2004

Brad Goodrich

2005

Cash Myers

2006

Joe Beaver

2007

Cash Myers

2008
Cash Myers

ANIMALS IN THE ROUND-UP AND HAPPY CANYON HALL OF FAME

BUCKING HORSES

1969
War Paint
Midnight
Long Tom
No Name
Philip Rollins

1970
Roosevelt Trophy
Five Minutes to
 Midnight

1971
Badger Mountain
U-Tell-Em

1972
Sam Jackson

1973
Bill McAdoo

1974
Blue Blazes

1975
Miss Klamath

1980
Necklace

BUCKING BULL

1978
Sharkey

BULLDOGGING HORSE

1985
Peanuts

HAPPY CANYON PERFORMERS

1977
Domino (horse)

1986
Molly (horse)

1988
Shorty (horse)

1990
Monty (horse)

2000
Beauregard (elk)

2005
Cataldo (horse)

ROUND-UP AND HAPPY CANYON HALL OF FAME PRESIDENTS

1968–1971	Dan Bell
1971–1972	Jack Hodgen
1972–1975	Lester King
1975–1977	Pat Folsom
1977–1979	Bob Hales
1979–1981	Ralph Currin
1981–1982	Joe Daley
1982–1984	Bob Hawes
1984–1985	Joyce Hales
1985–1988	Joe Daley
1989–1990	Stan Timmerman
1990–1991	Pat Terjeson
1991–1992	Joe Daley
1992–1998	Jack Sweek
1998–2003	Bonnie Sager
2003–2004	Bill Dawson
2004–2006	Tim O'Hanlon
2007–2009	Matt Duchek

ROUND-UP AND HAPPY CANYON HALL OF FAME HONOREES

1969
Clarence Burke
Lee Caldwell
Yakima Canutt
Henry Collins
George Fletcher
Roy Raley
Gene Rambo
George Strand
Til Taylor
Herb Thompson

1970
Carl Arnold
Fay LeGrow

1971
Allen Drumheller
Hugo Strickland
Lawrence Lieuallen
Mabel Strickland
Pete Knight
Phillip Bill

1972
E. N. "Pink" Boylen
Jackson Sundown

1973
John Hales
Melissa Parr
Tim Bernard

1974
Bill Switzler
Bob Crosby

1975
Elsie Fitzmaurice
 Dickson
Shoat Webster

1976
Berkeley Davis
Dr. Joseph Brennan

1977
Eliza Bill
Lew W. Minor
Marion Hansell

1978
George Moens
Monk Carden

1979
Finis Kirkpatrick

1980
Montie Montana

1981
Harley Tucker
Ike Rude

1982
Chauncey Bishop
Clarence Bishop
Roy Bishop

1983
Dan Bell
George Doak
Karl Doering

1984
Art Motanic
Clark McEntire

1985
R. A. "Bob" Fletcher
Everett Bowman

1986
Pat Folsom
Sid Seale

1987
Bob Hales
Ella Lazinka Ganger

1988
Bob Christensen Sr.
Mildred Searcy

1989
Bob Chambers
Jack Duff

1990
Doris Swayze
 Bounds
Verne Terjeson

1991
Gerald Swaggart
Tessie Williams

1992
J. David Hamley
J. J. Hamley
Lester H. Hamley
Don McLaughlin
William Minthorn
Bill Severe
Duff Severe

1993
Floyd "Bus"
 Howdyshell
Leonard King

1994
Herman Rosenberg
John Dalton

1995
Bertha Kapernik
 Blancett
Bob Hawkins
Don Hawkins
Wray Hawkins
Everett Shaw

1996
The Currin Family,
 Ron Sr., Judy,
 Mike, Ron Jr.,
 Tony, Steve &
 Jennifer
Dick Oliver
Tom Simonton

1997
Lawrence G. Frazier
Jim Rosenberg
Dick Truitt
The Elgin Stagecoach
 Team: Odie Payne,
 Billy Hindman,
 & Sonny
 Weatherspoon

1998
Larry Mahan
Harry Vold
Bob & Betty Byer

1999
Main Street
 Cowboys
Beryl Grilley
Jim Shoulders

2000
Bill McMacken
McKinley & Susie
 Williams
Paul Cimmiyotti

2001
Robin Wesley
 (R. W.) Fletcher
Esther Motanic
Bonnie McCarroll
Jack Sweek

2002
Frank Tubbs
Guy Allen

2003
Wallace Smith
Pat Gugin
Raymond "Popcorn"
 Burke

2004
Casey Tibbs
Dr. Richard Koch
Jesse Jones Jr.

2005
Ron J. Hudson
William G. "Wilbur"
 Shaw
Walt Arnold

2006
Harry Charters
Marie & Louie Dick
Jack Hodgen
Slim Pickens

2007
C. M. "Mort" Bishop
John S. "Jiggs" Fisk
Phillip Morris Lyne

2008
Bonnie Tucker
 Blankenship
Christian "Sonny"
 Davis
Fred Hill

BIBLIOGRAPHY

Beckham, Stephen Dow. *Oregon Indians: Voices from Two Centuries.* Corvallis: Oregon State University Press, 2006.

Bernstein, Joel. *Wild Ride.* Salt Lake City, Utah: Gibbs Smith, Publisher, 2007.

Boylen, E. N. *Episode of the West: The Pendleton Round-Up, 1910–1951, Facts and Figures.* Pendleton, Ore.: Master Printers, 1975.

Burbick, Joan. *Rodeo Queens and the American Dream.* New York: Public Affairs, 2002.

Campion, Lynn. *Rodeo: Behind the Scenes at America's Most Exciting Sport.* Guilford, Conn.: The Lyons Press, 2002.

Canutt, Yakima, and Oliver Drake. *Stunt Man: The Autobiography of Yakima Canutt.* New York: Walker, 1979.

Carroll, R. D. *Shoat: A Champion Roper.* Barnsdall, Okla.: Evans Publications, 2003.

Clancy, Foghorn. *My Fifty Years in Rodeo: Living with Cowboys, Horses and Danger.* San Antonio, Tex.: Naylor and Company, 1952.

Collings, Ellsworth, and Alma Miller England. *The 101 Ranch.* Norman: University of Oklahoma Press, 1971.

Crockatt, Ernest L. *The Murder of Til Taylor: A Great Western Sheriff.* Philadelphia: Dorrance, 1970.

Crosby, Thelma, and Eve Ball. *Bob Crosby, World Champion Cowboy.* Clarendon, Tex.: Clarendon Press, 1966.

Flood, Elizabeth Clair, and William Manns. *Cowgirls: Women of the Wild West.* Santa Fe, N.Mex.: Zon International Publishing, 2000.

Fredriksson, Kristine. *American Rodeo: From Buffalo Bill to Big Business.* College Station: Texas A & M University Press, 1985.

Furlong, Charles Wellington. *Let 'er Buck: A Story of the Passing of the Old West.* New York: G. P. Putnam's Sons, 1921.

Grafe, Steven L. *Peoples of the Plateau: The Indian Photographs of Lee Moorhouse, 1898–1915.* Norman: University of Oklahoma Press, 2005.

Groves, Melody. *Ropes, Reins, and Rawhide: All About Rodeo.* Albuquerque: University of New Mexico Press, 2006.

Hassrick, Peter H. *Wildlife and Western Heroes: Alexander Phimister Proctor, Sculptor.* Tempe, Ariz.: Third Millennium Publishing, 2006.

Jordan, Bob. *Rodeo History and Legends.* Montrose, Calif.: Rodeo Stuff, 1994.

Jordan, Teresa. *Cowgirls: Women of the American West.* Garden City, N.Y.: Anchor Press, 1982.

Jory, Doug, and Cathy Jory. *From Pendleton to Calgary: An Oral History of Rodeo.* Bend, Ore.: Maverick Publications, 2002.

Kendrick, Robb. *Still: Cowboys at the Start of the Twenty-First Century.* Austin: University of Texas Press, 2008.

Kesey, Ken. *Last Go-Round: A Real Western.* New York: Viking, 1994.

Laegreid, Renée M. *Riding Pretty: Rodeo Royalty in the American West.* Lincoln: University of Nebraska Press, 2006.

LeCompte, Mary Lou. *Cowgirls of the Rodeo: Pioneer Professional Athletes.* Urbana: University of Illinois Press, 1993.

Lindmier, Tom, and Steve Mount. *I See by Your Outfit: Historic Cowboy Gear of the Northern Plains.* Glendo, Wyo.: High Plains Press, 1996.

MacNab, Gordon. *A Century of News and People in the* East Oregonian, *1875–1975.* Pendleton, Ore.: East Oregonian Publishing Co., 1975.

McGinnis, Vera. *Rodeo Road: My Life as a Pioneer Cowgirl.* New York: Hastings House, 1974.

McKinney, Grange B. *Art Acord and the Movies.* Raleigh, N.C.: Wyatt Classic, 2000.

Porter, Willard H. *Who's Who in Rodeo.* Norman, Okla.: National Cowboy Hall of Fame, 1982.

Proctor, Alexander Phimister. *Sculptor in Buckskin: An Autobiography.* Norman: University of Oklahoma Press, 1971.

Roach, Joyce Gibson. *The Cowgirls.* Denton: University of North Texas Press, 1990.

Ruby, Robert H., and John A. Brown. *Indians of the Pacific Northwest.* Norman: University of Oklahoma Press, 1981.

Rupp, Virgil. *Let 'er Buck! A History of the Pendleton Round-Up.* Pendleton, Ore.: Pendleton Round-Up Association, Master Printers, 1985.

Schnell, Fred. *Rodeo! The Suicide Circuit.* New York: Rand McNally, 1971.

Smith, Wallace. *Oregon Sketches.* New York: G. P. Putman's Sons, 1925.

Stratton, W. K. *Chasing the Rodeo: On Wild Rides and Big Dreams, Broken Hearts and Broken Bones, and One Man's Search for the West.* Orlando, Fla.: Harcourt, 2005.

Wallis, Michael. *The Real Wild West: The 101 Ranch and the Creation of the American West.* New York: St. Martin's Griffin, 2000.

Webber, Bert, and Margie Webber. *I Shot the News: The Adventures of Will E. Hudson, First Newsreel Cameraman in the Pacific Northwest.* Medford, Ore.: Webb Research Group.

Westermeier, Clifford P. *Man, Beast, Dust—The Story of Rodeo.* Lincoln: University of Nebraska Press, 1947.

Western Legacies Series, multiple contributors. *A Western Legacy: The National Cowboy and Western Heritage Museum.* Norman: University of Oklahoma Press, 2005.

Wills, Kathy Lynn, and Virginia Artho. *Cowgirl Legends: From the Cowgirl Hall of Fame.* Salt Lake City, Utah: Gibbs Smith, Publisher, 1995.

Wooden, Wayne S., and Gavin Ehringer. *Rodeo in America: Wranglers, Roughstock, and Paydirt.* Lawrence: University of Kansas Press, 1996.

IN MEMORIAM

MATTHEW J. JOHNSON
June 1952–November 2008

Matt Johnson was the grandson of Floyd "Bus" Howdyshell, the official Round-Up photographer from 1939 to 1977. Howdyshell also worked for the *East Oregonian* for twenty-five years, leaving in 1952 and starting Howdyshell Photos, a Pendleton business Matt carried on after Howdyshell's death. Also a Round-Up enthusiast, Matt photographed the event annually from 1975 to 2008 and augmented the Howdyshell Collection with his own work.

In a 2008 interview with Michael Bales, Matt recalled his grandfather teaching him photography as a boy. The two often worked together in Howdyshell's home basement, which served as a darkroom. "We'd have two hundred negatives hanging from clotheslines. Those are some good memories."

Matt Johnson died on November 15, 2008, as this book he helped to create went to press. Pendleton and the Round-Up will miss him.

▶ Overleaf: George Fletcher in the 1911 bucking contest.

By O. G. Allen in Low Collection.